# ·THE·
# FIRST
# SIN OF
# ROSS
# MICHAEL
# CARLSON

# ·THE·
# FIRST SIN OF ROSS MICHAEL CARLSON

## A Psychiatrist's Personal Account of Murder, Multiple Personality Disorder, and Modern Justice

## Michael Weissberg, M.D.

DELACORTE PRESS

Published by
Delacorte Press
Bantam Doubleday Dell Publishing Group, Inc.
666 Fifth Avenue
New York, New York 10103

Library of Congress Cataloging-in-Publication Data
Weissberg, Michael P.
    The first sin of Ross Michael Carlson : a psychiatrist's personal account of murder, multiple personality disorder, and modern justice / Michael Weissberg.
        p.    cm.
    ISBN 0-385-30536-2
    1. Carlson, Ross Michael.   2. Murderers—Colorado—Denver Metropolitan Area—Biography.   3. Insane, Criminal and dangerous—Colorado—Denver Metropolitan Area—Biography.   4. Parricide— Colorado—Denver Metropolitan Area—Case studies.   5. Multiple personality—Colorado—Denver Metropolitan Area—Case studies.   6. Forensic psychiatry—Colorado—Denver Metropolitan Area—Case studies.   7. Trials (Murder)—Colorado—Douglas County.   I. Title.
HV6248.C179W45   1992
364.1′523′092—dc20
[B]                                                                    91-39563   CIP

Book design by Robin Arzt

Manufactured in the United States of America
Published simultaneously in Canada

July 1992

10  9  8  7  6  5  4  3  2  1

RRH

*And I saw a beast coming out of the sea. He had ten horns and seven heads, with ten crowns on his horns, and on each head a blasphemous name . . .*

*—Revelation 13:1*

# ACKNOWLEDGMENTS

I could not have written this book without the help of many people. Unfortunately I have the room to thank only a few. My cousin, Peter Trachtenberg, was the first to encourage me to pursue this project. Chief Deputy D.A. Bob Chappell and Investigator Brian Bevis of the Arapahoe County District Attorney's Office were part of this story and provided me with an abundance of material. Bob made important comments about an earlier draft. I am grateful for the openness two of Ross Carlson's friends, Michael Batagglia and Jim Peelor, showed as they shared their thoughts about what happened and the frankness with which Craig Truman, Carlson's first attorney, and Robert Kingsley, Carlson's last judge, told me what they could within professional constraints.

The Reverend Harvey Potthoff and Dr. Dennis MacDonald, both of the Iliff School of Theology, graciously served as sounding boards for my ideas. Jean Otto of *The Rocky Mountain News*, George Lane of *The Denver Post*, and Mark Groth provided needed assistance. I also appreciated David Savitz's letter of encouragement and his article about multiple personality disorder. David was one of the two attorneys who so tenaciously defended their client until the end.

I am also deeply indebted to those who read earlier manuscripts. The Montana contingent of Mike and Sue Dailey and Joan Brownell made many useful criticisms, as did Sheila Carter in Denver. My agent, Regula Noetzli, gave me invaluable help as I shaped my ideas. And working with Brian DeFiore, his assistant Shawn Coyne, and the rest of the people at Delacorte was a dream. Finally, I want to thank my wife, Susan, for her intuitive sensibility, patience, and steady encouragement without which this book would never have seen the light of day. It is to Susan and my son, Nicholas, that I dedicate this book.

# HAVE YOU SEEN MICHAEL?

The first thing he said when he caught up to me was "aren't you the guy who examined Ross Carlson?" Instinctively, I was on guard. Ross Carlson still stirred strong emotions. I did not know what to expect.

It was February 1991, and I had just finished teaching a seminar at the Fitzsimmons Army Medical Center in Denver about violence and violent patients. As I walked to my car, I was approached by this tall young man with close-cropped dark hair and a handsome, open face, dressed in an officer's uniform. I recognized him to be someone from the class.

"You had your doubts about him, didn't you?" I gave a noncommittal answer. I needed to get back to my office and I did not want to get into a big discussion. Nevertheless, he persisted in a friendly, but intense sort of way. Clearly, he wanted to talk.

"Hello, my name is Michael Batagglia," he said as he stuck out his hand. "I was one of Ross Carlson's best friends. His attorney, Walter Gerash, wanted me to testify, but I wouldn't do it."

I stopped in my tracks. For the past year I had been writing down my experiences with Carlson attempting to make sense out of what happened. When Batagglia told me he was Carlson's best friend, the tables suddenly turned. Here was someone who had no stake in the outcome; no axe to grind. Our meeting was a complete accident and he was Carlson's friend. Now I wanted very much to hear what Batagglia had to say.

Michael told me he was a fourth year medical student in the Armed Services Medical School doing a psychiatry rotation at Fitzsimmons to be close to home. I asked if he would like to tell me more about Carlson at lunch in the next few days. With a smile, he agreed.

That night, when I called to arrange our meeting, Michael's mother told me he was out lifting weights, something I later learned he had spent long hours doing with Ross. When Michael called back, we made arrangements. But he did not hang up; clearly, he wanted to talk. After eight years, his words tumbled out.

"I felt terrible that I did not call him afterward, but it was hard for me to do. Ross was the first person I met in high school and right away we started to hang out together. We would have lunch a couple of times a week but my other friends wondered what I saw in him. For instance, after he saw *American Gigolo* he went out and bought five hundred dollars worth of fancy clothing. Everyone picked on him for his expensive Italian outfits. But he wasn't violent. He was so strong from hours of weight lifting he could have torn those people to shreds, but he never did it.

"I thought he always had a strange relationship with his parents. I can't define it but he never invited me over to his house although he always came over to mine. Sometimes he looked like he was spacing out but he never lost track of conversations. He was always Ross.

"Right before graduation, it must have been the spring of 1982, Ross told me that he wanted to blow up his parents' house to get the insurance money. 'Ross,' I told him, 'that is really crazy.' Another time he told me that he wanted to falsify documents and live his life all over again.

"The last time he called, it was August 1983. I didn't call back. I don't know why. Afterward, Gerash called. He wanted me to testify. I thought long and hard about it. Gerash called many times. I finally told him I could not do it. What I would have to say would not have helped him at all." Michael had told me a lot in a short time. We finalized our plans to meet at noon the following Saturday.

On Saturday, Michael got right to the point. "It was financial. No doubt about it. It was financial. During our senior year we often went to lunch at Southglenn Mall or sat in my 1978 Corvette and he would tell me things. Like once he wanted me to do a credit card scam with him. He had it figured out to the last detail. Get a false name and false card. In one day, buy lots of cheap items which we could sell for cash. I told him no. I don't know if he ever did it.

"No, Ross was not a religious person. Or, at least, not obviously. What he talked about mostly was girls and getting laid. He never talked to me about religion. Not once."

I asked Michael what he knew of Ross's parents. "I never met them in all those years. But because I knew that I was coming to meet you for lunch, I asked my girlfriend, Christie. Mr. Carlson was Christie's fifth grade teacher. She remembered when Mr. Carlson once told the class that 'my son could not do this math problem.' Christie thought that was an odd and insulting thing to say. She also remembered that in the fifth grade, Mr. Carlson lost it with a student in the cafeteria. I don't know what the student did, but Mr. Carlson started to shake him for it. Ross was real secretive about his parents.

"Maybe he withheld things from me. I don't know . . . Why did Ross want a gun? Ross had a good reason to have a gun. He sometimes hung around with some pretty dangerous people. With those people, he would need the gun for protection . . .

"His other attorney, Savitz, called me several times. I told Savitz that 'it was another one of his schemes. It just got out of hand.' After a while, Savitz stopped calling.

"The cyborg stuff, that was total bullshit. I was sure he was faking it. This is a guy who would do anything. Blow up a house. Do a credit card scam. It was always extremely well thought out. He always had all the details. Ross was a poor kid who probably thought this was another of his 'deals.' Only this time the 'deal' got out of hand.

"When you saw him," Michael finally asked me, "did he ever show any remorse? I always wondered about that . . . I always wondered how people manage not to care. After he did it, I never called him although I meant to . . ." He looked pained.

I remembered Michael's name in Carlson's letters. "Have you seen Michael?" Carlson asked, or "Have you heard from Michael?" I did not tell that to Batagglia.

"He always wanted to be what he wasn't. But Ross was a smart guy. He was industrious. He was not a yo-yo. He was definitely not a bozo. Ross was the type of person who could have been successful in any business . . . maybe he even could have been a lawyer." Batagglia said the last with a smile on his face. Soon afterward, we shook hands good-bye.

My chance meeting with Michael Batagglia was a blessing. It was a relief to talk with someone who had nothing to prove, no angle to sell, no tactic to try. Batagglia was not a witness for either side. We were not in a court of law; we were just two people talking, wondering what happened and what went wrong.

# 1

## THE CRIME

# · C H A P T E R ·
## O N E
# BODY HEAT

**August 18, 1983**

The Thursday morning the couple was found began like any other Colorado August day, only hotter. To the west of Denver, in the direction of the fourteen thousand foot peaks of the Continental Divide, the air was crisp and clear. But the cool of this early August morning would not last long. The sun, which now climbed the eastern sky, had already driven out the shadows and high desert chill of dawn. You could tell it would be another hot day, over ninety.

Heat was beginning to build in the earth, on the asphalt and wood-shingled roofs of the tract houses which sprawled to the south. On a day like today heat could kill. Already, the whoosh of rainbirds could be heard as they pumped out scarce water in the never ending battle to retain the lush, green patches of lawn in favor of tumbleweed and thistle—the natural state of this high desert plain.

By 7:20 A.M. the sun had been up for over an hour. The morning air was already warm when the bodies were spotted by Roger Gribell, a construction worker on his way to work. Gribell stopped his white pickup. At first glance, the man and woman looked peaceful; there were no signs of a struggle. They lay side by side as if they had fallen asleep on a date.

The searching bright yellow light from the rising sun provided details which could not be seen during the night. In life the woman had been pretty. She had very blond hair, cut medium length. She looked athletic and was approximately five foot two inches tall, and weighed somewhere between one hundred five and one hundred fifteen pounds. She had chosen her last outfit carefully. She wore a comfortable blue pullover blouse, blue skirt with blue and white belt, tan hose, and the kind of cool sandals you can wear all summer in Colorado. She had been married: she wore a double-banded wedding ring. Only by looking carefully could you see the ugly, small bullet hole in the back of her head.

The woman had not died right away. The key sign of her death struggle was the pink froth which now caked the skin around her mouth. She clutched a damp tissue in her right hand and her left arm looked as if she had tried to reach her companion as her life slipped away. She did not succeed.

The man matched the woman. He, too, was neatly dressed in a tan-and-blue pullover shirt, jeans, brown belt, brown socks, and brown tasseled loafers. Close to six feet tall and about one hundred eighty pounds, with brown hair cut short. He did not have a hair out of place except for the small hole where another bullet had punctured his skull. The man also wore a wedding band on his left hand. It was odd to see that his Seiko continued to run even though he had been dead for over eight hours. It later puzzled the police that though the man had been in good shape and could have put up a fierce struggle, he just lay there and died.

After making sure he saw what he thought he saw, Gribell called the police.


### August 17, 1983

Twenty-four hours earlier, Ross Carlson slept late in his bedroom on the second floor of his parents' brick-and-wood two story home in Littleton, Colorado, a comfortable town a few miles south of Denver. Ross had just quit his job selling shoes, and classes at Metropolitan State College had not yet begun. This morning the nineteen-year-old Ross could have lazed in his queen-size bed if he had wanted. But Ross had to get up; he had errands to do.

Ross moved with the easy grace of an athlete as he walked from his exceptionally neat room to the bathroom. Ross was tall, six feet, and powerful, his body well muscled by many hours of lifting weights. He entered the shower and, as he did every morning, thoroughly scrubbed his face. Afterward, he took the antibiotic for his skin though there was hardly a sign of the acne which still worried him. He then went downstairs to the kitchen and popped a piece of cold pizza into the microwave, his usual breakfast. Ross's mood mirrored the big blue Colorado sky; he later said he felt "calm and collected." He had the whole day ahead of him.

Rod and Marilyn Carlson were also still at home this morning; Littleton public schools were in recess, so for the moment they, like their son, could take advantage of the last long days of summer. Marilyn, who had a masters in education, taught kindergarten; Rod taught the sixth grade. They would soon have to begin another school year. But for now, the popular teachers could savor a few more days of rest.

After breakfast Ross chatted with his parents. Later, as often happened, neighborhood children might drop in for milk and cookies and a chat with Marilyn and to play with Ragamuffin, the Carlson's little dog. But first Marilyn was going to Marina Square—an upscale shopping center—to meet a friend for lunch. Rod planned to spend the day getting the yard in shape: Carlson's landscaping was the neatest in the neighborhood and perhaps in all of Littleton.

Rod also planned to pick up a United Airlines ticket for a quick trip to Minneapolis and his twentieth reunion at Roosevelt High. He knew he had to buy his ticket by midnight to qualify for a reduced fare. Therefore, he had to get to Stapleton sometime that night, at least a thirty minute drive. The reunion was going to be on Saturday, August twentieth.

As Ross passed the laundry room door he saw his parents' insurance portfolio and deed for the house lying on the counter. He knew why the papers were out; a real estate appraiser was coming today. The Carlsons hoped to obtain a second mortgage to pay off their new car and for Ross's college tuition. Though he had not yet decided whether he wanted to go to Pepperdine College in California, as his parents wanted, or would spend another year at Metro, Ross knew his parents planned to borrow money to help cover the costs. Rod and Marilyn were schoolteachers and their income was solid but not extraordinary; like many families, they needed the extra cash.

Ross dressed. At 10:30 A.M. he called Susan Keller, an ex–girlfriend. Ross wanted Susan to follow him to a stereo store at the Tamarac Square shopping mall and then give him a ride home. Ross wanted to buy a new stereo for his Oldsmobile Cutlass. Since Susan had plans she had to say no, but told Ross she would call when she got home. Then Ross called David Bassler but Bassler's mother, Shirley, told Ross that David was still at work. David would be home at four.

After she hung up, Susan Keller later told the police, she wondered why Ross needed another stereo since she knew Ross already had an AM-FM cassette. But, at the time, she did not think much of it since she knew Ross was always buying things and always had the best.

Almost every summer afternoon thunderheads sweep across the peaks of the front range and spill over the plains. Most days, dark cloudbursts, lightning, and the rumble of thunder interrupt the torpid heat of Colorado summer afternoons. Today would be no exception.

Ross was out during the afternoon cloud buildup when Kenneth Cortez telephoned. Ken chatted briefly with Rod Carlson and then hung up.

When Ross got home he made two calls. First he made a hurried return call to David Bassler. He told David that the psychology experiment planned for that night in a remote part of town was called off. Ross had promised Bassler fifty dollars for the deal. It had sounded like an exciting evening; an exchange of black bags, a fake drug bust with guns, and a shooting but now it was off.

Ross's second call was to Ken Cortez. But it was already 4:30 and by this time Cortez was out of the office. When Carlson finally reached Cortez at home they agreed to have dinner and take in a movie to honor Cortez's *A* in a summer calculus course. But Cortez's grade was an excuse; the two friends got together a couple of times each week. At first they decided on dinner at 6:30 but Ross later called Ken and asked to change it to 7:00. Ken agreed.

Ross went to his closet and chose his clothes carefully. He was meticulous about his blond, blue-eyed good looks. Tonight, as always, he wanted to look good. He chose a dark blue pinstripe three-piece suit and an expensive, off-white shirt. He knew that his burgundy tie and matching handkerchief would go well with the outfit. Of course, he wore black shoes.

About 5:30 Rod and Marilyn returned from the small Dairy

Queen on South University Boulevard where they had taken an afternoon break. A few minutes later Ross said good-bye to his mother, who had just finished setting the patio table for supper. Rod was still in the yard, in T-shirt and shorts, when Ross left and walked the few blocks south to Kenneth Cortez's house.

## At the Movies

"It seemed to me to be dinner out, an evening at the movies," Ross later said. Movies were a passion for Ross. One particular movie, *Body Heat*, fascinated him. Since the movie had been released in 1981, Ross had seen *Body Heat* as often as he could. But tonight it was *War Games* playing at Tamarac Square which was Ross's destination.

When Susan Keller came home at six, she called Ross to see if he still needed a ride to Tamarac. Marilyn answered the phone and told Susan that Ross was out for the evening. Susan spoke with Mrs. Carlson for a moment, left a message, and hung up.

Sometime later that evening, Rod called his mother in Minneapolis to make the final arrangements for his trip which was three days hence. Today was Wednesday; Rod planned to leave Denver on Saturday and to arrive in Minnesota by 3:30 which would give him plenty of time to reach the reunion festivities.

Ross arrived at the Cortez home at six, just as Susan talked to his mother. Ross was earlier than Ken had expected and Ken, who was still in the shower, was not ready. So Ross shot the breeze with Ken's parents.

Ken and Ross left for dinner sometime between 6:30 and 6:40 in Cortez's '77 Honda Accord. They drove north out of their neighborhood toward Interstate 25 and the Denver Tech Center. The afternoon thunder had receded; the sun was on their left, casting eastward the long shadows of late afternoon. A little more than an hour remained before the sun would set behind the jagged peaks of the Rockies. Usually, the thunderclouds had disappeared by this time of day. But this evening they lingered in the west. Lightning would dance on the horizon all night long.

It is a fifteen minute drive from South Forest Court to the Canterbury Inn. After some small talk, Carlson turned to his friend. This was not going to be one of their normal nights out, Ross told

Ken. Ross had something other than movies on his mind. Something big. And he needed Ken to cover for him.

Ross had told Ken before about big deals and scoring big. A few days earlier Ross told Ken and another friend, Cheri Mettille, about a plan to rip off a drug dealer. Ross estimated that one hundred thousand dollars might be in the jackpot. At first, when Ross started in again, Ken thought Ross was bullshitting, blowing smoke. But tonight Ross began to seem different. As he drove, Ken started to realize that Ross was for real.

Ross asked again: would he cover? Ken had been Ross's schoolmate and friend for years; he spoke to Ross on the phone every day. More to the point, Carlson had used Cortez to cover before in other ways. So when Ross asked again for Ken to provide an alibi, Ken agreed.

A little before seven, the two arrived at the Canterbury Inn, an expensive restaurant known for its prime rib and fake English ambience. They were seated immediately. Andy, their waiter, later recalled that Ross wore a gold chain across his midsection and also noted the three-piece pinstripe suit. Ross seemed relaxed and chatted throughout the meal. Both men ate beef but ordered nothing from the bar.

During dinner, a client of Cortez's came over and chatted about stocks and other financial matters. The friends finished dinner at eight but dawdled over coffee for another fifteen minutes before deciding to go. Ross buttoned his suit jacket as he stood up to leave. He then paid for the entire meal with his credit card. Cortez did not realize it, but Ross was beginning to establish his paper trail alibi for the night.

They again headed north. On the way to Tamarac, Ross told Ken what to do. "If somebody asks where I have been," Ross said, "you tell them I was with you." By now Ken was worried about Ross's safety. What if Ross was having an affair with a married woman? What if Ross really was involved with a drug deal? Ross always seemed to have extra cash and now Ken became alarmed that his friend might be in some sort of danger. Or that he was involved in one scam too many.

Ken pressed Ross. What was he up to? Why keep him in the dark? But Ross said nothing.

Cortez began to waffle on his earlier promise. He would not cover for Ross unless Ross told him who he was going to meet. Again, Ross refused.

Finally, as they approached the theater, Ross told Cortez to pull into a bank parking lot. Ross jumped out, went into the all-night teller, got a deposit envelope and piece of paper, and returned to the car. Ross then wrote a name on the paper, sealed the paper in an envelope, and stuffed the whole thing into the Honda's glove box. "Only open this if I don't return," Ross ordered. Ken stopped his questioning and agreed to the deal.

Laura Branca, who worked tickets that night, had dated Ken and also recognized Ross when they arrived. Laura later told police that Ken and Ross arrived about nine. Ross—as if he wanted to be noticed—asked Laura whether they would have any trouble getting tickets for the last, 9:30, showing of *War Games*. No problem, Laura said, Wednesday nights were slow. Ken and Ross then left. They window-shopped Tamarac and ran into many friends as they cruised the mall.

Ten minutes before show time they returned to the theater, bought their tickets, entered the auditorium, and sat down. The movie started at 9:30. But, as the lights went down, Carlson got up. Ross whispered his last instructions to Ken; he had a deal to do. As Ross left his seat he told Cortez he would meet him after the movie at the car. Ross then headed for the rear exit.

Ross had planned it so Laura would only see him go into the theater, not out. Ross left unnoticed by Laura or anyone else. He went directly to his Oldsmobile Cutlass which he had parked nearby. He checked the trunk for his black bag and then quickly unlocked the door. He then hopped in, put the key into the ignition, and turned the engine over.

It was a little past 9:30. Ross had two hours before the movie was over.

## Cottonwood Road

Ross eased the car out of the lot and turned west on Hampden and then south on Interstate 25, going back the way he had just come thirty minutes before. But a few miles down I-25 there is a two-lane exit which loops to the left and heads northeast; this is the beginning of Interstate 225. Ross took this exit. Ten minutes later he entered the parking lot of the Ramada Renaissance Hotel and International Athletic Club. He found a space, parked, got out, and took the black bag with him.

I do not know whether Ross entered the Club or the Ramada to change. But when he emerged into the parking lot, Carlson had on a pair of jeans, red plaid shirt, and blue jacket. In place of his black loafers were heavy brown boots. He was ready for work. Ross then waited patiently.

Right on schedule, a big dark blue fancy sedan, a 1980 Cadillac Seville, pulled into the lot. Two people sat in the front seat and they were looking for Ross. The car stopped when they spotted him. As Carlson walked to the car, he carried his black bag. Except for a scratch on the right front door, the car was in perfect shape. After hellos, Carlson got into the back seat.

The Cadillac headed south on Parker Road past the empty spaces of Cherry Creek State Recreation Area, quickly leaving the lights and traffic of suburban Denver behind. If people in the cars driving north noticed the occupants of the Cadillac as they passed they would have seen nothing out of the ordinary; just three people in a car having a talk, two in the front and one in back. They could not have seen Carlson open the Triolite bag and take something out.

The Cadillac turned right on Arapahoe and headed west. It crossed Cherry Creek and passed the Valley Country Club. The car then slowed as it approached Jordan Road where it made a sharp left and headed south toward the empty spaces of Douglas County. Houses were becoming less frequent; the smell of rangelands was in the cooling night air. The sky was still cloudy, but by now the lightning had moved its silent dance miles to the west where it continued above the peaks of the Rockies.

The Cadillac crossed the northern boundary of Douglas County; soon it began to slow. To the east was Cottonwood Road, now a dead-end road since the bridge over Cherry Creek had washed out. Carlson knew they were almost there.

The Cadillac swung slowly east on Cottonwood, traveled a quarter of a mile, and then stopped. The car now sat in the middle of nowhere but Carlson had been here before. They had driven thirteen and one-half miles since the Ramada Renaissance.

Carlson opened the rear door and got out. He had added something to his outfit. Carlson now wore a pair of gloves, rubber surgical gloves. And the reason for surgical gloves on this August night became immediately obvious. As Carlson stood in the overcast damp darkness, he held a silver-barreled Rossi .38 Special revolver in his hand and pointed it at the people in the car.

Carlson later said he felt as if things were "speeding up," as if he had been "shot from a cannon." His mind was "doing two hundred miles an hour." He was, he later said, exhilarated. And the gloves? Simple. They were to protect him from the powder burns and blood.

Carlson told the couple to get out and ordered them to lie on the ground. They obeyed. There they lay, faces in the cooling earth, heads to the south, the soles of their shoes four feet from the shoulder of the road on the north. As Carlson stood behind them, the man was to his left, the woman to his right. They lay completely still.

The woman began to cry softly into the white handkerchief she held tightly in her right hand. At the end she was the only one to speak; "This is hell. I don't want to live. Just go ahead and shoot me." The man said not a word. Nothing.

It was like watching himself in the movies, Carlson later said. He walked toward the man first. Carlson stood a little behind and to the left of the man as he raised his hand in front of him; the hand in which he held the gun. Carlson aimed the Rossi .38 Special and squeezed the trigger. *Bang.* The bullet had to travel only two feet. The man jerked as the bullet crashed into his skull, shattering the bone and lacerating the soft gray and white matter of his brain. His vital control centers destroyed, the man's heart and breathing stopped almost immediately.

It must have seemed like an eternity to the woman before Carlson turned his attention to her. But it only took five seconds for Carlson to line up his second shot. He squeezed the trigger again. *Bang.* Carlson should have taken longer and been more careful.

This time Carlson's aim was a little off. The bullet entered low and burrowed through the woman's upper neck and then tore through her throat; as it exited it fractured her jaw and carried away the right side of her mouth. The woman did not die the way the man did. Instead she drowned in her own blood, her lungs acutely distended as she violently gasped for air that could not penetrate the bloody fluid which had quickly filled her lungs.

As the woman lay dying, Carlson scooped up her purse and shoved it, along with the pistol, into the black bag. He ignored the man's wallet which was in the man's right rear pocket and the checkbook in his left. Carlson was on the move.

Carlson got into the Cadillac and retraced his route back to the Ramada. But he had a problem. The couple had brought a dog with them, a gray miniature schnauzer. Carlson had to take care of the dog before he returned to the theater; he had to hurry since now he had to make another trip. He had not planned on this extra time.

When Carlson arrived at the Ramada, he entered the north lot of the hotel. He hurried to the third bank of parking spaces, made a sharp right turn, and braked the car to a stop. He parked so quickly that he took two spots and didn't notice that the right rear fender and wheel of the big Seville hung over the painted white line. Instead he reached down and removed the floor mats, folded them neatly, and put them into his bag. No dirt from Cottonwood could be traced to the Cadillac. Carlson then made sure that the driver's window was down and the keys left in the ignition. The gas tank was three-quarters full.

Carlson hurried to his Cutlass and put the dog in. He reached over, got his suit, and reentered either the hotel or club. When he emerged, moments later, he was again dressed like a banker in his elegant three-piece suit. He had put his work clothes back into the bag. It was after 11:00 P.M.

Carlson then drove back to Littleton. He made little noise as he put the dog in his yard and his Oldsmobile in the garage. He then headed north in his parents' '76 Chevy truck. At 85 Meade Lane he pulled over. Houses in this part of wealthy Cherry Hills Village are built on two acre lots; there were plenty of promising hiding places for his bag. Carlson found the spot he was looking for.

Carlson hid the black bag in tall brush at the base of a pine tree surrounded by dense evergreen bushes and other trees. The cache was approximately fifteen feet due west of a split rail fence on the east edge of the Norgren property. He had done odd jobs for the Norgrens; Carlson knew the area well.

Inside the bag were Carlson's blue jeans, red plaid shirt, his brown leather boots, gray flashlight, one pair of leather and three pairs of rubber surgical gloves. There would be no blood on his three-piece suit. Also inside was, of course, the revolver with two spent shell cases in the cylinder and a black holster both stuffed into one of the boots. Carlson's blue windbreaker was also hidden in the bag. In the jacket's left pocket were another five live rounds of ammunition; a pair of used surgical gloves were in the right. The woman's blue purse, an old blue nylon wallet with a forged driver's license for a Ross Michael Karlson, and the Cadillac's floor mats made up the final contents of the bag.


## Frank Christianson

When the movie was over Ken Cortez walked toward the front of the theater. He had still not seen Ross. Ken spoke briefly to Laura about her plans for college while he kept his eye out for his friend. Ken then went out into the parking lot. Ross, as he said he would, stood by the car.

Ken asked Ross if he was all right. "Yeah, it's done," Ross said simply. To Ken, Carlson seemed subdued but normal. Cortez remembers that Carlson's clothes were crisp and spotless. Upon getting into the Honda, Carlson opened the glove box, pulled out the envelope, and ripped it up into small pieces. "You won't need this anymore," Carlson said as he tossed the paper out the window. The envelope and its contents scattered on the parking lot ground. At that moment Carlson must have relaxed because, as Cortez later told reporters, when they pulled away from the theater Carlson began to sing a little tune. But Cortez could not remember which one.

At 11:46 Ross and Ken stopped at the Tenneco on East Arapahoe Road to buy beer. Carlson paid and kept the receipt. More paper. They then went to Cortez's house. Cortez was tired and he hinted he wanted to go to sleep. But Carlson wanted to stay a little longer. After a couple of beers, Cortez finally dropped Carlson off at home.

But Ken did not go straight back to his house. Instead, he doubled back to Tamarac to find the envelope and the name. A few minutes later he pieced together what he found. He could not understand it. Carlson had written the name "Frank Christianson" on the paper, a man Cortez did not know.

When Carlson entered his house he went into the kitchen. He placed the remaining beer into the refrigerator and put the empty twelve-pack next to the trash can in the garage. He then climbed the stairs to his bedroom. He emptied his suit pockets and was careful to save the ticket stub for *War Games* dated 8/17/83 and purchased at 9:22 P.M. Carlson then hung his dark blue, pinstriped suit neatly in the closet and went to sleep.

The man and woman lay in the dark. Around midnight, the last of the clouds disappeared overhead. The temperature dropped. It was cool compared to the heat of the day, in the fifties. Far to the west, the lightning continued over the mountains until dawn. By the time the sheriff's deputies arrived the temperature was already in the sixties; Thursday was going to be a scorcher.

# SUSPICION

**Thursday, August 18**

Ross Carlson slept through the night. About seven thirty in the morning, just about the time that Roger Gribell stumbled over the dead couple, he heard his doorbell ring. It was two of his mother's teacher friends looking for Marilyn; they, apparently, had planned to meet for breakfast.

Carlson let them in and then he went upstairs for his mother. She wasn't in, he said; perhaps she was out shopping for breakfast. Ross phoned Sandberg Elementary School but no one at the school had yet seen Marilyn. She must have forgotten the meeting, Ross told the women. The two teachers went to Winchell's Donut Shop without her.

At 7:40 A.M., Investigator Gary L. Robinson of the Douglas County Sheriff's office was called to Cottonwood Road on a report of a double homicide. This was Robinson's first homicide investigation. He arrived at 8:05 and was met there by Captain Michael Acree. Many deputies were already involved and combing the area. The checkbook and wallet which Carlson overlooked in the dark were spotted quickly. One deputy, working carefully so not to disturb the ground around the couple, removed them from the man's back pockets. The last check was dated August 16, 1983. It was for twenty dollars and made out to the Roosevelt High School Reunion, Class of 1963.

When Investigator Dempsey heard the name of the victim, he gave a start of recognition and mentioned his concern to his partner, Deputy Gary L. Younger. They then left the murder scene and arrived at the Carlson home on 7009 South Forest Court at 9:30.

At the house they were let in by Ross. He was in the middle of his usual breakfast of pizza and was reading the paper. Younger asked Ross where his parents were. "I don't know," Carlson said. Ross then told the officers of the earlier visit by his mother's colleagues. Ross said he thought that his parents had gone to do some last minute shopping before the breakfast.

The deputies' job was to make sure that the dead man and woman were, in fact, Ross's parents and to tell Ross that his parents were not coming back. Younger asked Carlson for a picture of Rod and Marilyn. While he waited, Deputy Younger saw the portfolio which contained the deed for the Carlson residence. Carlson told Younger that yesterday the house had been appraised for a second mortgage; his parents were going to borrow forty-eight thousand dollars to send him to Pepperdine, a college at Malibu Beach, California.

Ross gave Younger a snapshot of his parents, sitting and smiling at a restaurant table. When Younger saw that they were, in fact, the dead couple on Cottonwood Road, he asked Ross to sit down. He then told Carlson that there had been a double homicide and that the murder victims were likely his parents. Younger later wrote that Carlson looked like a person who had just heard horrible news.

At that moment the phone rang; it was Ken Cortez, making his usual morning call. Only this time, Cortez was worried about "Frank Christianson" and the "deal." Ross told Cortez that police officers were with him; there had been an accident. Cortez, even more alarmed than he had been the night before, left work to come over.

### Alibi

After he hung up the phone, Carlson told Younger that he had last seen his parents at 6:00 P.M. the previous evening. He had no idea where they might be now. It would not be uncommon, he said, for his parents to make plans and not tell him. They often went out for a late dinner and/or drinks.

Carlson said that he had walked over to Cortez's house after saying good-bye and he and Ken Cortez had gone to the Canterbury Inn for dinner to celebrate Cortez's getting an *A* on a calculus test. Then, Carlson said, they saw *War Games* at Tamarac. Afterward, they drove to a Tenneco store for some beer which they drank at Ken's house. When he got home at 1:00 A.M., Ross said, the front door was locked and the lights were on as usual. He entered quietly so as not to disturb his parents. Ross then slept through the night until he was awakened by the first visitors of the day.

Younger asked Carlson about the cars. Younger knew that the registrations were found in Rod's wallet and the cars were not parked outside, nor in the garage. Did Ross know where the 1980 Cadillac and '76 Chevy truck were? His parents probably had the Cadillac, Ross said, and he had not seen the pickup for two weeks. The truck might be at a garage or perhaps his father had loaned it to one of his friends.

Younger hurried to call in a statewide bulletin for the 1980 Cadillac. Likely, when found, the driver of the stolen car would know something about the murders. But, by now, the officers knew something was not right with the story. Ross appeared cooperative and upset. Nevertheless, as soon as Investigator Dempsey had seen Carlson, he knew why he had recognized the Carlson name. He had arrested Carlson eleven months before.

### Dynamite

The dynamite episode, Dempsey had thought the year before, was straightforward. Now he was not sure. In September 1982, Dempsey learned that an officer of the Illinois State Police, who had written an article about explosives for *Soldier of Fortune* magazine, received a letter from a J.N.T. asking for three sticks of dynamite and blasting caps. The letter read in part:

> *Sir, I am in need of some advice. I hope I can, so to speak, shoot straight with you and trust the subject of this letter will go no further. I will come right to the point. I am in need of three sticks of straight dynamite and three electric blasting caps for a project.*

The dynamite, J.N.T. said, was for "nonviolent" reasons. The Englewood, Colorado, return address was a postal box, Dempsey learned, leased by a Ross M. Karlson.

A trap had been set. During the sale, J.N.T. asked if Dempsey could find him a "hot" .38 caliber handgun and ammunition. Yes, Dempsey said. When J.N.T. handed over forty dollars for the dynamite and caps, Dempsey signaled to his backup that an arrest could be made. After a brief escape attempt, J.N.T. was caught. In his wallet was a driver's license which identified J.N.T. as Ross Michael Carlson. J.N.T. stood for Justin Nicholas Time, a name, the police later kidded, made up just in the nick of time.

Why did Carlson want dynamite? Dr. Gregory Wilets, the psychiatrist who treated Ross Carlson when he was placed on probation, said that Carlson was suicidal and wanted to blow himself up. Now, Younger and Dempsey asked Carlson—who gave no hint that he recognized Dempsey—to come with them to the Arapahoe County Sheriff's department.


**Suspicion**

As they were about to leave, Ken Cortez drove up and spoke briefly with his friend. "Keep to the story," Carlson urgently whispered. The two officers and Carlson then left, but Cortez stayed. Investigator Keith Schooler, one of the officers who had also arrived that morning, was busy interviewing neighbors when he noticed Cortez hanging around clearly upset.

To Officer Schooler, Cortez looked as "one suffering from great anxiety." But he was not helpful when Schooler approached him. No, he was not aware of trouble between Ross and his parents. No, he hadn't noticed anything strange. Yes, he and Ross were at the movies last night. Schooler arranged to meet Cortez at the Arapahoe County Sheriff's department at 3:00 P.M. Cortez then went home, severely disturbed by what he had seen and what he had learned.

However, at 1:45 P.M. Cortez came back, again agitated. Once again, Schooler attempted to get Cortez to talk. "Was there something you want to say?" No. Although Schooler tried to talk with Cortez, he left, saying he had to get back to work. He would meet Schooler at the sheriff's office later.

Shortly after noon, Younger, Dempsey, and Carlson arrived at the Arapahoe County Sheriff's department where Carlson repeated his story. Listen guys, it was dinner followed by a movie and a few beers. That was all. The deputies had nothing.

At 2:30 P.M. Carlson went out into the hall to make some telephone calls. When he returned, Carlson said he wanted to go home. So far, the deputies could not hold him. Investigator Dempsey walked Carlson out to his police car, the two men got in, and they began to drive back to Forest Court. But one of the calls Carlson had made was to his psychiatrist, Dr. Wilets. Twenty minutes later, Wilets returned Carlson's call. By then, Dempsey and Carlson were almost at the Carlson home.

When Wilets learned of the murders from a deputy he became frightened. Carlson had been suicidal in the past, he told the deputy. He also knew that Carlson had just had a fight with his parents. It crossed Wilets's mind that Carlson might have, in some way, been responsible for their deaths. Wilets told the deputy to get Carlson back because he might be in danger of committing suicide. Dispatch quickly radioed Dempsey. Just moments before he was to drop Carlson off, Dempsey turned his cruiser around and headed back.

When Carlson was brought back in, he was told by Younger that his parents had been positively identified; there was no longer any question about who they were. This time, according to Younger, Carlson did not bat an eye. Instead, Carlson asked Younger what would happen if he tried to leave. Carlson was told that he was being held for a mental health evaluation.

## Cortez

At 3:00 P.M. Cortez showed up at the sheriff's office and promptly ran into Ross in the hallway. Out of earshot of the others, Carlson told him not to "spill the beans." But Cortez confronted his friend and asked the question which was, by now, burning in his mind.

"Did you kill your parents?" Cortez asked.

"No," Carlson said, he was not the one who had done it.

"Ross, do you know who did it?" Cortez kept on.

"I can't tell you," said Ross. His parents, Carlson said, had found out some deal he was going to do and tried to break it up. They failed and got shot. "They tried to Lone Ranger it," Carlson said. Cortez asked yet again, "Who shot them?" But Carlson would not say.

Since Schooler had not yet returned, another officer began the interview with Cortez. Cortez said he wanted to tape the entire thing and was told that was fine. Cortez, dressed in a two-piece gray suit and a shirt and a tie, seemed agitated. But he held to the alibi.

They were then joined by Captain Michael Acree. Cortez told the two men that he and Carlson had gone to dinner and a movie and that after the movie they went out and bought some beer. Cortez said that Carlson had been with him the whole night from six to one in the morning. Cortez got this all on his recorder.

But Cortez was keyed up and the officers pressed. Cortez was obviously nervous and the two men knew about the dynamite. The officer asked Cortez for details, and to go over the story again and again. This proved to be too much for Cortez and he began to leak some of the details. The big one, of course, was that as soon as the theater lights went down, Carlson got up, told Cortez he had "a deal" to do, and left by the rear exit.

At that, the first officer left; he wanted to search for the missing cars. Acree continued the interview. Cortez then told the captain that after the movie he found Ross waiting and that they went to a Tenneco station, bought a twelve-pack, went to Ken's house, had a couple, and then Ken drove Ross home. Cortez added that Carlson seemed just fine when he returned.

But Cortez did not add what he thought was the key detail. It was only after he was asked to take a lie detector test that Cortez finally told Acree how he had pressed Carlson to write down the name of the man he was to meet: Frank Christianson. He did not reveal that name for one simple reason. He was frightened that Christianson was still on the loose; that Carlson—and Ken—might still be in danger.

About the time that Cortez revealed Christianson's name, the black and silver 1976 Chevrolet pickup truck was found on the southeast corner of Tamarac and Eastman. Coils of clean, white rope were behind the rear seat. Three-foot lengths of freshly cut rope lay behind the seat on the passenger's side.


### Prime Suspect

Carlson was confronted with his lie. He was now the prime suspect; the police were sure he was connected with the killings, but they couldn't prove it. Yet. They had Cortez's statement but they had nothing to physically link Carlson to Cottonwood Road. It was then that Carlson said he wanted to call an attorney and all questioning stopped.

At 9:05 P.M. Ross tried to reach Cortez, but Ken was not home and Ross spoke, instead, to Ken Senior. Ross said that Ken "had said some things that could hurt him." He wanted Ken "to change his story. It would help a great deal." Ross went on to say, "It would be like getting an early Christmas present." Mr. Cortez did not know what Ross was talking about. To him, Ross sounded calm, like nothing much was out of the ordinary.

Carlson then called Dr. Wilets again and begged him to get him out. "I just want one hour out of the station," he said. Carlson wanted just one hour "alone" with Wilets in his car. He again pleaded with his doctor. "Dr. Wilets, just do me this one big favor— get me out of here." Then he added, "You know I am not exactly the all-American boy but you don't think I did it, do you?" Luckily, Dr. Wilets did not take Carlson for a drive. His prudence may have saved his life.

Later that evening, Carlson was contacted by a junior partner of Walter Gerash, one of the most celebrated—and certainly the most flamboyant—defense attorneys in Denver. How Carlson got to Gerash so quickly is still a mystery. Later, law enforcement officials speculated that Carlson had long planned to use Gerash if his alibi turned sour.

But fame did not come cheap. Gerash would take the case only with a steep retainer, which, according to news articles, was said to be somewhere between seventy-five and one hundred thousand dollars. Carlson did not have the money so, for now, he would have to depend on Craig Truman and the Public Defender's Office.

A little after nine, a call came in that Cortez had panicked and was now hiding out at a friend's house. Cortez had just contacted a deputy and asked for an escort; he said he thought he might be killed. He told the deputy that he was still frightened of Frank Christianson though, when pressed, Ken said he didn't know who or where Christianson was. But Ken also admitted that he was scared of Ross Carlson if he were released that night.

## Admission

Toward midnight, Carlson was examined by a sleepy mental health worker of the local mental health center, who was unimpressed with the seriousness of Carlson's suicide potential and wanted to send Carlson home. Dr. Wilets, alarmed at this turn of events, decided to come in. He arrived at the jail a couple of hours later with his partner.

It was now in the early morning of August 19. Carlson told the two psychiatrists that he had suicidal thoughts since the age of five and repeated the story that he had planned to kill himself with the dynamite. Since the dynamite episode, Carlson said, he had felt "paranoid" and that he was "being bugged." He said he thought that "robots had placed him on this planet." The psychiatrists placed Carlson on a mental health hold and he was transferred to the Colorado Psychiatric Hospital at 4:00 A.M. Friday, August 19, and evaluated on the emergency service which I run. He then was admitted to our inpatient ward for further observation and treatment.

# EVEN MONKEYS FALL
# FROM TREES

**Friday, August 19**

When Dr. Wilets called our hospital to arrange for Carlson's admission, Wilets told the resident on duty that Carlson had been suicidal on and off over the past year. It began, Wilets said, in September 1982 when Carlson had tried to buy dynamite to kill himself. On the recommendation of Carlson's lawyer, Wilets recounted, he began treating Carlson the day after his arrest. Then like any middle-class kid following a first offense, Carlson was placed on probation.

In his first report to the court, Wilets said that Carlson was no longer dangerous to himself. Furthermore, "To the best of my knowledge," Wilets said, "he never planned to harm anyone else." Carlson even referred a friend to Wilets because he thought Wilets was such a "good psychiatrist." When Carlson wanted to take a summer break, Wilets agreed.

At the end of July, Wilets got a frantic phone call from Marilyn Carlson. She had found some expensive clothing which Ross could not account for. Then Marilyn listened to Carlson's answering machine and heard an older woman call. At the meeting with Wilets, Ross told his parents that these were gifts for going out with women. His father accused Ross of being a gigolo.

Wilets resumed treating Ross and last saw him on August 2. Carlson missed the ninth and Wilets was delayed on the eleventh and by the time he arrived Ross had already gone home. They rescheduled for Tuesday the sixteenth, but before that session Marilyn called and said that Ross was sick. The next day was Wednesday, the night of the murders.

Ross Carlson was admitted to our psychiatric unit, 8 East, under a mental health law which allowed us to keep him for up to three days. Any time during those seventy-two hours Carlson could be released—or certified for a longer, thirty day stay. Although the doors were locked, 8 East is a psychiatric unit, not a jail. It was not unusual for patients to slip out. This ward was not designed for murderers. When he arrived, Carlson was searched—as all patients routinely are—and his clothes locked in the utility room. Among Carlson's possessions were one record album, one cassette radio player, thirteen tapes, and two stuffed animals.

## The First Examination

Carlson did not look like a murderer nor did he look like his parents had just died. In fact, upon admission, the resident described Carlson as "well-groomed, smiling, and composed." She also found "little indication of depression or grieving" and no abnormalities in Carlson's mental state. He knew who he was, where he was, and when it was. When asked to explain what "you can't tell a book by its cover" meant he said, "Insides can't be judged by the cosmetics outside." When asked the meaning of "Even monkeys fall from trees" he replied: "Anyone can make a mistake."

He denied being suicidal—contradicting what he told Wilets at the jail—but also said that he was "not free to talk about anything because of the possible legal implications," the advice he had just gotten from Walter Gerash's partner the night before. He then added that he knew he was "a prime suspect" in double murder. That was all.

When the resident, who now had to perform a physical exam, asked Carlson to take off his shirt, he removed it dramatically and stood with his chest protruded and stomach tucked in as if he were a Marine at attention or someone at a beach party muscle show. Later the resident wrote Carlson had a great need to be admired. When she left, she thought Carlson wanted her to stay.

## Mr. and Mrs. America

Carlson was big news in the hospital in the morning. When the resident presented the case to me and told me he was admitted, my first thought was that Ross Carlson was hospitalized because he was the distraught child of a cruelly murdered couple. No wonder he was suicidal.

On the front page of *The Denver Post* under the headline SCHOOL-TEACHER COUPLE FOUND SHOT TO DEATH I read the story of the death of an "all-American couple" who were "found Thursday morning shot to death—execution-style on a dirt road in Douglas County."

"Neighbors," the report said, "obviously shaken by the news and passing information around the cul-de-sac, described the Carlsons as conservative, nondrinking churchgoers . . . 'They were Mr. and Mrs. America,' said [a close friend] . . . 'Just look at their house on the corner. It is the neatest on the block. In fact, it's about the neatest in the whole subdivision of 400 homes.' He went on to describe Ross Carlson as 'a good-looking, popular boy who had everything he wanted.' "

## Thirty Days

On Friday evening, Carlson was interviewed by Dr. Joe Horn, a soft-spoken psychiatric resident from Arkansas, who was assigned to Carlson's case. Dr. Horn had to decide whether Carlson could be discharged when the seventy-two hours were up. He asked Carlson about the murders. All he remembered, Carlson said, was that he had found out about the murders while eating breakfast at home. "I can't imagine why anyone would want to harm my parents. The murder was such a waste." He had, Carlson told Dr. Horn, just lost his "most prized possessions."

But when Carlson told him that "I would have no qualms about suicide," Dr. Horn was relieved. This was all he needed to prolong Carlson's stay. When Dr. Horn asked for more, Carlson got a "blank expression on his face." Carlson then told Horn that he had been advised that anything he said could possibly be used against him. "I can't talk about anything but the weather."

Dr. Horn filed a thirty day certification on Friday night. If it went uncontested and was not prolonged, Carlson would be discharged no later than Sunday, September 18, unless, of course, Carlson decided to become a voluntary patient or the certification was extended. Carlson slept well that first night in the hospital.


## Investigation

The police were busy on Friday, Carlson's first day in the hospital. They learned that on Wednesday, Rod had called his mother in Minnesota telling her about his class reunion. He then told his mother that he and Marilyn were going to go out to dinner. After dinner they were to meet Ross at a health club, the one next to the Ramada Renaissance Hotel.

The police were contacted with bits of information. Investigator Schooler was told some odd things by Cheri Mettille, one of Carlson's slew of girlfriends. When she met Carlson in October 1982, Ross told her that he was sixteen but that he was in the process of legally changing his age so that he could be "older." Ross also told Mettille that he had a twin brother who beat him so badly that his parents sent him to live with an aunt in Arizona. This brother, Justin Nicholas Time, had grown into a "muscular, successful businessman," according to Carlson.

Mettille also told Schooler that Carlson always "needed money" and that nine days before the shooting said that "If you want something bad enough, you'll do anything to get it." Mettille asked Ross whether he would kill for it. Ross told her "No, I don't think I could."

Later, Captain Acree met at the District Attorney's office with the other investigators and Chief Deputy D.A. Robert Chappell, the prosecutor assigned to the case. Their problem was simple. While Carlson was in the hospital, they had to build their case. But unless they found something to tie Carlson to Cottonwood Road, they could not arrest him. They knew they had to scramble because Carlson would not stay in the hospital forever.


## Saturday, August 20

The next day, *The Denver Post* ran a first page follow-up story accompanied by Carlson's picture, shirt collar open, with a slight smile. This was the first time I saw who Ross Carlson was. He was a nice-looking kid but to me his face was too perfect and his lips were a little too full.

Carlson was "in protective custody at the University of Colorado Health Sciences Center," said the reporter. But this was the first time I learned of the dynamite and it finally dawned on me that we might have a killer upstairs. I felt queasy. Why would a son kill his parents? He must have been abused, I thought, and was just protecting himself.

The reporter described Carlson as a 1982 Heritage High School graduate who was currently studying psychology at Metropolitan State College. Carlson, "an· avid weight lifter," was called by acquaintances "an extremely handsome teenager and an average to above average student." "He was a real friendly guy who liked people," said one eighteen-year-old friend. "He dressed nice—a real classy guy," said the student.

An uneasy note crept in at the end of the article. A teacher at Heritage High, who did not want to be identified, said Carlson exhibited "erratic behavior . . . teachers used to talk about how strange Ross was. There was definitely something different about him."

Carlson slept until 9:15 A.M. When he awoke, he was cheerful despite the fact that the one task he had to accomplish that day was to decide what clothes his parents would be buried in. Carlson was visited by a friend's father who told the nurses that he worried about Carlson's "comfort." Carlson was "well thought of" by his friends, he said, and he thought Carlson was being mistreated. The police, he said, needed a "scapegoat." That evening, Carlson walked out of the day room when a TV news report about his parents came on.


## Leads

On Saturday—the day Rod was to fly to Minnesota and his reunion —while Carlson chose his parents' outfits, the police attended to the tedium of checking out leads. The manager of the Tamarac Square Theater identified the ticket receipt from Carlson's bedroom. It was bought at 9:22 P.M. for the 9:30 to 11:30 P.M. showing. The manager confirmed that it was easy for someone to buy a ticket and then leave by the rear doors without being noticed.

The woman who sold tickets corroborated Cortez's version of events. Laura Branca had seen Carlson and Cortez around 9:00 P.M.; at 11:30 P.M. she had spoken to Cortez who told her that Ross was waiting for him out by the car. Laura also said that Carlson had come in to the theater earlier that summer while she was working there—perhaps when *War Games* was already playing. Ross had spoken to her and she was positive that he remembered her from the days when she dated Ken Cortez. So Carlson probably had seen *War Games* before August 17.

The 1980 Cadillac was found on Saturday afternoon in the lot north of the Ramada Renaissance Hotel. It had been parked quickly; the keys were in the ignition and the driver's window was down. It was a setup to be stolen. The radio was tuned to a station which played "easy listening" music.

Officers also checked memberships at the International Athletic Club. Neither Rod, Marilyn, nor Ross was listed. They also found no leads at the three restaurants in the motel but guessed that sometime between 9:30 and 11:30 on the night of August 17, Ross Carlson had been there.

**Lucky Breaks**

But the news of Saturday was Wayne Heatley. He was the first of what Chief Deputy D.A. Robert Chappell soon started to call the "lucky breaks" of the case. Heatley, an old friend of Carlson's, called the sheriff's office with news that excited the deputies. Heatley thought he knew the murder weapon.

Three months before, Heatley bought Carlson a revolver and two boxes of ammunition. It was a double action revolver, nickel-plated with a blue cylinder, Heatley remembered. Heatley thought that it was a Rossi. Investigator Robinson accompanied Heatley to 937 South Sheridan Boulevard where they met with Elwyne Martin, who confirmed Heatley's story. Martin sold the Rossi to Heatley on May 17, three months before the killings.

As Ross had waited in the car, Heatley bought the gun with one hundred and fifty dollars of Ross's money. When Heatley handed over the gun, Ross told Heatley to tell no one. His parents would take it away, Ross said. Heatley watched Ross put the gun and bullets into a black bag. At the time he bought the gun, Carlson still faithfully attended his sessions with Dr. Wilets. He was not telling Wilets anything.

**Memorial**
On Sunday, August 21, a memorial service was held for Rod and Marilyn. Carlson insisted that he go. The psychiatric staff thought this might be a good opportunity for Carlson to do "grief work" and Carlson left the unit accompanied by a university police officer and a ward attendant.

Four hundred teachers, friends, students, and family gathered for the afternoon service. The Carlsons were described as "dedicated educators whose lives were devoted to teaching." Afterward, Carlson showed "a lot of emotion." To the attendant, Carlson seemed genuinely upset. The service, the attendant thought, had put Ross in touch with the fact that his parents were "really" dead.

That evening, a visit with his grandparents, aunt, and uncles lasted from 8:30 to 9:45 in the evening. The nurses commented that Ross was tearful during the meeting but that night Carlson slept well. The next day Carlson wrote a note thanking the staff for allowing him to go to the memorial service. "It meant," Carlson wrote, "a great deal to me!"

**The Black Bag**
Another call came in to the police on Monday. A Loretta Norgren told police that Carlson had done maintenance and landscape work for her family since he was fourteen years old. Recently they discovered Carlson had stored what looked like stolen goods at their house at 85 Meade Lane. In July her daughter, Kim, found several expensive suits in the basement closet, sizes thirty-eight to forty-six. She also found boxes in the barn area. The Norgrens told Ross to remove his things, the goods which precipitated Marilyn's crisis call to Dr. Wilets in mid-July. Kim saw Carlson remove a black bag. This was the second black bag which had been spotted. Heatley said Carlson had put the gun into one as well. Now the police began to look for it.

**Routine**
By now Carlson had been in the hospital four days and had developed a routine. His day was punctuated by the many telephone calls he would make and receive. He had a steady stream of visitors, often young women. Once a nurse saw that he had his arm around

one while he secretly touched the hand of another. Carlson erratically attended ward groups. When he did, he said nothing about himself. One day he announced, "I am doing my best to appear as normal as possible here." He began to blame Dr. Wilets for his hospitalization.

Carlson always had a book by his side. Almost every evening he would exercise vigorously. "A good healthy body keeps a controlled, healthy mind," he told a nurse. He appeared to sleep well, usually retiring around midnight and getting up around 9:00 the next day.

## August 24

One week after his parents' death, Carlson told Dr. Horn that he had finished grieving—"I am now going to bed with dry eyes these days" even though Wednesday was the day Rod and Marilyn were buried in Minnesota. That evening, Carlson spoke with his pastor. On the surface, Carlson was calm.

Earlier that day, Investigator Robinson picked up Carlson's probation records. Carlson last checked in with his officer on July 18, one month before the killings. Ross, the officer had written, was "cooperating in the program."

Investigator Robinson also learned that the Carlsons had applied for a second mortgage on their home for forty-eight thousand dollars just seventeen days before their death. Rod had mentioned that some of the money was for Ross's education and some of the money was to be used to take care of "his son's obligations." On the day of the murder, the house was appraised and the loan approved.

## Back Door Man

Wednesday evening Dr. Wilets wrote an order that if Carlson should "escape" or be "discharged" he, Dr. Wilets, must be notified immediately. Clearly, something frightened Dr. Wilets. Wilets also said that Carlson experienced "rapid shifts in ego states." He moved quickly from rage to depression to being overly polite. Wilets said that he "never in the year I have worked with him witnessed such intense anger and rage." Wilets reiterated his order to be notified if Carlson should get out.

After meeting with Wilets, Carlson told Dr. Horn that he was

being "mistreated." Carlson said that he had been told by his lawyer not to fight the mental health certification but he had an urge to
"tear somebody up." He also said that if he wanted to he could
escape. Around 5:00 P.M. Carlson was seen, for the first time, checking the lock on the rear fire escape door. He had already been
warned to stay away from them; now, he was told never to do that
again. Ross then spent the evening reading and on the phone. Afterward, he exercised in his room and slept all night.

The next day, Friday, the eighth of his hospitalization, the police
found out about other Carlson attempts to buy guns. A Jim Peelor
said he met Carlson in high school and had taught Carlson karate.
Peelor, who had a gun collection, said Carlson many times asked
him to buy an unregistered or "hot" gun for him. Carlson wanted a
.357 Magnum or a .38 Special. Peelor told Carlson about the Rossi,
but according to Peelor, Carlson was not interested because it was in
a gun shop. He did not want a record made of the purchase.

## Search

No record was found somewhere else too. On Friday Investigator
Robinson learned that the Colorado Bureau of Investigation lab did
not find blood on Carlson's three-piece suit—the suit Carlson wore
on the night of the killings. But Robinson had one piece of good
news. The bullets removed from the bodies were fired from a Gar-
cia-Rossi revolver and both bullets came from the same gun. The
bullets were .38/.357 caliber, at least one hundred twenty-five
grains, semijacketed with six lands and grooves with a right hand
twist.

The police were now certain they knew who the murderer was,
which gun he used, and who had it until the night of August 17. But
the police had to find the gun. Despite the ballistics, Cortez, Heatley, and Peelor, they could do nothing. They needed the Rossi to
tie Carlson to the crime. There was not enough to charge Carlson
and the thirty days would soon be up. On Saturday, August 27, with
the news about the gun fresh in their minds, Captain Acree and
Investigator Robinson led search teams along the roadsides of the
most probable route Carlson took from Cottonwood Road back to
the theater. Nothing was found.

That morning Carlson refused to meet with Dr. Wilets. He was
"imprisoned," Carlson said, and blamed Wilets. Carlson, clearly,

was itching to leave. Dr. Wilets met with Carlson on Monday. Afterward, Carlson saw Craig Truman, his public defender. On Tuesday, August 30, Carlson stood near the doors. He was warned but the next day did the same thing. Now the staff was alarmed, not only about Carlson's suicide potential but about fears that he would escape. They decided to watch him more closely. On September 2, Carlson requested an increase in hospital privileges so that he could take walks outside. He was refused.


## Football
Sometime during the week of September 4, eleven-year-old David Trigg, while he played with his father, kicked a football into his neighbors' yard. The neighbors happened to be the Norgrens, for whom Carlson had worked. David hustled over the fence, through the bushes, very dense underbrush, and weeds. He stopped short when he stumbled on the black bag lying at the base of the tree, well hidden from view. David told his father, a Seventeenth Street lawyer, about his interesting discovery. Mr. Trigg, in good lawyerly fashion, told his son to leave the bag alone. The bag was not his business. But the picture of the black bag, lying in the weeds, stayed in David's head.

On Monday, September 5, Carlson met with his public defender, Craig Truman, for an hour. By now it was clear that the police knew that Carlson had done it, but they could not prove it. However, Truman had to plan for any eventuality. One possible defense, if Carlson were tied to the shootings, was to plead him not guilty by reason of insanity.

The next day, however, Carlson was upbeat. "I am," he said, "just waiting until they turn me loose." He now spoke even less with other patients and staff. Why? Because, Carlson said, "My lawyer told me not to talk with staff much." Later that week he did speak. When asked what happened to his parents, he teared up and said, "They were going out to eat or to a movie and they picked up a hitchhiker and something happened and then they were gone."


## Dr. John Macdonald
On Monday, September 12, Carlson had his first of four meetings with Dr. John Macdonald—the dean of forensic psychiatry in Den-

ver, and a professor in our department. Craig Truman, Carlson's attorney, chose Macdonald and Sy Sundell to see Carlson because he knew Chappell would believe these two psychiatrists if they said that Carlson was insane.

Truman met Macdonald at his office and walked with him to the psychiatric ward where he introduced him to Carlson. Truman urged Carlson to be candid, to tell Macdonald everything and told Ross that these evaluations were strictly confidential. Macdonald met with Carlson again on September 13, 14, and 15.

After his second meeting with Dr. Macdonald, Carlson became agitated. He told the nursing staff that he intensely feared going to prison. "I won't last seventy-two hours in jail." He said that he would be "beaten up" by inmates. He then added, "Someone who fears my talking may come in and blow me away." He wouldn't say who, because it "would be worse for me in the long run" if he did. Something that Macdonald said clearly frightened him. Nonetheless, at 7:30 that evening, Carlson's suicide precautions were dropped. It was becoming increasingly clear that if the police would not take him, Carlson would soon go home.

## Celebration

The next day, Carlson was excited about the change in his status. He was now able to wear his street clothes instead of pajamas. As usual, he spent much of the day on the phone. Carlson also attributed his bright spirits to something Truman had told him. "At this point," Truman had said, "the police have nothing to file charges with and they probably cannot come up with anything at all." That evening, with one of his girlfriends at his side, he ordered pizza to "celebrate."

The results of Macdonald's evaluation were confidential. So after Macdonald met with Carlson for the last time, Macdonald passed on to Truman what he found. Macdonald never put anything into writing and he did not tell the ward staff a thing.

## Discharge

Dr. Horn and the staff were in a box, unclear about what they should do next. I was not directly involved in Carlson's care, but what I heard made me uneasy. The thirty days were quickly coming to an end; we could not keep Carlson forever. The police had to do something. By law, we had to discharge Carlson when we thought he was no longer a danger to himself or others. A discharge date would have to be set. Dr. Horn picked Wednesday, the twenty-first of September, three days beyond the thirty and exactly five weeks to the day from the shootings.

That evening Carlson was seen close to the doors as furniture was moved in and out of the ward. Later he tried opening one of the fire escape doors. When confronted, Carlson said, "I wanted to check the fire escape door because Dr. Macdonald and I meet there and an unlocked door would not be good." Carlson was put back into pajamas.

Discharge was still Wednesday. For some reason, that night Carlson had trouble falling asleep. The next morning, Saturday, September 17, Carlson was visited by Truman. Carlson demanded his clothes back. The staff told him that he would have to stay away from the door.


### David Trigg

For the past week, many leads had been followed but not much was happening; there were no more lucky breaks. Then on Friday, the day Dr. Horn decided to let Carlson go, Investigator Robinson met with Nancy Trigg. Nancy had dated Carlson during the summer of 1980. Trigg told Robinson that Carlson seemed to like his parents, but mainly talked about himself. Carlson's goal, she said, was "to be a millionaire before he was twenty-one." When Robinson asked Nancy whether she had seen the black bag, she said no. Then Robinson left.

When brother David came home from school, Nancy described her conversation with the investigator. When she mentioned the bag, the picture of the bag he saw while playing flashed through David's head. David told his sister what he had seen almost two weeks before. He retraced his steps and showed Nancy the bag, which still lay hidden on the Norgren property. Nancy Trigg called Robinson back.

At 7:25 P.M. Robinson arrived at 85 Meade Lane and was led to the bag. It lay fifteen feet west of the split rail fence on the east edge of the Norgren property and twenty feet north of the split rail fence on the south edge of the Norgren property, right where Carlson had left it four weeks before. It was four days before Carlson was to leave the hospital; Carlson could have destroyed it easily when he got out.

## Yom Kippur

The circle closed. On Saturday the black bag was opened. In it were the Cadillac's floor mats, the .38 caliber Rossi, ammunition, Marilyn's purse, Ross Karlson's phony driver's license, surgical gloves, and Carlson's clothes, his red plaid shirt, jeans, and brown work boots. Carlson was tied forever to Cottonwood Road. Robinson, with the help of Chief Deputy D.A. Bob Chappell, prepared a warrant for Ross Michael Carlson's arrest.

The bag was the flaw in Carlson's plan. He had been too sure of himself, too certain he would get to the bag before it was found. But anyone can make a mistake; even monkeys fall from trees. At 11:30, Saturday night, Robinson, Captain Acree, and two deputies came to 8 East and, thirty-one days after he executed them in cold blood, arrested Ross Michael Carlson for the murder of his parents. He was charged with murder in the first degree—two counts. Robinson advised the cuffed Carlson of his Miranda rights. Carlson remained silent. Then Robinson transported Carlson to the Douglas County Jail. Nothing was said to or by Carlson during the forty-five minute trip. In Carlson's cassette player was an album by a group called "The Police."

When I heard of his arrest, I thought the timing was appropriate. Ross Carlson, raised by his parents to be a devout Baptist, likely was not aware that the day his black bag was opened, the day he was trapped, the day he was arrested, was the most holy day of the Jewish year: the day of atonement, Yom Kippur.

A front page article in *The Denver Post* on September 20 announced Carlson's arrest. "The discovery of a gun in a black suitcase hidden in weeds, along with statements made by friends," read the lead paragraph, "led to the arrest of a 19-year-old Littleton man in connection with the slaying of his parents . . ." Later that morning, Robinson examined Carlson's belongings from the hospital and found the keys to the Chevy truck and Cadillac. He also found a letter from Psi Chi, the National Honor Society of Psychology, which invited Ross Carlson to join.

## The Perfect Crime

For Chief Deputy D.A. Robert Chappell the Carlson murders were superlative. This was, Chappell said, the closest thing to a perfect crime he had ever seen. It took a lot of police work and a big chunk of luck to find the bag four days before Carlson could get to it. It was total luck that "some poor jerk," in Chappell's words, did not steal the Cadillac which sat at the Ramada for three days, window down, keys in the ignition, begging to be stolen, only to be caught halfway to Kansas and accused of the double homicide.

Deputy D.A. Chappell always would have known that Carlson did it. But Carlson would have been sitting pretty with half a million from his parents' insurance and the sale of the house. Carlson told Nancy Trigg that he wanted to be a millionaire by age twenty-one; by August seventeenth he was halfway there.

Chappell could have suspected Ross forever but he could do nothing about it without something to tie Ross Carlson to Cottonwood Road. So when David Trigg remembered the black bag full of incriminating evidence the situation changed one hundred and eighty degrees.

Bob Chappell thought his case was now the tightest "murder one" he had ever seen. It was two counts in the first degree, a prosecutor's dream. Chappell could prove premeditation. Investigators had uncovered months of Carlson's planning: the gun, the gloves, the site, the movie, the alibi. Chappell had the timing, he had the route, he had the bodies, and he had the weapon. And most important, he could tie the Rossi .38 Special to Ross Michael Carlson's hand fifteen different ways. No problem. Open and shut. Next case.

Deputy D.A. Chappell is from Nebraska. Straightforward; he attacks head-on. In the courtroom he likes to slug it out toe-to-toe; in Chappell's world, the man with the best case wins. In Carlson, Chappell knew he had the best case. If Chappell needed a thousand pieces to complete Carlson's jigsaw puzzle he already had 999. But soon after it began, Chappell found out he was wrong. Somewhere along the line, the best case he was ever given on a silver platter turned sour. It started to stink and he tried to figure out why.

# WELCOME TO THE CIRCUS

# ·CHAPTER·
## FOUR

# ENCOUNTER WITH ANTICHRIST

**December 1987**

I popped the tape into my VCR, punched on the power, sat back, and watched. It was now four years after Carlson's arrest. This, D.A. Bob Chappell told me with a smirk, was the evidence that Ross Carlson had multiple personality disorder, MPD. Against my better judgment, I had reentered the fray. I now had to review Carlson's record of the past four years.

There had been hundreds of hours of testimony in front of three judges. Thousands of pages had been generated with ten thousand copies. Ross Carlson, if he did nothing else, was doing a lot for the economy of Colorado. He had already fed a lot of people for a very long time.

Black, blue, red, magenta, green, cyan, yellow, white. The test pattern's eight vertical splits covered my screen. I heard expectant clatter behind the electronic curtain of color; chairs were shifted, microphones clicked into place, and shoes shuffled on what sounded like a hard tile floor.

Suddenly a quick, close, head shot. I recognized his deep-set blue eyes, his sharp and handsome, almost too pretty, face. He was an alert, blond version of Tom Cruise, except his features were a little more angular; they were more like a hawk, a bird of prey.

Noise came from Carlson's right. As he turned, his blue-eyed stare was so hard that too much white showed around his eyes. But his hands stayed crossed calmly in his lap, and his right leg remained draped languidly over his left knee. Except for the intensity in his eyes, Carlson looked as if this were a talk show and he the guest of honor. Except, this was not a talk show.

The noise came from Dr. Robert Fairbairn—one of Carlson's chief defenders and my colleague at the university. Bob Fairbairn set up this interview which took place on a fine spring day, Friday, April 6, 1984, behind the bars of the Douglas County Jail.

This would be the second time I consulted to the state hospital at Pueblo on Carlson. The first was in 1984, seven months after Fairbairn made this tape. Then, I met Carlson within the walls of the red-bricked maximum security building which housed the criminally insane. Carlson was as impenetrable as the electric locks, bars, gates, and maze of caged yards which kept the citizens of Colorado safe. After the third time we met, I wanted nothing more to do with Ross Carlson, his lawyers, or his case.

His lawyers, the high-profile Walter Gerash and cocounsel David Savitz, were hard on those who doubted that Carlson suffered from multiple personality disorder. But there was a more basic reason I wanted out. Behind his seductive good looks, I thought Ross Carlson was brutal and I had to admit to myself I was scared. So in 1984, I made my recommendations, wrote a short note, signed my name, and hoped I was off the hook.

Just weeks before I sat down to watch this tape, a judge came down hard on the state and again accused the hospital of "warehousing" Carlson and ordered it to devise a new treatment plan for Carlson's MPD. My department chairman then asked me to set up a panel of experts to help the state's doctors, and now I had to face Carlson again.

My eyes fixed on the screen. Bob Fairbairn was about to begin. Ross Carlson had said little to me; I wanted to see what he would say to Fairbairn. I thought Carlson would be more cooperative; Fairbairn was hired by the defense and I had just read Fairbairn's report.

When he first met Carlson on February 26, 1984, thirty-nine days before he made this tape, Bob Fairbairn scoffed at the notion that "this good-looking young man" was possessed by the devil, an idea first put forth by the other defense expert, Dr. Ralph Fisch, a specialist in multiple personality disorder and a forensic psychologist at the University of Denver. Ralph Fisch had told Bob Fairbairn that he had discovered that "satanic forces" had destroyed Ross Carlson; that Ross Carlson as Ross Carlson had long since "disappeared."

The devil. Satanic forces. I guessed that Fisch was hinting that Carlson might have been exposed to satanic ritual abuse. There are some who believe there is a worldwide multigenerational conspiracy to worship Satan through perverted sex, and animal and human sacrifice. Fisch sounded like a believer.

Nevertheless, at first Fairbairn felt Ross made a "vivid positive" impression. Ross offered Fairbairn a "steady" and "firm" hand; Fairbairn saw before him "a tall, graceful, yet powerful man with muscular arms and shoulders." When they spoke, Fairbairn was struck by Ross Carlson's "intelligence and ready smile." Ross Carlson was attractive and friendly, "like a graduate of a military academy"; certainly not like the devil.

But four separate meetings with Carlson convinced Fairbairn that something was wrong. Fairbairn said he almost missed the diagnosis of multiple personality disorder, just as so many doctors had done before. Ralph Fisch, Fairbairn wrote, was the first to catch on to Carlson; and now Fairbairn believed that Fisch was right. Fairbairn then arranged this April 6, 1984, interview to collect the evidence to quiet the skeptics and dispel their doubts.

I watched as Ross looked expectantly to his right, in the direction of Fairbairn's shuffling. Fairbairn eased into it. "What is your understanding of this deal today . . . me, the cameras, both of these other guys? What is your understanding?" Fairbairn's voice had an accent which could be British if one did not know he was from Canada.

Ross Carlson was smooth. "Well, I assume that this will be of some possible benefit for me to understand the way I am." A possible benefit; no kidding, I thought. By now, this tape was the cornerstone of Carlson's defense.

"Who am I talking to today?" Fairbairn asked, as he leaned over the yellow foolscap pad which seemed to rest on the laps of almost every psychiatrist and lawyer involved in the case. "Who am I talking to now? Is it Justin?"

After a pause, "Justin" nodded. I scribbled furiously on my own yellow pad.

"I thought it was Justin." Fairbairn already had one alter personality on tape.

Now one of Carlson's two silent attorneys who sat behind Fairbairn, as if uncomfortable at this emergence of Justin, spoke from beyond the right side of the screen. It was the more famous of the two, Walter Gerash. "Would you prefer that we leave the room now?" Gerash's voice was low, tinged with the accents of the streets of New York. The other lawyer, David Savitz, remained silent.

Carlson slowly shifted his gaze in the direction of the interruption. "No" he answered in his measured way. "No, I would be more comfortable if you would leave but by the same token if that would disrupt you . . ." He was being very polite.

Fairbairn jumped in, cutting off Carlson. "You can handle it," he told Carlson. Fairbairn's reassurance seemed directed at the two lawyers as well. Fairbairn clearly wanted to keep the two men in the room as long as he could.

The camera panned back. This wide shot revealed Bob Fairbairn, who now leaned ever so slightly toward Ross. Fairbairn was tall, slender, in shirt sleeves and khakis. In his fifties he was, as always, elegant; hair smooth and silver, like his voice.

The wide shot also showed me a full view of Carlson as Justin. Like his doctor, Justin was impeccable. He was dressed in a pink button-down oxford and black pants, but unlike Fairbairn he wore no tie. Carlson looked very much like he did when I saw him in the state hospital at Pueblo. But now I saw that something was wrong with his face.

Bob Fairbairn began to stall and stare. "How do you feel?" he asked again. About a ten second pause was followed by another noncommittal response. Fairbairn seemed fixated by Carlson's eyes.

"What happened to your eyebrows?"

"I don't know." The cameraman, also interested, moved in for a tight shot of Carlson's face; his blond hair made it hard to spot the mutilation above his eyes. From temple to temple, where his eyebrows once were, lay a smooth ridge of skin and bone.

"I woke up," Carlson said, "and they were gone."

"What might have happened?" Fairbairn repeated.

"I believe it was either Gray or Norman or possibly Blue . . . I don't know." Carlson looked perplexed. "We make the best with what we have," he sighed. "That's just the way things are."

Fairbairn heard the opening. "We?" Fairbairn asked. It was the "we" of multiples. "Who is we?" The room was dead still.

Carlson looked at the floor. Finally, after what seemed like an eternity, he answered. "We are not really big on going into this with the camera here." I could see a shadowy smile play at the edges of Carlson's mouth; his smile said otherwise.

Fairbairn pushed. The two lawyers again made noises as if they wanted to leave. It seemed that no one wanted to look at something as private as bare skin where eyebrows should have been or at whatever Carlson might say or do next. "No, keep it rolling," Fairbairn told the cameraman.

"We? Who is we?"

"The Unit."

"Which is?"

"Myself, which is Justin, Steven, Gray, Blue, Michael, Stacey, Black, and Norman." Justin exhaled deeply.

"Can they hear us now?"

Justin lifted his left hand in a manner of what seemed studied indifference before he spoke. "I don't know."

I sat forward in my chair. "Tell me, Justin, what kind of guy is Justin?" Fairbairn asked.

"Ah," Carlson took another breath, "I enjoy nice surroundings, nice things, good food. This is not the Savoy, the Ritz, or the Astoria," he nodded toward the cream-colored, institutional walls. But this was not irony. In multiples, each personality is different. In Carlson's world, Justin appeared jaunty, personable, and tactful but seemed not to joke.

Off camera, someone struck a match. I then saw Fairbairn take a deep drag on his cigarette and fix his eyes intently on Justin as he exhaled. "Justin is looking uptight." Fairbairn's voice became even more gentle if that was possible. "How old are you?"

"Sixteen."

"Where were you born?"

"We or me? We were born as a unit in Minneapolis."

I looked at my watch. The tape had been running for ten minutes.

"You know your situation is pretty serious," Fairbairn said, stating the obvious. "Why are you here?"

"Presumably," Justin replied, "they have me here because of . . ." Justin paused a couple of seconds—he again looked perplexed. "Presumably they have me here for two counts of first degree murder."

"Is there some doubt about that?" Fairbairn's voice rose at the end of his question.

"Yes, I doubt it very seriously"—Justin smiled—"I frequently don't think this situation is real."

Fairbairn seemed suddenly frustrated. "I need to talk to Steve. Can you bring up Steve?"

Ross's eyes began to look odd, spooky. It seemed so theatrical, so unreal, except that Justin began to show the classic signs of an hypnotic trance. I could see the Spiegel eye roll that typically heralds a personality switch.

Justin's eyes looked left and right, up and down. I thought I saw his pupils dilate and contract. Carlson turned his head toward Fairbairn and then rocked it from side to side. Justin was spaced; then he blinked as if awaking from a deep sleep. All this took seventeen seconds. Someone was back.

Fairbairn spoke first. "Hi."

Carlson answered comfortably, "Hello, how are you?" His voice was suddenly lower, more resonant, more serious, and more boring than Justin. He slumped in his chair.

"Who am I talking to?" Fairbairn asked, but he already must have known.

"Steve."

Carlson looked at the camera. "What's going on here?" The personality of Steve appeared to have no clue. Fairbairn patiently explained that this session had been planned for days but Steve said he had no knowledge of it.

Fairbairn gestured with both of his long, elegant hands. He seemed excited, probably by getting another personality on tape. "How old are you?"

Steve smiled indulgently. "Do we really have to go on with this?"

But Steve was coy and took little prompting. "I'm forty-two," he said. "I find there are some advantages to my age," he added by way of explanation. "I am more satisfied with how things work. It is true that I'm more tired and I'm eternally going to the rest room . . . basically I need to urinate more frequently." Steve droned on as if Fairbairn were the student and he, Steve, the teacher. "But it is a trade-off with youth, it is a fair exchange for the wisdom I have received throughout the years."

Fairbairn had described Carlson's personalities as cardboard people; Steve, Justin, and the rest. It was like putting a nickel into a nickelodeon, Fairbairn said. A record runs out and another record comes and plays a different tune. But unlike Fairbairn, I thought that the nickelodeon probably knew what it was doing. Suddenly, Steve stopped. Some leather straps near Fairbairn had caught his attention. He looked at Fairbairn. "I've a sneaking suspicion that we are going to try and get Black."

"I guess you don't remember we spoke about that," Fairbairn said, sounding nervous. Steve kept talking. "I don't want any time stolen," he said. Imperceptibly, Steve now sat more erect. There had been a shift in mood; Steve's words now had an edge. I thought I could hear an echo of menace in his voice. Despite my incredulity about his performance I, too, felt a twinge of nervousness. Then just as quickly as it came, the menace was gone.

"There are people who say you are faking all of this," Fairbairn persisted, "that it is all a big act."

Steve nodded. Yes, he was aware that a haze of doubt hung over him in Colorado's legal and medical communities. There was nothing he could do to dispel those doubts, Steve said reasonably.

I was one of those psychiatrists who thought that multiple personality disorder had become a fad. Once thought to be rare, it was the hot new illness in American psychiatry, especially among a group of psychiatrists and psychologists who seemed to "discover" a large number of patients with the disease. Up to five percent of the population could have it, they said. I was not so sure. Some of these cases, I thought, were induced in susceptible, suggestible individuals by the very doctors who then set out to treat them.

I was also leery of a self-serving mental illness revealed by a criminal after he was caught. I had heard that criminals could be taught to act like multiples by unwitting examiners and that multiple personality disorder could be faked. Proponents of multiplicity said that this was not possible. They said that multiplicity was a disease of secrecy and might only be discovered during a criminal proceeding. Carlson was for real.

The personality of Steve continued to talk in his conciliatory and superrational way. "Disbelief is a common reaction. I suppose I would feel the same way." The mood had shifted. There were more pauses. Something had been acknowledged and ignored. The straps and the charge of fake hung in the air.

I watched as Carlson intertwined his fingers in front of him; he now sat slightly forward in his chair, feet squarely on the floor. "I have adapted a way of survival . . . through divergent personalities," he said with no emotion. "We all have to survive." He sounded irritated, perhaps with the camera, the strangers and invasion of privacy, the straps or the doubters, and the charge of fake. He exhaled as if he had been through this before. The tape had run for twenty-seven minutes.

Fairbairn wanted to move on. "Could I talk to Blue?" he asked. I watched to see if Carlson again switched on demand. He responded quickly. "I don't think so." I did not hear doubt in the tone of his voice, though his words were less direct.

"Could we try?" By way of explanation Fairbairn added, "Blue telephoned me yesterday." Suddenly, on cue, the eye roll started again. I could see Carlson's deep-set blue pools swing back and forth six or seven times. His head still faced Fairbairn but Carlson appeared to see nothing. A few seconds more, someone else had pushed out.

Blue huddled in the chair; so much so that he seemed smaller than Steve or Justin. As he turned his head to his left, I thought I saw him flinch as if he expected danger. Head down, he chewed his left thumb as he peered around and looked terrified. His lips began to quiver and I heard whimpers coming from behind his hand. Another pause.

The eyes rolled again, this time only once or twice. Steve was quickly back, erect, face thrust forward. Blue had been out for only a moment. Steve sighed as he noticed a taste of salt in his mouth. "We always have a salt taste when something unusual happens," he said in that bored monotone. Odd experiences, I knew, often accompany switches.

Multiples also complained of holes in their memory as if they went to sleep several times a day. Only they didn't look asleep and didn't remember anything when they awoke. Now Steve complained that time had been misplaced, time stolen, time was lost.

By now Bob Fairbairn's confidence seemed high; it must have been getting close to lunchtime, but apparently lunch could wait. Fairbairn wanted more.

"What are our chances of getting Norman?" Fairbairn asked. He wanted to march through them all. Norman, I knew, was one of the personalities Fisch and Fairbairn thought was at Cottonwood Road.

Carlson put him off. "I'm not terribly thrilled with his behavior as of late." An understatement.

"Let's try," Fairbairn persisted. Fairbairn wanted it all. He wanted to get closer to the killer, to Black.


## Antichrist

The psychologist, Dr. Ralph Fisch, the other mainstay of Carlson's defense, was the first to stumble upon Ross Carlson's dim memory that he was just a bystander at Cottonwood Road. Carlson, Fisch discovered, watched the killer, a man dressed in blue, pull the trigger. It was "like a movie," Carlson told Fisch; as he stood there and watched his parents being shot, Carlson said he could not stop the man in blue.

In this dissociated experience, Fisch uncovered Carlson's double, the double who Carlson called Antichrist. Antichrist, Fisch guessed, was an amalgam of Norman and Black, two of Carlson's most aggressive personalities. Now Fairbairn wanted to call Norman and Black out.

For a moment, I wondered why Carlson chose the name Antichrist for his killer, psychopathic core. Carlson was raised in a home awash in fundamentalist Christianity. A multiple or not, Antichrist was, I thought, a perverse choice. But I stopped thinking about Antichrist as I became aware of a new note of tension which had crept into Bob Fairbairn's voice. He suddenly shifted in his chair. Fairbairn knew about Antichrist and that Antichrist had killed. If I were Fairbairn, and sat just five feet away from Carlson, I too would have been tense.

Carlson wanted to put a stop to the proceedings; Norman and Black could wait. He asked for a cup of water. Off camera there was clatter as someone hurried to comply with Carlson's request. For a split second the camera swung wildly. Walter Gerash then blocked the lens as he brought Steve a plastic cup. No chance for sharp edges here; no opportunity for a suddenly improvised weapon. The blond Tom Cruise was, after all, in jail accused of murder. Carlson took a long drink and then surveyed the scene. He carefully set the cup down behind him and slowly faced Fairbairn. He was ready.

**Norman**

Suddenly the strain of the interview seemed to have gotten to Fairbairn. Perhaps he felt that normal psychiatric tactics would not work. Out of the blue, Fairbairn became dangerously provocative. "I want to talk to Norman," he snarled.

"That is going to be tough," was Carlson's firm reply.

"It is a tough business," Fairbairn shot back, mocking and attacking. "I'm not fooling around." Such aggression did not suit Fairbairn's almost too gentle manner but it was perhaps this dissonance which finally caught Carlson off guard.

He looked pissed. His eyes rolled and his body stiffened as he switched. I noticed the power in Carlson's neck, shoulders, and arms.

"What the hell is that thing doing here?" Norman glared at the camera. "What are you guys up to?" He scanned the room. He greeted Fairbairn's suddenly reasonable voice with disdain. "Fuck you, you're nuts, buddy, I'm fine. There ain't nothing wrong with me."

I watched as Fairbairn's tough act was overrun by the street punk heat of Carlson's Norman. Fairbairn giggled anxiously. Carlson leaned toward his right in the direction of Fairbairn and raised both of his arms. For a moment Norman's hands were aimed directly at the soft underside of Fairbairn's throat only a short lunge away. But Norman did not attack; a second later his hands landed silently in his lap.

Norman's mock attack happened so quickly that it did not seem to register with Fairbairn. I looked at my watch. Thirty-five minutes into the tape one part of Antichrist had appeared. Fairbairn lit up his second cigarette in twenty minutes, leaned back, and feigned a nonchalance he could not feel. Fairbairn may not have seen the threat but he was clearly on edge.

Norman thrust his face toward Fairbairn. "You are pushing me. I don't like people pushing me."

"I'll back off," said Fairbairn.

"Smart move," responded Norman, his eyes still on his interrogator.

The tension lowered when Norman asked for a cigarette. Fairbairn looked gratefully at Norman as he handed one over. Fairbairn struggled with the match but finally succeeded in lighting it. Norman, I remembered, was the only personality who smoked. Ross Carlson said he hated cigarettes.

The lit cigarette dangling from his lower lip, Norman was still puzzled by the camera. "I don't need no defense," Norman said when the camera's purpose was explained. "I haven't done anything wrong."

The tough character of Norman looked out of place dressed in Carlson's clothes; he was a preppie Sylvester Stallone or Stanley Kowalski. "Get me out of this joint. The food is shit. They have fucked up, trumped up charges against me."

But the longer Norman talked the more empty his words sounded. He looked sad, depressed, and alone. Fairbairn's voice turned soft. He wanted Norman to go and for Steve to reemerge.

This time the eye roll lasted for only two seconds and as quickly as Norman came, he was gone. Steve had lost more time. Puzzled and smiling, Steve complained that he just missed part of his life.

There was another pause. Fairbairn's thin long frame slumped far back in his chair, his once crisp white shirt wrinkled from the morning's work. He looked worn out; forty-five minutes of nonstop tension had taken its toll. The conversation was tired.

Carlson began to read from the pad on which he kept his life in order. He complained that his medicine hindered his thinking. He could not keep conversations in place. He could not tell the difference between what he had been told and what he had experienced. Like the conversation, the picture on my screen began to wander. The cameraman must have been tired and hungry too.

Fairbairn wanted to arrange the afternoon session before they broke for lunch. "In a few minutes I am going to ask you to accept some restraints," he told Steve.

A tight shot showed Steve as he took another drink. I could see his eyes above the white cup. "I'm not thrilled about it. If you are going to try to contact Black, you won't get anywhere." I watched as the tape was about to run out. Both doctor and patient looked relieved that they would have a chance to refuel; it had been a long morning. Bob Fairbairn, Carlson, and the two lawyers must have wanted to get out of the claustrophobic, windowless room and stretch their legs in the air outside. But, of course, the prisoner could not leave.

The session ended fifty minutes after it began. As I turned off my VCR and removed the tape, I realized that I had just seen some things which I would have to think about, things I would have to explain.

# ·C H A P T E R·
## F I V E
# SCARS

I put the tape back in, punched on the power, and the test pattern came back up on my screen. I was amused when I noticed eight vertical splits; eight colors for Carlson's eight personalities. The attorneys were gone; it was only Carlson, Fairbairn, the cameraman, and me. Carlson sat in the center of the cinder-block room. Which personality was it? As if on cue, Carlson handed a piece of paper to Fairbairn.

It was an "architectural drawing." Fairbairn held up the paper so the camera could record the straight lines. The drawing was so perfect that it seemed machine made. Only Steve drew; the rest of Carlson's personalities could not draw a lick. So it was Steve. If Carlson went free it would be because the judge believed what he saw on this tape.

## Two Scars
Fairbairn needed history, not drawings. He pointed to the wide, raised scar on Steve's left wrist. I knew why he asked about the scar: child abuse was crucial to Carlson's defense.

Severe child abuse, often incest, is found in almost all multiples. In fact, alter personalities are created to defend against parental attacks. Children dissociate and split off personalities as if to say "it was not me who was beaten or sodomized. It was Justin, Steve, Norman, or Black." This is how multiples are born and how they learn to survive. To prove that Carlson was a multiple, therefore, the defense had to find abuse.

Fairbairn asked about the burn.

Carlson put his notebook away. He then moved his hands together in front of his stomach and tilted his head before speaking. I noticed that, like his father's photo, no hair was out of place. He then began the story which I knew Fairbairn had heard before.

Carlson had accidentally pulled a pot of boiling macaroni water on himself when he was nineteen months old. The two-inch scar was the only remnant of the accident. Fairbairn suspected there was more behind the macaroni story. He leaned over and held the young man's left wrist with his own long-fingered hands. He gently turned it so that the camera could record the fat, raised, angry scar.

"Do you have any memory of that? Does anyone? Does Gray?" Steve did not remember the burn or anyone dumping hot water on him, accidentally or on purpose.

In 1984, I also did not find abuse. Carlson said little to me and his record revealed less. Carlson's scarred wrist, however, reminded me of another scar I read about when Ross's mom wrote to the probation department after Ross's arrest for buying dynamite.

The first thing she said about her son was that he was born with a defect. "Ross," she wrote, "was born with a spot on his head . . . that skin had never grown over." Her doctor was so alarmed that he kept Ross in the hospital for nine days after his birth. Tissue grew in and covered the hole. Nevertheless, this scar was something Marilyn, for some reason, emphasized. It was the scar which I could still see at the top of Carlson's head.

But this scar was not abuse; the hole was nature's or God's work, not man-made. The lack of abuse could be fatal to Carlson's defense because a multiple who has not been abused does not exist. I knew that Fairbairn would come back to abuse over and over again and so would I.

### Christopher Columbus

Fairbairn cleared his throat three times, quickly. His hands were now in motion. "Do you understand why we are getting together again this afternoon?"

"Yes. The restraints."

Fairbairn, well over six feet tall, now stood. He towered over Carlson.

Carlson, alert to shifts in mood, sensed a hesitation in his doctor. "It might be best if there is trouble with Black," he said helpfully, "to give me a mathematical problem. It will engage me. I think that will work best . . ."

Self-consciously, Fairbairn picked up the three-inch locking leather restraints, the kind used to restrain psychotically disturbed patients. He kneeled on Carlson's right. Doctors did not usually apply restraints in the hospitals Fairbairn worked in—only nurses did and it showed in Fairbairn's clumsiness. He took an inordinately long time to put on the first wrist cuff.

Carlson offered to help; it was an uncomfortable moment and the camera pulled back as if to look away. "They have to be fairly tight, but I don't want to hurt you," Fairbairn said, knee still on the ground. He finally attached the cuff to the locking leather belt and wound the whole thing around the right metal armrest of the chair.

By now, Fairbairn's sleeves were rolled up as he worked on the other wrist, the burned one, and both of Carlson's ankles. As Fairbairn struggled, Carlson tried to converse in his monotone but Fairbairn made only distracted remarks in return.

He had been thinking about the truth. A lot of people thought the world was flat, Carlson said, and that Christopher Columbus was a liar. The metaphor was obvious. He, like Columbus, did not lie. The earth was round and he had MPD.

Finally, he was shackled, each wrist and each ankle connected to the chair. Fairbairn took a small key, the size that is used for mail boxes, and locked the young man in. It took five minutes. If this had been an emergency, Fairbairn would have been in big trouble a long time ago.

Sitting in the institutional metal chair, legs apart, each arm on an armrest, Carlson slowly surveyed the room. His eyes took in everything. Though tightly restrained and helpless, he was still in charge. I had to admit to myself that Carlson had a commanding presence.

**Antichrist in Blue**

Fairbairn relaxed and could be solicitous now that Carlson was safe and secure. "Why are you here," he asked, "what have you been told, and what do you remember?"

He took in a breath. "One morning I woke up," he said in his helpful way, "and some police were at my door. They said that my folks had been harmed in some way." He paused and picked his words carefully. I wondered how he would handle his attempts to have Ken Cortez lie. "I don't recall anything after that for a while." Time lost. Carlson shook his head and closed his eyes as he strained to remember. Time lost. A convenient way, I thought, to dispense with the messiness of Cortez and his alibi. Time lost, I had to remind myself, was also a hallmark of MPD.

"They got kind of nasty," Carlson resumed. "They made a number of accusations . . ." Then another, longer pause. "They told me I killed my folks and that I had disappeared from one place for a while and reappeared here and there . . . all over the place. That doesn't sound like me." He looked puzzled. "That isn't like me at all."

Fairbairn continued. "We've met maybe half a dozen times for quite a few hours," Fairbairn said as he drew in his breath. Fairbairn jabbed the air with his right index finger for emphasis. "Fairly early when we were reviewing the murder you remembered a movielike moment, standing there watching your shoulders firing the gun." He then stopped and pointed his index finger, thumb cocked back, at Carlson's head as if shooting Carlson between the eyes. But Fairbairn's charade was unconscious, perhaps generated in response to Norman's mock attack. "Was that Steve or was that someone else?"

"It wasn't me with the gun," Carlson said. This was the heart of his defense; Ross wasn't there. Steve wasn't there. I saw that small smile reappear around Carlson's mouth. It was the double—Antichrist—who killed Rod and Marilyn Carlson on Cottonwood Road. It was the man in blue.

Both seemed oblivious of where they were and what they were doing. It was an odd tableau, this chat between a preppie tied down by leather straps and his silver-haired psychiatrist. But the restraints had been on for ten minutes, and the afternoon session was twenty-five minutes old.

## Black: 3 × 7

Finally Fairbairn cleared his throat, as he did when he was about to do something worrisome. Despite the precautions, he was, I guessed, uncomfortable. Fairbairn asked about Black.

"Black shuts down," Carlson said, "whoever threatens the unit. I don't know him very well," he told Fairbairn. "It is mostly speculation more than anything else."

He gave an example: "If you came after me with a hammer, for instance, Blue would kick in to begin with."

"Then what would happen?"

"Then there would be Gray and, in rapid succession, there would be Black. You would be disarmed immediately." Carlson sat with legs and arms wide, and stared at Fairbairn as his last words came out. "I don't really like discussing it."

I knew from Bob Fairbairn's testimony that he believed Carlson's father came at Ross with a hammer. This time Fairbairn did not want to stop at abuse; he wanted more personalities. The tape was running and the afternoon was wearing on. "Let's bring back Blue." Fairbairn knew that Blue showed up before Black.

Carlson paused. Then came the familiar, darting eye roll; another switch on demand. A tight camera shot showed Carlson's face and the pink oxford of his right shoulder. He looked at the lights, the camera. He did not understand the shackles. His lips formed a grimace and he seemed about to duck.

"You look awfully scared," Fairbairn told the boy. The camera panned back. But just like that, Blue was gone. In his place, something odd was happening.

Whoever now inhabited Carlson's body took three enormously deep breaths. Carlson's neck and shoulder muscles, substantial from years of weight training and karate, bulged. The grunts and growls reached a crescendo. There was no doubt who this was; Black was out.

Fairbairn watched. Black, six feet tall and powerful, rocked back and forth, his face contorted in anger and upper lip curled in a snarl. Then as I watched with disbelief, Black snapped the leather restraint which held his right arm and raised halfway out of his chair. The other restraints still held but the broken one, the first one Fairbairn put on, dangled uselessly from Black's right wrist.

Black slowly swung his gaze from Fairbairn and looked straight into the camera and seemed to talk directly to me as I sat watching in my living room. Pointing at me with his free hand, Black snarled: "Don't you ever dare lock me up." I felt uneasy because, depending on what I decided after I examined Carlson again, that is what I thought I might have to try to do.

Suddenly, Black swiveled his head in Fairbairn's direction. "Take these off of me NOW!" he demanded, and waved the broken strap in Fairbairn's face.

Fairbairn gathered his wits and remembered the cue about a math problem. "Three times seven, three times seven," Fairbairn said in a too even tone, his outward calm covering what must have been fear inside. The math did its magic as Black, pulled up short, seemed to deflate before my very eyes and slowly relax. I checked my watch. Black was out for a total of sixty-four seconds. As quickly as he had come, Black, part of Antichrist, was gone.


## Ross Michael Carlson

Carlson looked sheepishly at Fairbairn as if he realized he was the cause of the consternation he saw in Fairbairn's eyes. He had lost time and saw the broken restraint and quickly guessed what happened. "There is nothing you can do which can restrain Black," he reassured Fairbairn. "Nothing. Can we do away with these other restraints now, please?"

Fairbairn was ashamed. He was shaken that he did such a poor job with the restraints. Carlson, reversing roles with his doctor, tried to soothe Fairbairn. "Don't feel bad," he repeated. "There is nothing you can do to restrain me." He flicked an unseen speck from his left leg as the last of the leathers was removed.

"I'm embarrassed," Fairbairn said.

"There was nothing you could do," Carlson repeated, "I think he can break handcuffs too. Black can escape from anything; only thirty men and a bullet can stop him."

Fairbairn, suddenly alert to a new tone or inflection, stopped the apologies. I, too, noticed a change in Carlson; a liveliness not typical of Justin or Steve. I had not seen a switch.

Fairbairn took a long look at Carlson as if he could see who was there. "What's your full name?" Fairbairn finally asked. "Ross Michael Carlson," Carlson answered with some wonder in his voice. There was a pause as Ross gazed around with a grin on his boyish face. "It's real nice," he finally said with tears and a smile.

Ross Carlson's joy was short-lived. He looked perplexed as he pulled at his hair and touched his chin as he struggled to scan his memory. "I have been locked up for a long time, haven't I?" This seemed more a statement of fact than a question. His left hand rested on his temple; he then moved it to his top lip where he distractedly rubbed it back and forth.

"Why are you here?" asked Fairbairn, as he broke the silence.

Ross's pause seemed longer than the twenty seconds it took. Like Fairbairn, I wondered what he would say. "I don't think I should tell you. I don't think I should think about it because it seems like it's awfully serious if it is what I think it is. It's awfully serious . . ." His voice trailed off.

"Yes it is serious," Fairbairn answered in his slightly British way.

Ross's jaw then dropped as if he suddenly remembered something. "Tell me this," he asked, "where are my parents?" "Your parents are dead." As he heard Fairbairn, Ross looked appalled. His left hand at his mouth, he turned his head away and gasped for air. He drew in a sudden sob and covered his face as his body convulsed with this apparently new information.

Fairbairn, alarmed, leaned toward Ross, almost touching him. "Do you want me to hold your hand? I don't want to leave you alone like this." Carlson was seductive but I startled at Fairbairn's adoration, warmth, and tenderness. Ross Carlson, after all, killed his parents.

On the screen, Fairbairn's tenderness lasted only seconds. This time I saw the dart and roll as Ross Michael Carlson disappeared. Fairbairn slowly sat back in his chair. I wondered what would have happened if Carlson had said yes to Fairbairn. But now Justin was back and I would never know.

"You'll have to excuse me a moment." Carlson's voice was again tactful and measured but emotionless. Justin wiped away the tears which had wet Ross's cheek.

I was distracted by a noise behind me. "I can't believe this." The voice belonged to my fiancée, Susan, who had quietly walked in. "Carlson looks so phony." As an afterthought she said: "What happens if Carlson gets out? If you testify against him, will he come after you?" This had crossed my mind. A little knot formed in my stomach as Susan walked from the room. On the screen the tape was still running but not much was happening. It was now after three in the Douglas County Jail. Someone whistled in the jail house hall. This afternoon session was forty-five minutes old.

Fairbairn had enough, said good-bye, and walked out. The last picture I saw was of Carlson alone, seated in the middle of the room. My television suddenly covered with snow as the camera was turned off. For a couple of moments, I sat and stared at the empty screen.

I knew Fairbairn was happy. He had been able to call out five of Carlson's eight personalities—Justin, Steve, Blue, and the two Antichrist personalities, Norman and Black. He had also caught a glimpse of the birth personality, Ross, and demonstrated that Ross Carlson did not even know that his parents were dead. On the night of August 17, Antichrist pulled the trigger. Antichrist was the killer; in a very real sense, Ross Carlson was not even there. Fairbairn had it all on tape; the tape, I knew Fairbairn hoped, would key Carlson's defense.

I shut off my VCR and worried. This was the man I had to examine again. Furthermore, Deputy D.A. Bob Chappell had all but told me that he hoped I was going to turn "this thing" around because if I didn't, Carlson could soon be back on the streets. As I imagined Carlson walking out from behind locked gates, Susan's words came back to me. Abused or not, a multiple or not, Carlson was a killer.

I knew that Carlson had his act down pat and had had nearly four years since he made this tape to perfect it. Now my job was to wade through the records of these years to find out what happened. Yet a small thought played at the back of my mind. Wouldn't it be odd, I thought, if despite all of his obvious phoniness and theatricality, Carlson turned out to be a multiple after all?

# ·CHAPTER·
## SIX

# DOUBLE

Something big had happened between Wednesday, August 17, 1983, when Carlson killed his parents and Friday, April 6, 1984, the day Fairbairn made his tape. For nineteen years no one suspected that Ross Carlson was a multiple; now he had the symptoms and signs of the disease. It seemed staged but that was how MPD always looked. Even real MPD is a theatrical disease suffered by suggestible, theatrical people. Nevertheless, how had Carlson gotten so far in eight short months?

## Chappell's Bad Luck

Something else changed in those eight months, even before Carlson's multiplicity was discovered. His first lawyer was public defender Craig Truman. Something Carlson said had made Truman explore pleading Carlson not guilty by reason of insanity—NGRI. Perhaps it was that a son who killed his parents must be crazy. I did not know.

Truman chose two psychiatrists who Chappell would believe should they find Carlson insane so there would be no dispute and a deal could be made. Both John Macdonald and Sy Sundell evaluated Carlson. Their conclusions had not been made public four years later. But Truman decided against the insanity defense.

I twice asked Macdonald what he thought. "Michael," he told me both times, "you know I can't say," but I had long since guessed. Since the defense never called on Macdonald or Sundell to testify I figured that meant their testimony would hurt and that the two doctors thought Carlson was a fake.

## Money
By November 1983, six weeks after Ross's arrest, Craig Truman was gone, John Macdonald was gone, Sy Sundell was gone. I suspected that Ross Carlson did not like what any of them had to say. Carlson replaced them with Walter Gerash.

To get Gerash, Carlson had to pay and therefore needed to gain control over his parents' estate, estimated to be worth up to five hundred thousand dollars in insurance and real estate. Gerash's partner—who talked with Carlson just the day after the murders—said he met with Ross Carlson "because I felt that here was this young man, obviously in pain and in trouble."

But altruism aside, Gerash required a retainer, according to news articles, in the one hundred thousand dollar range. Carlson's money was tied up because in Colorado a murderer cannot benefit from his crime. So while Ross Carlson checked the fire escape doors, Walter Gerash hired attorney David Savitz to help shake the trust money loose. Obviously, five hundred thousand dollars could buy a lot of defense. It was a strange situation: the money of Rod and Marilyn might set their killer free. Savitz went to court. Gerash got his retainer.

On November 12, Gerash sent a local psychiatrist to see Carlson. He told Gerash "there was a possibility" that Carlson suffered from a mental illness which had interfered with Carlson's ability to tell right from wrong. As I read through these early records of Carlson's case, it occurred to me that the defense might have decided to develop Carlson's insanity defense well before they had their experts fully lined up.

On Tuesday, November 29, 1983, Ross Carlson, described as looking confident and at ease, entered the Douglas County Court House, flanked by his new defense team, David Savitz and, of course, Walter Gerash. Carlson was scheduled to enter a plea—

widely thought to be insanity—but Gerash asked for a postponement. They may have needed time to find other experts to buttress
their case. They were given until December 19. Ross Carlson had
until then to be found insane.

The two lawyers then searched for experts who would agree. It
did not matter that Macdonald and Sundell did not find Carlson
insane. The lawyers knew there were plenty of others to be hired
now they had the money to do it. Ralph Fisch first saw Carlson on
December 7 and Bob Fairbairn the following February.

This is how it often works. Lawyers develop a plan and then find
experts who, because of temperament, prejudice or other reasons,
tend to side with one side or another. This is why experts are often
called "hired guns." No doubt I would be called a hired gun and,
perhaps, worse.

### Unwitting Cues

I'm not sure how Walter Gerash got Ross Carlson to psychologist
Dr. Ralph Fisch but Carlson saw Fisch on December 7, twelve days
before they had to enter Carlson's plea. In those twelve days, not
only did Fisch decide that Carlson was insane when he killed his
parents, he added something which, from that moment, radically
redefined Ross Carlson and his case.

It was during their last interview on December 9, that Fisch discovered the double which convinced Fisch that Ross Carlson was a
multiple. Fisch, I thought, was the key. I had to learn how he decided that Ross Carlson had MPD just in time for the December 19
court date.

Doctors write reports and give their "scientific" conclusions,
often in just two or three pages, but these reports cover many hours
of examinations. To grasp how conclusions are reached, however,
transcripts or recordings of examinations are necessary. The specific
ways evidence was collected is important because many sources of
bias may shape the outcome.

Fisch examined Carlson in the Douglas County Jail on December
7, 8, and 9, 1983, for a total of seven hours. For some reason, Fisch
then waited three months to write his final report but he gave Gerash a verbal reading of what he found almost immediately. Unfortunately, Fisch taped only his last interview. What actually went on
during their first two long sessions when Carlson told Fisch about

Justin and Antichrist, I can really never know. I was thankful, however, to have this forty-four page transcript. It was one of the strang-
est things I ever have read.

Testing. Testing.

Testing. Testing.

FISCH:         Testing, testing, 1 2 3 4 5 6 7 8 9 10 (pause) ah . . .
               there are two of you. Imagine one of you is sitting on the
               lap of the other.

I almost fell out of my chair. Here it was on page one. If this were
not a leading instruction—"there are two of you"—I did not know
what would be. This was why, in forensic work where the stakes are
high, exact transcripts are crucial. I read on. Fisch then began something he called his Eidetic Imagery exercise; a technique meant to
help recapture some of Carlson's forgotten memories. Fisch asked
Carlson to visualize his parents in a variety of settings and Carlson
dutifully complied.

For example:

FISCH:         . . . picture your parents running in an open country-
               side.

Carlson laughed. Apparently, this instruction was too silly for
Carlson to imagine. Running was not something he could visualize
them doing, he told Fisch. Fisch persisted.

FISCH:         Are they both running?
CARLSON:       Ah . . . that I can't imagine. Ah . . . it's something
               that my parents wouldn't do. I just can't picture my . . .
               I don't think I have ever seen my mother run. I have
               seen my father run, but . . . he always runs in a suit
               and, you know, ah . . . Florsheim shoes. So, to see him
               actually run in a country setting seems too far out.

Fisch insisted. He wanted Carlson to tell him how his parents ran.

FISCH:         As you see your parents running, do their limbs appear
               to be stiff or relaxed?
CARLSON:       Kind of stiff.
FISCH:         Whose limbs appear more stiff? And whose limbs appear
               more relaxed?
CARLSON:       They are equally stiff.

Stiff. No kidding, I thought. Fisch then moved on to their eyes.

FISCH:         Are your mother's eyes extremely brilliant, very brilliant,
               or just brilliant?
CARLSON:       I'd say brilliant.

FISCH:      Pardon?

CARLSON:    I'd say, I'd just say brilliant.

Then Fisch asked Carlson to "set aside that picture" and to imagine he heard his parents' voices, voices which had been silent for almost four months.

FISCH:      Now, hear your parents' voices. Do the voices seem meaningful, or are they merely patterns of sound in the air?

CARLSON:    There are consistent sound—the things they ask me to do. Ah . . . I hear things like—brush your dog, take out the trash . . . type things . . . commands . . . I guess. Ah . . . my mother has a Margaret martyrdom-type sound to it. "It's okay. You do what you need to do. I'll take care of all the dishes by myself." Ah . . . God, I sound great there, don't I? Ummm . . . but my mother used to use guilt very expertly, to move me to action . . . I like . . . I try to be a person of my word. I really . . . the only person I break my word to is my-self . . .

FISCH:      Continuing to listen to your parents' voices, do they give you any feeling or tell you any story?

CARLSON:    I still get a very strong sense that I am being held in some kind of contempt. Ah . . . a feeling of "You lazy scumbag. Why don't you do any work?" That's, that's what I get . . .

*I am held in contempt; lazy scumbag.* I knew that Fisch would use this to argue that Carlson was abused.

Then Fisch did something strange. He asked Carlson to set aside that image and look at him again. Fisch pointed his nose around the room and sniffed. Sniff. Sniff. Sniff.

FISCH:      I'm sniffing the air in here and you can tell by facial expressions whether I like the air or not. Now see your parents sniffing the air in the house in the same way.

CARLSON:    Um-hum . . . since my father I don't really think con-cerned himself about the air, but for the sake of this, I'll give it a shot. Uh . . . he seems to think it is fine. And my mother quite frequently smells strange odors—all the time. It was really annoying. She had us run around and check all the gas things and check the house, and seems like at least once or twice a week—to find out if there was some strange odor. And there never was.

I thought that was an interesting lead about Carlson's mother. She sounded anxious and worried. Fisch changed the subject. Apparently, he was searching for something else.

FISCH:    Okay, now look at your parents' skin. Concentrate on their skin . . . Describe how you feel when you look at their skin.

CARLSON:    I'm irritated. I picture their skin as kind of being a bluish tint. To me, the only thing that could represent would be coolness. Sick. The blue skin is unhealthy.

They have blue skin because they are dead, I wanted to tell Fisch. Fisch then asked Carlson to imagine how his parents ate. "Do they swallow easily?" he asked. After they swallowed and drank they chewed. I thought this grotesque, but I was also vaguely amused. How did Fisch get a multiple out of this?

Then on page twenty-eight—with sixteen pages to go—it got downright macabre.

FISCH:    Okay, now look at me again. Imagine that my upper skull has been surgically removed and that you could see my brain. You can touch my visible brain with your finger and feel the temperature there. Now, picture your parents in a similar way. Touch their brains alternately— their imaginary brains with your finger.

CARLSON:    Um-hum.

What could Carlson be thinking? If he had looked closely he would have seen his parents' brains oozing out on Cottonwood Road. But Fisch meant to lead him through an imaginary postmortem examination of his parents.

FISCH:    You will similarly feel a temperature there. Describe the temperature of each parent's brain. Is it cold, warm, or hot?

CARLSON:    Fifty-eight degrees—both of them.

FISCH:    Why do you say that?

CARLSON:    That's just the feeling that I get . . . personally I would think that would be cool.

Fifty-eight degrees. That was close to the ambient temperature as his parents cooled throughout the night on Cottonwood Road. Fisch continued to move through the anatomy.

FISCH:    Imagine that a window has been carved in each chest and that you can see their hearts beating there—see their hearts beating. And describe how each parent's heart beats.

I wondered what the judge would think when he read this transcript, if he did. Would it confirm in him the idea that psychiatrists and psychologists were crazy?

FISCH:    Is there any sign of any anxiety in the heartbeats?

CARLSON:  Yeah, in both of them.

FISCH:    How would you describe them?

CARLSON:  Startled.

Was Carlson joking? His parents must have been more than startled, I thought, when they saw their son had a gun in his hand and it was pointed at their heads. They must have really been terrified when they heard, just for a split second, the gun explode.

FISCH:    Now look at your parents' intestines. Do they appear healthy or unhealthy?

CARLSON:  Both unhealthy . . .

FISCH:    All right. Now see your parents' genitals. Touch the genitals of each parent and describe the feelings of temperature there.

CARLSON:  I still get a coldness.

FISCH:    Describe how each parent reacts to the touch.

CARLSON:  Indifferently.

With this, Fisch was done with his weird Eidetic test. But he had, he told Carlson, a few more questions. So far, I did not see anything remotely resembling a multiple other than Fisch's first instruction "there are two of you."

I then glanced to the bottom of the page; there were only nine pages left. But Fisch now switched gears.

FISCH:    Do you recall ever having any visual hallucinations?

CARLSON:  Visual as opposed to mental hallucinations?

FISCH:    Visual or auditory, but primarily visual. In your mind. *Or even at the time when you were shooting your parents?*

Here it was: Fisch made, I thought, his second mistake. Asking about hallucinations is a normal part of the exam. When, however, he told Carlson what kind of hallucination—"primarily visual"—and suggested when Carlson had them—"at the time when you were shooting your parents"—he was unwittingly cuing Carlson about the answer he was looking for. Talk about planting a seed.

At first, Carlson did not get it. So Fisch repeated his question. Then Carlson responded with:

CARLSON:    The only hallucination I can come up with is . . . I was standing off to the side here. With a movie camera—taking pictures of the entire event. Ah . . .

FISCH:    Which event? When you shot them?

CARLSON:    Yeah . . . that's it. I had the tendency once in a while to be outside of myself. I take kind of over the shoulder shots of it . . .

When he described this "tendency once in a while to be outside of myself" Carlson described a dissociative experience, a normal part of any traumatic event—even murder. Nevertheless, Fisch, with an interest in MPD, seemed intent on finding an hallucination in Carlson.

FISCH:    Have you ever had a visual hallucination of yourself?

CARLSON:    A visual hallucination of myself?

FISCH:    Where you actually kind of saw yourself?

CARLSON:    Oh yeah.

Finally, Ross Carlson caught on to the answer Fisch was looking for. Oh yeah, of course I had an hallucination of myself, he told Fisch, where I actually kind of saw myself.

FISCH:    In a very real way? As if you had kind of a double?

CARLSON:    Um-hum

I was so agitated when I read this that I had to get up and walk around. Not only had Fisch unwittingly led Carlson to the idea that he had a hallucination of himself as he shot his parents on Cottonwood Road, but Fisch then named Carlson's hallucination of himself: Carlson's "double." This was the same double, which Fairbairn assumed was real when he interviewed Carlson four months later. The hallucination named "the double," born out of Ralph Fisch's mouth on December 9, 1983, had by April 6, 1984, taken on a life of its own.

Psychiatrists and psychologists are not radiologists of the mind who, after taking pictures of what is already there, leave the scene relatively undisturbed. Our activity—unlike the radiologist's—can influence what we "discover." How we reach diagnoses—and how we influence patients—is important in all parts of psychiatry but especially in criminal work. Fisch clearly, if unwittingly, delivered the double to Carlson. Who, I wondered, had interviewed whom.

Fisch continued. He clearly wanted to give his "discovery" sub-

stance, and now unknowingly taught Carlson where the double was
and what the double did.

FISCH:    Do you recall if you ever had an hallucination of yourself
          at the time you shot your parents?

CARLSON:  Well, I guess I was watching the entire event.

FISCH:    But, you didn't see the double of yourself involved with
          your parents?

CARLSON:  Well, I would have had to have . . . I was watching it
          from outside of my own body. Ahhh, you know, I was a
          spectator . . .

FISCH:    In other words, if I understand you right, you say you
          would have had to have seen your double?

CARLSON:  Yeah. The double . . .

FISCH:    So, it was one of you standing away or watching the
          scene, and then your double was doing the enacting of
          the scene. Is that right?

CARLSON:  That's correct.

Fisch then began talking about the double in the third person,
each word making "the double" a separate person and more real.

FISCH:    Ummm—that's interesting.

CARLSON:  Any significance to it?

FISCH:    I think it is interesting. I'm just curious . . . your
          double then shot your parents? Is that accurate?

CARLSON:  Um-hum. Um-hum.

FISCH:    Is there anything else you can recount about your
          double shooting your parents?

CARLSON:  Ahhh—bodily, he seemed very at ease and very relaxed.
          But inwardly, I think very confused and uptight.

FISCH:    As your double was shooting your parents, did . . .
          your double notice anything unusual or different about
          them?

CARLSON:  . . . no, no . . . Uh . . . my mother said, and I quote,
          exact quote on this, kind of like running the tape back,
          "This is hell. I do not wish to" or "I don't want to live
          any longer. Just go ahead and shoot me."

FISCH:    She said that?

CARLSON:  That's correct.

FISCH:    She actually said that to the double? That almost sounds
          like they wanted you to kill them.

CARLSON:  There was no fight put up. I mean, if someone were to

FISCH:      do that to me . . . well, I don't know. I would think
            . . . that I would take the gun out of their hand.

FISCH:      They didn't plead for their lives?

CARLSON:    No . . .

FISCH:      Have you discussed this [idea of the double] with any-
            one else—another doctor?

CARLSON:    No . . .

FISCH:      . . . had you ever thought about it before I spoke about
            it? It seemed to come to your mind . . .

CARLSON:    Uh uh.

FISCH:      . . . very clearly, didn't it?

As I read and reread the transcript, I found nothing spontaneous about Carlson's double, the double which so convinced Fisch of Carlson's multiplicity. So much for the "scientific basis" of the psychiatric interview. I knew that I would try to read this interview into the court record when I got the chance.

It looked like the big thing which had happened to Ross Carlson between August 17 and Bob Fairbairn's tape was Ralph Fisch. If Ross Michael Carlson were found Not Guilty by Reason of Insanity, he would only be the second person in the history of the United States to be so as a multiple. The first was the Ohio rapist, Billy Milligan, who was found NGRI on the basis of multiplicity in 1978. Ross Carlson's defense was breaking new ground and it looked like Ralph Fisch was unwittingly leading the way.

# RIP VAN WINKLE

Ten days after Fisch's discovery Ross Michael Carlson pled not guilty by reason of insanity. On the night of August 17, Ross Michael Carlson, the defense said, was mentally ill and did not know right from wrong. How the defense would explain Carlson's alibis, I did not know.

Walter Gerash also told the judge that he would likely ask him to move the trial outside of Douglas County after he conducted a poll to see what Douglas County residents knew of the murders, because he did not think that Carlson could receive a fair trial so close to home. Gerash then announced he would attack the constitutionality of Colorado's new insanity statute. Deputy D.A. Robert Chappell was in a bigger fight than he had first thought.

## Insanity

It is a tenet of law that unless a defendant intentionally chooses to commit a crime, he is not morally blameworthy and should not be punished. In its broadest application, people who are mentally ill and therefore lack *free will* or *sufficient understanding* of their actions will be found insane. Mental illness, per se, is not enough.

It was clear why Walter Gerash was unhappy with the new Colorado insanity statute. Before July 1983, Ross Carlson, if judged to be mentally ill, could have claimed he had an "irresistible impulse" to kill his parents and lacked the free will to control himself. After July 1983, Colorado only used the straightforward right-wrong test. Ross Carlson would be convicted of the murders if he knew what he did was wrong, even if mentally ill and unable to resist his impulse to kill. Irresistible impulse no longer cut it in Colorado.

Colorado's tighter law was due to a shooting by another Colorado, John Hinckley. On March 30, 1981, John Hinckley stalked and shot President Reagan, his press secretary Jim Brady, and a secret service agent, Tim McCarthy. After a highly publicized trial, Hinckley got off as Not Guilty by Reason of Insanity, NGRI, because though Hinckley knew that trying to kill someone was wrong, he was so delusional that he could not prevent himself from pulling the trigger, or so his experts testified.

In the outcry which followed, irresistible impulse as a defense was rejected in state capitals across the United States. The difference between an irresistible impulse and an impulse not resisted is no sharper than the difference between twilight and dusk, it was said over and over again. The insanity test in Colorado, as elsewhere, was made much more rigorous.

Thus, *if* a jury thought Ross Carlson knew it was wrong to kill his parents *when* he pulled the trigger twice on August 17, no matter how "crazy" or "abnormal" he was, Carlson, in the eyes of the law, was sane. If sane, Carlson would then be prosecuted for murder, two counts.

It would be hard for Carlson to prove that he did not know right from wrong given his months of planning, split second timing, and his alibi. Bob Chappell could not believe that Carlson stood a chance of being found insane in any court in Colorado. Chappell thought he had it licked. It was Carlson's tough luck that he did not kill his parents one month earlier.

The judge on the case, Richard Turelli, set the sanity trial for the spring. If found sane, Carlson's murder trial would follow within weeks. Ross Carlson was then sent to the state hospital at Pueblo for evaluation by the state's psychiatrists. When Carlson was admitted to the state hospital at Pueblo on Tuesday, December 20, among his personal belongings were some business cards with his name and address and a Bible.

## Motions

When Judge Turelli dismissed the defense's challenge of the new Colorado law, Bob Chappell was sure he held most of the cards because it would be hard to squeeze Carlson into the narrower NGRI box. Even if Carlson were mentally ill, it would be hard to find him insane because of his obvious planning. Then on the eleventh of February, a psychiatrist at the Colorado State Hospital, Alan Fine, also found that Carlson was sane. So far, all Walter Gerash had was the double.

The defense remained busy. First, on February 23, they filed a motion to have Carlson freed on bond to live with the conservator of his trust or transferred to a psychiatric facility because he was "deteriorating" in jail. Carlson, the lawyers said, was entitled to be freed since the evidence against him was circumstantial and that no eyewitnesses to the shootings or any confession would be introduced. It was rejected.

Then on March 28, Turelli turned down another motion to move the trial saying that Carlson could get a fair trial in the county. Gerash responded by saying that the results of his "scientific" telephone poll of two hundred residents of Douglas County indicated that it could take "weeks" to seat a jury. These had been fruitless motions which stood little chance of success.

## Fisch Food

I had already noticed that Ralph Fisch waited three months to write his report. That gave Fisch a lot of time to think about Carlson; a lot could happen in three months. When I looked more closely, I found that a lot did. In those three months Fisch received six telephone calls and one collage from Ross Carlson. These confirmed Fisch's suspicions of Carlson's multiplicity.

The calls went like this. Carlson called Fisch at his office and left a message. When Fisch called back, Carlson said he had no memory of ever having called. It must have been someone else; perhaps it was the double. This happened six times. Then on February 22, 1984, came *the* phone call.

"He was very agitated, very nervous, very excited," Fisch later said. Ross Carlson then told Fisch: "I'm experiencing blackouts during the day . . . there is disorientation. I don't know whether I have done an activity . . . I can't account for it . . . I yelled at someone . . . that is not like me . . . I'm scared and I'm trying to piece things together . . . Steve is trying to figure it out. He is smart . . . Then there is Blue and Gray . . . they control me . . . I'm splintering." I wondered who was feeding whom? During this latest call, Carlson gave Fisch the whole assemblage—Blue, Black, Gray, and the rest on a silver platter.

In case Fisch did not get the point, three days later Fisch received a collage from Carlson which mapped out all of his personalities in visual form. Carlson had cut out magazine pictures and pasted them together on a sheet of paper. One he even labeled Gray. With these latest "discoveries"—the unbidden calls and unbidden collage—Fisch wrote his final report.

On March 5, 1984, Ralph Fisch said that, according to Colorado law, Carlson was insane at the time of the "alleged" commission of his crime. "The clinical interview," Fisch wrote to Gerash, who must have been delighted, "raises the issue of multiple personality in Carlson." Ross Carlson, Fisch explained, told Fisch about his "twin brother," Justin Nicholas Time—the alias Carlson used during the dynamite episode, a fact Fisch ignored. Fisch also found "a second and different personality, namely the Antichrist." While Justin was self-excusing and self-righteous and a law unto himself, the Antichrist was "starkly cool, sadistic, and unkind, hard-hearted, and constantly angry . . . with strong tendencies . . . toward retaliation toward others." A psychopath.

Finally, Fisch told Gerash that his interview "brings out" the phenomenon of the double in Carlson. Carlson, according to Fisch, had a "hallucination of himself committing the homicidal act; in such a manner, that he was a spectator or detached bystander watching himself do it, but carrying out the observation from an external vantage point. This phenomenon is a classic dissociative manifestation." Then there was the telephone call and collage which confirmed the diagnosis. There it was in black and white. On paper it looked scientific and unbiased, but I didn't believe it.


## Big Trouble

By the time of Fairbairn's taped April 1984 interview, therefore, Ross Carlson had new money, new lawyers, new doctors, and a new diagnosis. Bob Chappell, although he did not know it, was in deep trouble. He believed that when he had the opportunity to lay out the details of the murders, no jury in Colorado would find Ross Carlson insane no matter how ill he turned out to be. Carlson's planning was too cunning; clearly, Carlson knew right from wrong since he went to such great lengths to hide. Chappell had more details about this crime than he knew what to do with. It was there for every reasonable person to see: the planning, the alibi, stashing the black bag. Ross Carlson, Chappell knew, understood what he was doing at the moment he did it.

Therefore, in the eyes of the law, Carlson was sane. When judged to be sane, he would prosecute Carlson for murder and Chappell was sure he would get a conviction.


## Rip Van Winkle

In retrospect, Bob Chappell's thinking was clouded by what he knew of Carlson's one thousand percent guilt. Chappell, the straight ahead runner, told me he was outraged by Carlson and haunted by Carlson's confession to Dr. Alan Fine, the state hospital psychiatrist. "It was like this: Bang! Bang!" Carlson told Fine as he shot his parents in mime, his outstretched finger pointed slightly ahead and to the ground. "Bang! Bang!"

Because of his outrage, Chappell was about to be blindsided. First, Savitz and Gerash objected to having the two top forensic psychiatrists in Colorado, the ones that prosecutors like Chappell counted on to testify because the psychiatrists had first been hired by Truman and the defense. In the upcoming battle of the experts, Chappell now had only Alan Fine, the young state hospital psychiatrist assigned to evaluate Carlson. Chappell, so certain of Carlson's guilt, still did not worry about his lone expert; the facts would speak for themselves. If his psychiatrist only had one year of experience and the defense's had fifty, ironclad police work would win the day. Nonetheless, Chappell eventually asked Turelli to allow him to add another psychiatrist to his roster.

Turelli allowed Chappell to hire a second expert. But the psychiatrist who finally agreed to work with Chappell had also just finished his training. Chappell was going to field an inexperienced team. With some premonition, Walter Gerash said about his rival: "He woke up too late. Rip Van Winkle. He just woke up. He woke up too late . . ."

**Incompetent to Proceed**
Chappell's case sustained its second blow in May, just weeks before
the sanity trial was scheduled to begin. Gerash and Savitz must have
been aware that the police work was tight, the evidence against
their client overwhelming, and that proving insanity would be difficult. So when Fairbairn told them that it was "impossible" for Carlson to participate in his own defense because of his constant switching between Justin, Steve, and the rest, Savitz and Gerash jumped.

Carlson, they said, could not have a sanity trial because he could
not help in his own defense. Savitz and Gerash then asked the court
to find Ross Carlson incompetent to proceed. They were breaking
new ground. Billy Milligan was the only multiple so far to be found
NGRI; on an appellate level no multiple had yet been found incompetent to proceed.

Incompetence would buy more time. Furthermore, the test for
incompetence—preponderance of evidence—was easier to meet
than the test for insanity. The two attorneys told Judge Turelli that
Carlson's condition had "worsened" to the point that they did not
know "which personality" was out. Turelli agreed to schedule a
competency hearing before the sanity trial.

It was a clever tactic. If Turelli ruled Carlson incompetent, Carlson would be sent to the state hospital for treatment of his multiplicity. There, Carlson would "fuse" his eight personalities into
one. The defense then could risk a sanity trial because Carlson
would already have been labeled mentally ill (a tag he did not yet
have from the state). And then if Carlson were found insane, it
would be for an illness he no longer had since he had already been
"cured." Carlson, in no further need of psychiatric care, could walk
from the Douglas County Courtroom, a free man. The plea of incompetence might get Carlson out faster than any deal with the
D.A. Not a bad plan, if it worked.


**Chappell's Second Mistake**
Turelli set the competency hearing for June 4, eight days before the
trial was to begin. But as June 4 approached, Chappell decided to
strike back. He would, he thought, try to get rid of Judge Turelli.
This was Chappell's second mistake.

Judge Turelli, a young judge who—I was told—liked people to
"shake hands and make up," was originally assigned to the case.

Chappell worried that Turelli would not control Walter Gerash's courtroom behavior. Gerash had already spent one day conducting a hearing while lying on the courtroom floor, something which had made a big impression on Carlson, who wrote a letter describing the scene: "Walter's back has been giving him a great deal of trouble . . . He spent some time yesterday on his back with his knees pulled up to his chest on the floor of the court while in session. He really looked bedraggled . . ." And very much in charge of the proceedings.

**Eddie Day**
Therefore, instead of the competency hearing beginning on Monday, June 4, Chappell walked into court and asked for a new judge. The defense was outraged at this "delay tactic" but must have known what Chappell was up to. A retired judge would take over; Chappell hoped for one of the tough ones. On this one, Chappell outsmarted himself because he got Eddie Day.

Wherever Eddie Day presides, stories make the rounds about his gullibility and tender heart. One news story told of Eddie Day lending his 1969 maroon Cadillac DeVille to an acquaintance and convicted felon who said he needed to run some errands before turning himself in. The felon disappeared and Day's Cadillac was later recovered in Las Vegas. Chappell had heard these stories, too, and worried that Day had not learned from his mistake. Day, Chappell thought, could still be soft on defendants.

Therefore, as the June competency hearing approached, Chappell had lost his two big guns, was stuck with Eddie Day, and could no longer count on the facts of Carlson's plan and the way he carried it out to its deadly end to make his case. Those facts had to do with Carlson's frame of mind at the time he pulled the trigger on Cottonwood Road; Carlson's competence had to do with Carlson's mental ability to stand trial now. In the eight months since the arrest, Bob Chappell had been maneuvered further than ever from prosecuting Ross Carlson for two counts of murder one.

# "ASK JUSTIN"

It seemed like a good match, Ross Carlson and Walter Gerash. Gerash was so well-known as a criminal defense lawyer, a newspaper reported, that Carlson mentioned Gerash to a friend well before the murders. Chappell's investigator, Brian Bevis, told me that there was more to this story. Bevis guessed that Carlson—who had left little to chance—planned to hire Gerash as a fallback if necessary.

Gerash demanded attention by what he wore, what he said, what he did. He had toned down his courtroom dramatics since, as a reporter wrote, the days a "swashbuckling Walter Gerash" used to come to court wearing a cape and a wide-brimmed hat. But as he went on to say, "Any day Walter Gerash is in court is still a good day to watch."

Walter Gerash was a short man who looked vaguely bohemian in his blue beret or fedora, dark shirt, and even darker tie. This intellectual image fit with his past as truck driver, steel worker, union organizer, and champion of victims, the downtrodden, and the poor. Not *too* poor judging by the big retainer he required from Carlson.

He thrived on the media attention generated by Carlson, his colleagues told me. MPD was his type of dramatic defense. I counted over twenty stories in *The Denver Post* and ten in *The Rocky Mountain News* published before Carlson's first hearing. By the spring of 1984,

Carlson had become a big-time case, one of the biggest in the history of Colorado.

## Carlson One, June 1984

Ross Carlson was presumed competent and sane. Therefore, Walter Gerash had to convince Eddie Day that Carlson was mentally ill and did not understand the nature of the charges against him, or did not comprehend the courtroom proceedings, or could not help his lawyers with his case. After the defense put on their experts, D.A. Chappell would have a chance to undo whatever damage was done.

Therefore, Walter Gerash had to begin to accomplish two things on that June 6. One, he had to begin to convince Judge Day that Ross Carlson was mentally ill and, two, that Carlson was incompetent. Gerash brought multiple personality disorder into Eddie Day's Douglas County Court, right out of the chute.

## MPD Bait: "Ask Justin"

The night after the murders, Gerash said in his opening, Dr. Gregory Wilets, Ross Carlson's psychiatrist, asked Carlson who killed his parents. According to Gerash, Carlson told Wilets, "To find out who killed my parents you will have to ask Justin."

"Oh my God," Dr. Wilets said, reported Gerash, "I think he has multiple personality disorder. I missed it." This was the first I heard this. If true, Ralph Fisch was not the first to diagnose MPD. When Ross Carlson threw out the MPD bait, Wilets bit first and Fisch bit second. But I was puzzled. Why, if Wilets thought Ross was a multiple, didn't he write it in Carlson's hospital chart? Why, if Wilets thought he was a multiple, did not Gerash schedule Wilets to testify?

Then Gerash followed his "ask Justin" surprise by another unusual announcement. He said that he and David Savitz would testify in support of the very issue they were trying to prove. The two attorneys would become witnesses in their own case and tell Eddie Day, under oath, that Carlson could not cooperate in his own defense.

It was, Gerash said, a problem of amnesia. Ross Carlson did not remember what happened to him as a child, could not remember what happened on August 17, and Carlson could not remember witnesses who could help his case now.

Why was it, Gerash asked, that only his experts—Ralph Fisch, Bob Fairbairn, and a recently imported L.A. psychologist and expert in MPD, Bernauer "Fig" Newton—believed that Ross Carlson was a multiple? Because, Gerash answered his own question, MPD was missed by uninformed, inexperienced psychiatrists because it was a "secret" disease, a disease of "hiddenness."

## The Secrets of Abuse

Gerash then circled back to Carlson's amnesia and to child abuse, the abuse which, Gerash said, must be there. Gerash promised that when Carlson's personalities were fused—and Carlson's amnesia undone—the newly unified Ross Carlson would remember his parents' sadism.

It was like this, explained Gerash. Abused children who were adept at self-hypnosis created alter personalities to deal with the terrible reality of their lives. He then began the litany of abuse which he repeated over and over during the next days, weeks, and months. Ross Carlson was conceived out of wedlock. According to Gerash when Marilyn told her mother that she was pregnant, the mother said: "I wish you were dead." Then came the boiling macaroni-water story. It was no accident, Gerash implied; Ross's mom dumped the water on him on purpose.

It was not only his illegitimacy which turned the Carlsons against their son. This was a very bright couple, he reminded Day. At the University of Minnesota, Marilyn graduated fourth and Rod eighth in their classes. Ross was an intelligent and precocious child—at the age of four he campaigned for Hubert Humphrey and made little speeches for Humphrey all over the community. So the Carlsons must have been doubly devastated and angry, Gerash said, when they discovered his reading and spelling troubles, due to his as then undiagnosed dyslexia.

Gerash said that Carlson remembered some things. During his evaluation at the state hospital, Carlson told Dr. Alan Fine about feces filled diapers rubbed into his eighteen-month-old face by his father, when Ross had a potty accident, "like you would deal with a dog." Also, Carlson had been suicidal since he was three. Gray was a suicidal person, not as deeply as Blue, said Gerash, but very suicidal.

As Gerash jumped from one argument to another, I recognized that imbedded in his disorganization Gerash outlined his arguments. He repeated key phrases over and over again, as if repetition made his "facts" more believable and real. Gerash came back again and again to the amnesia and abuse and repeated what I started to call the Carlson mantra: "Carlson's secrets prevent witnesses for the defense, Carlson's secrets prevent witnesses to the child abuse." Ross Carlson's amnesia was the key.

### Three Women

Gerash, then, pulled out another surprise when he announced that he had, waiting in the wings, three witnesses who would prove that Carlson suffered from "different personalities" years before the murders.

"We will call Miss Littleton," said Gerash. Years ago, Gerash said, Carlson told Miss Littleton that he was "forty-two years old." That must be Steve, I thought. "We will call Sue Rhoads," Gerash went on, a classmate of Carlson's who worked at Courtesy Ford the day Ross Carlson came in posing as an oil man who wanted to "check out" a few cars. When Rhoads said hello to Carlson, he brushed her off. He said he did not know who she was. "We will also call Michelle O'Hagan," said Gerash. The sixteen-year-old would swear that Carlson "looked like he was thirty or forty" and tell the court "how six times she saw a dramatic switch of personality."

I was eager to read what these three women had to say. Carlson's MPD depended entirely on his own report. He was the one who told Wilets to "ask Justin"; he was the one who revealed that his father rubbed his face in feces, he was the one who told Fisch about Justin and Antichrist. If the three women told convincing stories, then Ross Carlson was a multiple *before* he killed his parents. This would end the speculation that Carlson was a fake or that his illness was induced by his experts' unwitting suggestions. He still might have been competent and sane, but at least he had MPD.

Gerash then told of the videotapes, the "dramatic proof" of Carlson's disease. Everyone, Gerash promised, would see the tapes, especially the Fairbairn tape. Everyone would "see in the film when the killer called Black comes out . . . and, for an instant, you will see Ross Carlson. And you will see," Gerash told Day, "Ross Carlson doing something on that film that we have never seen before. He finds out that his parents are dead. . . .

"In the interest of justice," Gerash ended, Carlson must be found incompetent. "Your honor," Gerash said, "right now there is no Ross Carlson." Then Gerash sat down.

Gerash took twenty-four pages to lay out his opening argument. Bob Chappell only took three. Chappell's argument was simple, logical, and short. Carlson's MPD depended on his self-report. He was a multiple because he said he could not remember the murders and then told Fisch about Antichrist, Justin, and the rest. Carlson, Chappell pointed out to Day, who knew this already, ran the risk of two life sentences. How could Carlson's claims of multiplicity—about the double, of Antichrist, Blue, and Black—be believed? He would do anything to save his skin.

## The Fallacy of Lies

At eleven that morning Gerash called his first witness, Susan Louise Rhoads, nineteen years old, and Carlson's classmate. She had been a receptionist at Courtesy Ford in 1980, three years before the murders, when Carlson came in to look at some cars. Carlson came across, according to Rhoads, "as being very successful, being quite the young professional . . ." He gave out his card and it was lucky he looked so rich, she said, otherwise the salespeople would not have taken him so seriously. "If they are going to sell him a car, obviously he has got to have the money for it." But when Rhoads said "hello," Carlson ignored her. "I don't know you," he said, and left.

At school a few days later Carlson denied to Susan that he was ever at the dealership. "He just didn't know what I was talking about." It was strange, odd, she said. "Kind of makes you wonder if it's you." But this, Rhoads said, was not a Carlson scam. What convinced Rhoads of Carlson's truthfulness was that Carlson's behavior looked so "real." To Rhoads, Carlson acted "anywhere from late twenties to late forties," quite a span. She did not think that anyone could "have lied that well."

Susan Rhoads did not know that studies have repeatedly shown that it is impossible to tell with certainty if someone is telling the truth, no matter how truthful they look. The appearance of honesty has little to do with truthfulness. But Sue Rhoads was impressed with Carlson's appearance; Sue Rhoads bought into what I call the fallacy of lies.

On cross-examination, Chappell went right to the heart of the matter. He got Rhoads to say that "Car salesmen don't want to waste time with a seventeen-year-old boy . . ." When Chappell followed this up by asking Rhoads whether she considered that the reason Carlson didn't know her was because she was "blowing his cover," she responded with a quick no and repeated that she did not think that Ross Carlson could lie that well. He was too convincing.

Chappell pushed. Didn't Carlson have a motive to lie? No, said Rhoads. Now I thought that either Sue Rhoads was herself lying or was very naive. This was not proof of MPD, this was Carlson on a scam. I wondered what the two other women would say.

The next witness turned out to be a fiasco for Gerash. Cynthia Ann Lebel, ex–girlfriend, and current "Miss Littleton," told Eddie Day that Carlson acted "older" than the other boys she knew but her testimony was vague. Soon Gerash was unhappy with her.

"Sometimes when he called," Lebel said, "he would say 'I feel older today.' And I guess that's when I asked 'How old do you think you are?' and sometimes his answer was 'forty-two.' " Feeling older was hardly being older. By now, upset with his second "star witness," Gerash asked Lebel whether "the District Attorney [told] her not to" talk and told her what to say. Miss Littleton held to her story. No, Carlson had never told her of his twin brother, Justin Nicholas Time.

Then Chappell asked Lebel whether he had coached her. Lebel, of course, said no. What she did, however, was to further hurt Carlson. Carlson, she said, explained that he felt older because things were "piling up on him." This was adolescent ennui, not MPD. Miss Littleton bombed as a witness for Gerash.

So far, Gerash had not delivered the forty-two-year-old Steve. Steve had not arrived from Courtesy Ford or with Miss Littleton. Sixteen-year-old Michelle O'Hagan—on occasion Eddie Day called her "hon" which befitted her age and Day's social background—was more difficult for Chappell because her story kept changing.

O'Hagan met Ross Carlson at Skate City when she was fourteen or fifteen. Carlson, it seemed, told Michelle that he had a twin brother Justin Nicholas Time who, Carlson said, was sent away by their parents at age three because Justin had been "mean to Ross." Ross dated a friend of Michelle's, Cheri Mettille, prior to the murders. O'Hagan said that Carlson had acted very old with Mettille, "probably around forty, I guess." Mettille was fourteen or fifteen at the time too.

Once, after Carlson failed to show up for a date with Mettille, Carlson told Mettille that he "didn't remember" the date. This, according to Michelle, only happened once but was proof of the existence of Steve. Again, I did not find Gerash's witness convincing and I doubted that Eddie Day would be convinced as well.


## Loose Lips

But Gerash must have been tickled by what Michelle O'Hagan said next.

GERASH:    On the day after the homicide were not you and your mother interviewed by the police at your house?

MICHELLE:    I wasn't there for the interview but I remembered the twin's name.

GERASH:    Pardon?

MICHELLE:    I remembered the twin's name, and the police came back to the house . . . and they told me that they thought that Ross had a double personality.

GERASH:    Had a what?

MICHELLE:    Double personality.

GERASH:    Who said that?

MICHELLE:    One of the officers that were there.

GERASH:    The day after the homicide?

MICHELLE:    Uh-huh.

Loose lips, sink ships, I thought. First, Wilets blurted out that Carlson must be a multiple after Carlson told him to ask Justin and now this. Either the deputies were astute psychiatrists and uncovered something in one afternoon which was not evident for Carlson's nineteen years or Ross Carlson was putting out that he did not kill his parents—just ask Justin—from the beginning.

Michael Watanabe, Chappell's assistant at that time, cross-examined Michelle O'Hagan. He stayed away from the police gossip.

How many people did the sixteen-year-old Michelle know over forty, Watanabe wanted to know. "A lot," she said, and then added that she knew what forty-year-old men "acted like." Ross, she said, was just like that. "They don't go jumping around and stuff like that," she added by way of explanation.

Michelle then elaborated. Ross "acted more mature." Not much of an elaboration, I thought. Then Michelle said that she saw Carlson "switch"—Gerash's word—as he would "like come into the room, and . . . he would act different." Michelle said she saw Ross Carlson "switch" six different times.

At the end of their time on the stand, I could not believe that Sue Rhoads or Cynthia Lebel hurt Chappell's case. Neither did O'Hagan, if I thought about what she actually said. Not one of the three locked MPD securely in place because what each said had plausible alternative explanations. But this was always the case with MPD, I was learning. Everything could be interpreted in light of what one believed about MPD. The rich oil man could have been forty-two-year-old Steve or just Carlson on the make.

**The Press**
The seduction of MPD grabbed the next day's headlines. *The Denver Post* carried on its front page, 'ASK JUSTIN,' CARLSON SAYS. Carlson's personalities conspired to kill his parents, according to defense attorneys Savitz and Gerash, the reporter wrote. The attorneys did not, however, know which personality fired the bullets that killed Carlson's parents. They believed, however, that it was forty-two-year-old Steve who was in court on Wednesday. They also said that videotapes, yet to be shown, would demonstrate dramatic switches between Carlson's personalities.

Then the editors, no matter what they thought of Carlson, ran the first of their box scores. Under the banner CARLSON HAS SEVEN PERSONALITIES, HIS ATTORNEYS CLAIM was a list of those who lurked inside of Ross Carlson's body: Justin Time, Blue, Gray, Black, Steve, Norman, and Stacey, who they were and what they were like. For some reason Michael was missing. "The defense contends," the newspaper reported, that "Black may have been involved in the murders."

The box score, in black and white, lent credence to the idea that Carlson was a shell—the defense's contention—inhabited by different people. The issue of Carlson's competence was nowhere to be found. This was turning into a circus. Despite Gerash's unspectacular three women, MPD was gathering a momentum of its own.

**The Other Side**
Thursday morning, June 7, 1984, Walter Gerash was sworn in and began his testimony. It was unusual to have an attorney testify on his client's behalf but Day said that Gerash would be "more competent than a psychiatrist" in judging whether Carlson could remember things or not since they worked so closely together. Eddie Day's ability to trust, I could see, had not appeared to have been influenced by his life on the bench.

A lawyer named Miller led Gerash and Savitz through their testimony. When asked whether he could communicate with Carlson, Gerash said, "No . . . because if one personality is out in the courtroom, he is amnesic . . . for . . . the other personalities . . ." We never know who is there. Furthermore, Gerash said, "we are bereft of witnesses . . . because this is a disease of hiddenness . . ."

I wanted to see how Chappell handled this. Chappell started slowly. He asked Gerash if he was aware that *before* he killed his parents, Carlson had talked about how impressed he was with Gerash. No, Gerash said, he had not heard that. Chappell then brought up Dr. Sundell and Dr. Macdonald whom Gerash would not let testify now. Chappell knew Day was well acquainted with Macdonald and hoped he would understand why Gerash did not plan to call him to the stand. But Gerash neatly dodged Chappell's question and must have brought a chuckle to the courtroom when he dismissed both as "Doctor Death and Doctor Death, Jr."

Then Chappell wanted to know who fed stories to the press. Which attorney told *The Denver Post* that the forty-two-year-old Steve was in court yesterday. "Was that you?" he asked Gerash. "I'm not forty-two . . ." Gerash flippantly replied. No, Gerash didn't remember telling them that. Chappell had better, Gerash said, ask Savitz.

This is how it went. Gerash gave not one inch until Eddie Day, who had sat silently behind the bench, suddenly chimed in. Maybe he meant to help Chappell who was not getting anywhere, or maybe he wanted to clear some things up for himself.

DAY:      Mr. Gerash, I only have one question. You made a statement at least twice, that I remember of, that Carlson cannot recount to you the events of the homicide.

GERASH:   That's right.

DAY:      Yet I have before me . . . one of the most detailed accounts of [Carlson's] actions from suppertime to bedtime that I have ever seen.

GERASH:    That's right.

DAY:    Where is the amnesia?

Good for Eddie, I thought. He, at least, is asking the right questions, questions which Chappell had yet to ask.

GERASH:    You have to realize that he has been told . . . he read over all the investigative reports . . .

DAY:    . . . meeting his parents and planning to tell them to go out and see whatever it was out in the remote area and the rest of that . . . could only come from him.

GERASH:    That's right . . .

DAY:    He couldn't have been told this. He could not have been told that he shot the breeze with Ken Cortez . . . [that he] drove to the Ramada Renaissance and waited for his parents . . . that he told his parents he would like to show them a mailbox that he built for the neighbors . . . that he pulled out a gun . . . and . . . "bang, bang," and all that. Now that's not amnesia . . .

GERASH:    Your Honor, you have to realize that one of the personalities or two of the personalities do have recall . . . Some of the personalities have knowledge of the events. They have been told not only by the other personalities, but they have been told by other people, and . . . by the investigative reports . . .

Eddie Day hit the nail on the head. The symptoms of MPD were vague and inconsistent. Someone had told Fine and Fisch about the details of the night of August 17. But if you accepted the diagnosis, then MPD explained everything. Carlson remembered something? It must have been Norman or Black at the scene of the crime who then passed on what happened to Justin or Steve. Neither Steve nor Justin and certainly not Ross was ever at Cottonwood Road. Despite Chappell's ineffective handling of Gerash, Eddie Day's doubt must have made Chappell happy.


### Thready and Upset

Cases do not only depend on facts, and the show had just begun. So far, Carlson sat at the defense table, sometimes looking spaced and, at times, appearing to nap. Gerash then startled the courtroom when he told Eddie Day that he feared one of Carlson's most violent personalities, Black, might disrupt the proceedings. Gerash, who said Carlson was "thready and upset," asked that Bob Fairbairn—who he called Carlson's psychiatrist—be allowed to sit at Carlson's side during the rest of the hearing to calm his patient down. Eddie Day agreed.

From then on, each day, Fairbairn sat at Carlson's side, helping his patient through the "trauma" of the proceedings. To me, this seemed like pure theater, but effective theater nonetheless because each time Eddie Day looked over, he would see Dr. Fairbairn, a kindly psychiatrist, ministering to this very sick young man.


**The Tape**
David Savitz followed Gerash to the stand. Savitz, led by Miller's questioning, went directly to the, as yet unseen, "dramatically convincing" Fairbairn April 6 videotape. How had they decided to make the April tape? Savitz told Dr. Fairbairn that unless the defense could show that Carlson's many "personalities indeed do exist, unless we could capture this by camera or by video that this disorder is so difficult to comprehend, that we are not going to get people to believe" it. Fairbairn, Gerash, and Savitz knew, the lawyer said, that if Carlson could show all of his personalities for Fairbairn's video, it would be very good for his case.

Savitz's admission, in open court, that the Fairbairn tape was the record of Ross Carlson's talent show, startled me. Perhaps Savitz did not understand that when Fairbairn asked Carlson to bring out his other personalities, Carlson showed the world that his switches were under his control. MPD on demand. Miller sensed the danger as well and tried to dispel it.

MILLER:    Did [the tape] appear to be contrived or deliberate?
SAVITZ:    . . . I came away from the afternoon session, before we recessed for lunch [with my] heart pumping. I was just keyed up. I was off the ground because I had experienced, in my judgment, something very vivid, very emotional, and very real, and in no way did it appear to me to be phony, contrived, or anything similar to that . . .

Vivid. Very emotional. Very real. In no way did it appear to me to be phony. It was real because it looked real; again the fallacy of lies.

Finally, Miller came to the crux of the competency hearing. Who was Ross Carlson and where was he?

MILLER:    Now the people of the State of Colorado have charged a person named Ross Carlson with two counts of first degree murder. Who are you defending? Who is this defendant?

SAVITZ:    I don't know.

I don't know. Carlson had forgotten who he was. Savitz did not know who he was. Fisch said he had disappeared and was overrun by satanic forces. This seemed to me like never-never land.

It was Chappell's turn to chip away at Savitz. First, Chappell got Savitz to admit that Ross had worked with him in freeing up his parents' money for his defense. "In other words," Chappell said, "Carlson could cooperate with his attorney. Why could he not cooperate now?" Then Chappell brought up Carlson's letters.

CHAPPELL:    Do you remember my repeated request for the Pam Digby letters?

SAVITZ:    Yes . . .

In a letter to Pam Digby, a school friend, Carlson wrote the news that "the trust officer feels that he can disperse [sic] funds for Gerash soon! Wich [sic] means I will have a *real* attorney! There has been some evidence uncovered in my favor."

CHAPPELL:    I would like Mr. Savitz to read one sentence from one of those letters . . .

SAVITZ:    "There has been some evidence uncovered in my favor."

CHAPPELL:    Mr. Savitz, you testified earlier that your client doesn't understand the nature of the charges and can't assist in his defense.

SAVITZ:    Correct.

CHAPPELL:    Mr. Savitz, isn't it true that your client does know evidence in his favor?

SAVITZ:    I'm sure a personality would understand perhaps a piece of evidence in our favor.

A personality but not Ross. Remember the night of the murders? That was knowledge, not memory. A piece of evidence uncovered in his favor? It was a personality, not Ross. If one accepted MPD, it answered everything. But, clearly, Carlson knew what was happening with the trust, his lawyers, and his defense. After only one mention, Chappell let it drop.

Chappell then pointed out that Carlson knew how many preemptory challenges his side would have when selecting a jury. I thought Chappell also scored when he asked Savitz if he knew that Carlson had enrolled in a course on wills, trusts, and estates which started just days after he killed his parents. No, Savitz said, he had not known that. Had Savitz questioned the diagnosis of MPD, Chappell asked, after he learned that Carlson had taken a psychology course in college? No, Savitz said, he did not.

Chappell also did well when he asked why the defense had been unable to find evidence of child abuse—other than what Carlson told them. And, Chappell pointed out, despite Carlson's supposed amnesia, there were two hundred twenty-five witnesses lined up for the murder trial on both sides already.

Nevertheless, when I finished reading their testimony, I realized that Gerash and Savitz were smart. They created an endless opportunity to work the system. Their war chest was deep as they pushed Carlson farther from a trial on the merits, two counts of murder one. MPD lent itself to a variety of explanations and excuses. It was a slippery and sticky diagnosis; it explained anything and everything.

Once applied to Carlson, it was very hard to wash off. There was little evidence of alter personalities before the murder? Simple. MPD is a disease of "secrecy and hiddenness." They could not find evidence for child abuse? Simple. Carlson would only remember his abuse once he was fused. Carlson's personalities knew something about one another? Simple. Memories always leak between personalities.

Chappell was on his heels from the beginning. Chappell, much more comfortable with the black and white of murder trials and, in his words, slugging it out toe-to-toe, had difficulty with the nuances of MPD. Even though Gerash and Savitz had to prove the presence of MPD, Chappell was thrust into the position to prove its absence.

When Savitz and Gerash finished it was time for the battle of the experts. The first expert for the defense was Dr. Ralph Irving Fisch.

# · C H A P T E R ·
## N I N E

# RAZZLE-DAZZLE

## Experts

Legal medicine is not medicine. It is a game, like chess, a battle of maneuver. But doctors are not the chess masters; the lawyers are. Doctors are pawns used to attack, defend, or cancel other experts out. Some of my friends refuse to do legal work. It makes them feel used and sleazy. I also know that legal work makes them anxious and scared.

In doctors' offices, patients come for symptom relief and are thankful for the help. In the legal arena the patient, who is not a patient at all but a defendant or plaintiff, comes to win. Where money or a sentence hangs in the balance, they may emphasize certain symptoms and neglect others. Experts may do the same. In this atmosphere, the truth can suffer.

Lawyers choose "their" experts accordingly, and want someone who looks the part of a wise, impartial doctor. Gray hair helps. In the criminal arena, doctors who usually work with prosecutors will, in civil cases, likely be lined up with the defense. Experts who defend the criminally accused will more often work with plaintiffs in civil suits. Lawyers know this. This was why Gerash called Sundell and Macdonald "Dr. Death and Dr. Death, Jr."; they usually worked with district attorneys.

Once in court, doctors are grilled as attorneys try to establish their dominance over unfriendly witnesses. The bully factor plays a part in all hotly contested trials. Needless to say, in the courtroom, doctors do not like lawyers. But there is a lot of money to be made; experts are sometimes paid outrageous sums for their opinions. That is why they are often called "hired guns."

Beginning on Friday, June 8, Gerash and Savitz rolled out their big guns: Fisch, Fairbairn, and Bernauer "Fig" Newton, a well known MPD expert, flown in from L.A. After that, it would be up to Chappell to see what he could do.

### Satanic Forces

By the time Ralph Fisch took the stand, Carlson had sat for two days getting emergency psychiatric aid from Bob Fairbairn. Every time Eddie Day looked down from the bench, he could see Carlson —who was floating, switching, and spacing out—being treated for an illness it was not clear that he had. If Carlson were paying for them all it would cost him a bundle to pay for an expert on the stand, an expert at his side, and two lawyers in the court.

Against this backdrop, Gerash led Fisch through his findings. Fisch—I remembered him to be short, professorial, his hair looking perpetually windblown—quickly startled those in court when he said that Ross Carlson was not the defendant. Ross Carlson had "disappeared," eaten up by "satanic forces," a long time ago.

While this brought a snicker from the prosecutor's table, Ralph Fisch was not joking. Today's multiples were yesteryears' possessed. This was Carlson's ultimate alibi: a routine case of demonic possession. "My hunch about Antichrist," Fisch said, "is that Antichrist is demonic, a devil, Satan, evil." It was Lucifer, Beelzebub, Satan, Antichrist at Cottonwood Road, not Ross Carlson.

### Three Month Delay

It was widely known that Carlson's calls and collage came between Fisch's December evaluation and his March report. The calls and collage, Gerash must have realized, could cut both ways and support the contention that Carlson was a multiple or was chumming with MPD bait. Probably that is why Gerash asked whether Fisch found indications that Carlson made himself appear sicker than he was.

No, Fisch said, Carlson was honest during his three day examination. He found nothing in Carlson's test results to suggest malingering. Then Gerash handled the telephone calls.

GERASH:   Well, what's so unusual about the phone calls? . . .
FISCH:    Apparently . . . he felt that he could talk to me . . .
          On the numerous occasions that he called me, I tried to
          call back as soon as possible . . . it was clear that he had
          no recollection of having called me . . . On February 22,
          1984, I received a call from Mr. Carlson . . .
GERASH:   What was that date again?
FISCH:    February 22, 1984 . . . [was] when he said "I'm experi-
          encing blackouts . . . I'm trying to piece things together
          . . . Steve, he's trying to figure things out . . . He does
          architectural drawings . . . He's great at karate. He's
          smart . . . then there is Michael, Blue, Gray . . . Blue
          is six . . . He gets real scared . . . Gray is real de-
          pressed and suicidal . . ."
GERASH:   . . . During your interview in December you were able
          to determine these personalities before, weren't you?
FISCH:    No. [In December, Carlson had] spontaneously provided
          me with a discussion of Justin . . . [and] . . . the
          Antichrist . . .

In December, Carlson "spontaneously" told Fisch about Justin and the Antichrist. Now Michael, Blue, Gray, Steven were "spontaneously" offered up. Why did not Fisch suspect that Carlson might be lying? Carlson was, after all, accused of a double homicide and was in a fight for his life.

There was another problem. How could Carlson spell it all out if amnestic for each personality? How did whoever was on the phone with Fisch know that Steve, for instance, was good at karate, architectural drawings, and was smart? Was this another example of the difference between memory and knowledge?

Then Gerash ran Fisch through competency. Could Carlson understand the charges against him? The nature of the courtroom proceedings? Could he assist in his own defense? Fisch said no to all three.

Fisch added that "Multiple personality is like a symphony orchestra without a conductor. All of the parts are playing, but they are not playing in unison." Fisch then repeated one of the lines which formed the core of the defense. "I am convinced," said

Fisch, "that Ross Carlson . . . hasn't got the slightest recognition of what the charges are and is . . . amnestic to the fact that his parents are dead . . ."

Gerash, whose style was to repeat and repeat—someone who knows him well says he beats dead horses to death and then stands them up and beats them again—asked again whether Carlson could cooperate in his own defense and got this from Fisch.

GERASH:    Let's say Mr. Carlson is sitting in court and Steve is out, and he stays for let's say fifteen minutes. Then he switches . . .

FISCH:    That's correct . . .

GERASH:    . . . can [that] happen slowly or quickly?

FISCH:    That can happen very, very quickly so that it is almost not observable, or [slowly] . . . As a matter of fact, I have been watching him through my testimony, and I think he has been switching during my testimony . . .


**Tapes in the Closet**

On Monday, in a change in strategy, Gerash announced that he would not show the tapes after all. The defense had decided, for "medical" reasons, not to show the court the "dramatic" proof of Carlson's illness—at least not for now. It would be "antitherapeutic" if Ross saw himself fragment, split, and switch; they wanted to save the tapes for the sanity trial, if necessary. Perhaps Gerash and Savitz thought the tapes exerted a more powerful effect when kept in the closet. Or perhaps they sensed they didn't need the tapes as Carlson switched and floated in living color, in front of Eddie Day.

The way Gerash introduced this change, I thought, cleverly reinforced the idea that Carlson was sick—the very thing that was under dispute.


**Dates**

On Monday afternoon it was time for the cross-examination. Chappell went over the critical dates. Fisch's interviews in December, the call February 22, collage on February 25, and Fisch's report on March 5.

CHAPPELL:   Did this collage . . . add anything to your basis for that conclusion or did you ignore it?

FISCH:      I didn't ignore it. I would say that it basically confirmed and supported my diagnostic conclusions about the multiple personality aspect . . .

Chappell's implication could have been damning, but he did not make it explicit. Perhaps he thought it so obvious that he did not need to. Chappell then went after Carlson's claims of amnesia.

CHAPPELL:   Was he able to describe to you the person who did the killing in December?

FISCH:      Well, he described [his double] where he described the murder scene and he described somebody doing the murder . . .

Fisch admitted that Carlson had remembered the shooting and said that Carlson had told him that "My parents made my life miserable . . . [but] I don't know why Antichrist killed them . . ." But Chappell again did not follow up. Perhaps he thought he had made his point. Or, I was beginning to think, as a prosecutor he usually put his case on first and was not good at the counter punching which cross-examination required. Chappell then moved to the crux of his case, in psychiatric jargon, to "secondary gain." Carlson had every reason to appear sick and had much to gain and nothing to lose.

CHAPPELL:   Okay . . . Now as I understand the sequence of events, you were the first to diagnose the defendant as multiple personality disorder?

FISCH:      To my knowledge, yes.

CHAPPELL:   . . . Did you do anything to get the defendant to tell you that there were two different people, Ross and Justin? . . . You didn't come out and say, is there a bad guy inside of you, did you?

FISCH:      I don't believe I did.

CHAPPELL:   Now, doctor, what do you call it when a child doesn't want to go to school and goes to mom that morning and says I feel sick I want to stay home? And then, after he is home and school has started, he feels much better and wants to play. What do you call that? . . .

FISCH:      Well, there could be many, many reasons for that kind of phenomenon . . .

Another good point, but again no Chappell follow-up. Perhaps

Chappell thought the MPD diagnosis would crumble under the weight of its absurdity. Chappell asked, instead, about the different size suits that Carlson had stored at the Norgrens, in whose yard Carlson had hidden the black bag. The suits were, Chappell was sure, stolen property, the result of a Carlson scam.

CHAPPELL:    On direct examination, you were asked about the business of different size clothing.

FISCH:    Yes.

CHAPPELL:    In possession of the defendant. Can you explain how that enters into confirmation of your diagnosis? . . .

FISCH:    Well . . . That would mean . . . that in his mind or in his amnesia different kinds of clothing could be used for different kinds of personalities . . .

Chappell's ridicule scored big with his investigator, Brian Bevis, who later told me he laughed out loud at that one. It was so crazy, different size suits for different personalities. They were stolen. But if Eddie Day accepted MPD then any explanation made sense.


## "The Patient Always Tells the Truth"

The greatest weakness in Carlson's defense was that Carlson's MPD depended entirely on his own report. The attack with the diaper. The personalities. His amnesia. Chappell saved it for last.

CHAPPELL:    Doctor, isn't it true that in order to reach your diagnosis of multiple personality . . . you have to believe everything that Ross Carlson has told you?

FISCH:    Well, I think the key word is believe . . . The weight of the data, the internal consistency of the data is what I believe.

CHAPPELL:    Have you made a judgment of whether Ross Carlson has told you the truth in his recounting of the murder scene.

FISCH:    Counselor, the patient always tells the truth!!!

Even in a murder case? At last, Chappell followed this one up.

CHAPPELL:    Dr. Fisch, are you familiar with the Rosenhan Study?

GISCH:    Yes.

CHAPPELL:    Can you describe that for the judge?

FISCH:    Well, in my recollection . . . people who were not patients entered a mental hospital and were judged by the staff to be severely mentally ill, when in fact they were not . . .

Rosenhan showed that his graduate students, with little training, could fake schizophrenia, be admitted to a hospital, treated, and discharged with not one psychiatrist catching on. What Fisch did not point out was that Rosenhan did the opposite, too, and demonstrated that real schizophrenics would be disbelieved if doctors were told ahead of time that they were fake. Rosenhan showed that you see what you expect and not what is really there.


## Fairbairn

Robert Fairbairn began testifying on Tuesday afternoon under the guidance of David Savitz. Since February 26, just days after the famous telephone call and collage, Fairbairn had seen Carlson twelve times and was present at three taping sessions. As he spoke, Fairbairn glanced frequently, with apparent concern, at Carlson who now sat without him at his side.

Savitz asked Fairbairn what Gerash asked Fisch. Could Carlson be a fraud?

SAVITZ:     Did you consider that Mr. Carlson may be a sociopathic or psychopath, just a cold-blooded killer?

FAIRBAIRN:  Yes [but] . . . a sociopath has a repeated history of delinquent behavior . . . in fact, Carlson was quite the contrary. Most of the time he was driven to excel, driven to be good, trying to conform with what his parents and his peers demanded of him, and that was atypical of a sociopath. And the second observation I made was his earnestness to relate, his puzzlement about his own condition, his desperation to find somebody who would understand him . . . A sociopath can be charming, but he is shallow, distant, and uninvolved . . . I can feel this young man's pain and confusion and his wish to have me help him understand himself. The sociopath would be unable to behave in this way . . .

Driven to be good? Why the dynamite, the guns, the petty thievery, the scams, a gigolo? Fisch believed everything that Carlson told him—"Counselor, the patient always tells the truth!"—and Fairbairn could "feel this young man's pain and confusion." But these were not firm grounds to make diagnoses. No way could

Fairbairn judge with certainty Carlson's truthfulness; again, the fallacy of lies.

During their first meeting, Carlson told Fairbairn that he thought his mind would "split into a thousand pieces." After nine hours of interviews Fairbairn said, "I remembered the offhand remark from Mr. Gerash that [MPD] was a . . . diagnosis of Dr. Fisch's . . ." Some offhand remark.


## Facts?

During their third interview, Fairbairn began to dig into Carlson's past. Fairbairn read to the court from his notes. "DOB, date of birth 5/28/64, that made him nineteen. Minneapolis, Minnesota, was where he was born. No siblings. My parents needed to get married. Folks in high school. Mother got pregnant. My grandfather, a Baptist minister. My grandparents threw my mother out . . ."

Then, Fairbairn continued, when Marilyn went to her mother to tell her that she was pregnant, her mother said: "I wish you were dead" and "I hope you have a child as rotten as you so you will know what it feels like." It appeared from Fairbairn's testimony as if he collected these quotes himself. But as I read this, it was not clear where this grandmotherly quote had come from and, apparently, it was not clear to Eddie Day either. I was glad to see that he interrupted.

DAY:          . . . I am not clear whether he is giving you this or
              where you are getting it from . . .
FAIRBAIRN:    . . . this information has been conveyed to me through
              two main sources—it is information the attorneys have
              gained from their investigator who interviewed the
              grandparents. That's one source.
Walter Gerash then interrupted.
GERASH:       In all fairness to the witness, your Honor, and as an
              officer of the court, my investigator, Mr. Tardy, talked
              to the maternal grandparents and got that information
              from them . . .
DAY:          The grandmother was willing to say that?
GERASH:       No, not the maternal grandmother but the paternal
              grandmother. They know about it . . .

Rod Carlson's mother apparently heard this story about Marilyn's mother twenty years ago and passed it on to Gerash's investigator,

Mr. Tardy, as fact. Then Bob Fairbairn picked it up from either Savitz and Gerash and spoke from the witness stand, as an expert, as if he had collected the information himself. When asked by Eddie Day how he had gotten this information, he did not really know; Gerash, for a moment, did not know either.

In this case, "facts" were bandied about whose origins were problematic. Did Wilets really believe that Carlson had MPD? If so, why did he not testify? Was Carlson abused? If so, where was the evidence?

## Memory versus Knowledge

But now Eddie Day persisted. He also wanted facts.

DAY:        All right . . . I have one other problem I wanted to clear up . . . I have heard here over the last six days that the one personality is amnesic as to what the other one does . . .

FAIRBAIRN:  Yes . . .

DAY:        . . . One personality, whoever it was, knows that he doesn't swear, but that he is swearing. So it seems to me that he has knowledge of the profanity propensities of this other personality, and knows that he is swearing . . . to me that doesn't look like he's amnesic as to what the other personality does . . .

FAIRBAIRN:  You share some of my confusion . . . The amnesia may be total. It may be partial. It may be variable. It can change from day to day . . .

DAY:        Does that explain then one other concern I have? . . . Does this explain then how this person, whoever it is, can search and find from magazines [pictures] . . . and put them into [the collage] in which all of these personalities are here . . . the whole picture [was] put together by somebody [who] . . . has some knowledge of the functions of all of these [personalities] . . .

FAIRBAIRN:  Yes . . . I will illustrate by a demonstration that was given at the course I took . . . "How many of you remember Pearl Harbor?" we were asked. Well, about forty people put their hands up. And then the instructor said, "How many of you were at Pearl Harbor?" One lady put her hand up . . . Now the forty people

|          | who put up their hands . . . had knowledge of Pearl Harbor but they had no memory of [it] . . . Now in multiple personality . . . [Carlson] has no memory . . . but picks up information . . . |
|----------|------|
| DAY:     | . . . Would you relate that to the collage and try to clear that up? [As I understand it] he has heard so much about all of these people and what they do when they are out . . . With that, he has put together a picture of all these people, so he can put it down on paper? |
| FAIRBAIRN: | Exactly . . . And he has been doing this for fifteen years. |
| DAY:     | Okay. All right. Thank you . . . |

The difference was clear. Anything which might incriminate Carlson was knowledge, not memory.


## Razzle-Dazzle

Then as if to emphasize Carlson's illness, Savitz asked Fairbairn to look over at his patient. This led to one of the day's few light moments.

| SAVITZ:    | Do you have an opinion as to your observations of the defendant during these last few moments of the proceedings? . . . |
|------------|------|
| FAIRBAIRN: | I think he is spaced out or is floating. He is not able to pay attention to what is happening in the court-room . . . |
| CHAPPELL:  | Your Honor, I would ask the record to reflect that the . . . defendant is sitting in the chair and appears to be asleep. |
| DAY:       | Let the record so show. I have observed that. |
| SAVITZ:    | That's his opinion, your Honor . . . |

One man's trance was another man's sleep; one man's true MPD was another man's fake. But all eyes were, once again, on Carlson. Imagining the scene, something I heard about camouflage came to mind. Some camouflage is meant to hide, to blend in; if the camouflage works the landscape is empty. But another type of camouflage shines and glitters to draw attention to itself. To beg attention is the plan, but what you see is not what is there. This kind of camouflage is called razzle-dazzle. Razzle-dazzle, I thought, fit Carlson. He begged for attention but what you see might not be what is there.

### Cross-examination

Fairbairn's testimony took two hundred and eight pages; Chappell's cross-examination a scant thirty.

Using Fairbairn's own notes, Chappell got Fairbairn to admit that Carlson understood what he was charged with and that he could be sent to prison. Carlson had told Fairbairn, in fact, and Fairbairn had written it down, that "realistically, the odds are they are going to send me to prison." Carlson also knew something that Fairbairn probably didn't: they had only had ten preemptory challenges during the jury selection process. This was a pretty detailed understanding of his legal circumstances.

Then Chappell ran into symphonies without conductors, again. Only this time, Carlson told it to Fairbairn. In the left-hand margin of Fairbairn's February 29, 1984, notes, Fairbairn wrote "almost like I feel I'm a symphony without a conductor."

CHAPPELL:    Is that a quote from the defendant?

FAIRBAIRN:    Yes.

CHAPPELL:    Thank you, doctor. I have no further questions . . .

Carlson had fed it to Fisch or Fisch had told it to Carlson. Carlson then gave it to Fairbairn. Chappell believed that the conductorless image, like the telephone calls and collage which came in the same week, was more razzle-dazzle. He was so sure that Eddie Day would agree that he didn't bother to follow it up.

### Fig Newton from L.A.

Though the defense had Robert Fairbairn and Ralph Fisch on their side, they left nothing to chance. Right before the hearing was scheduled to begin, the defense brought in a surprise witness.

Robert Fairbairn, the ex–ship's surgeon, was tall, smooth, and silky; Ralph Fisch, with twenty-five years and eight multiples under his belt, was a seasoned forensic psychologist. But Bernauer "Fig" Newton, flown in at the last moment from Los Angeles, was the most experienced hypnotist among the three and an old hand at murder trials and multiples. He was, according to the defense, their "star witness." I counted up the years of experience: the three defense experts had over seventy years between them; the prosecution experts had only three.

I had read one of Newton's papers on MPD and the law. Newton described a mild-mannered man who, though apparently incapable of such acts, sexually attacked several teenaged girls. Newton was called in and discovered that the man was, indeed, a multiple; he had an alter "psychopathic personality." Then just like Carlson, the man pleaded incompetent to proceed. The judge agreed and the man was sent to a state hospital where he was "successfully" treated.

On Thursday, June 14, Newton agreed that Carlson was a "sick, splintered" man. I was struck that splintered was the exact word Carlson used to describe himself when he first met Fairbairn. Carlson, Newton said, was so ill that he could not face a sanity trial.

Newton also chuckled when asked about the contention that Carlson was a fake. "One of the things I always ask myself in situations like this is 'Could I do this?' With my twenty years of experience with multiples, could I fake this? . . . I know I couldn't do it." Newton, apparently, had not read Rosenhan.

Gerash and Savitz seemed to realize that Eddie Day was stuck on the leaking "barriers" between personalities and was confused about what was "memory" and what was "knowledge." Such inconsistencies, Newton said, did not bother him. Newton was also certain that Carlson had been a victim of abuse and a "scapegoat" for a sick, sick family. It would take time to discover it, but the abuse, Newton was certain, was there.

On Friday, in an attempt to fend off the accusation of fake, Newton did agree that Carlson had been asked "leading" and "suggestive" questions by both Fairbairn and Fisch. "There is no question that it spoils a nice, clean record. We would like to have it otherwise," he said. But Newton said the errors "were not blatant" and that the leading questions had not contaminated the diagnosis. Though Newton had cautioned forensic evaluators to videotape all their interviews so that influences on the accused could be found, Fisch and Fairbairn had broken this rule. This lack of a record did not seem to bother Newton at all.

### Witnesses for the Prosecution

It was now Chappell's turn. On Friday, after Newton flew back to L.A. Chappell put on the first witness for the state, Norma Livingston, the psychologist who had done psychological testing on Carlson during his December evaluation at Pueblo. It did not take me long to figure out that Livingston did not like Carlson. He was a psychopath, she said, a fake. Carlson tried to make himself look sick, both on psychological tests and on the wards.

For example, when playing basketball Carlson was powerful and smooth. But as soon as he knew he was being watched, he became uncoordinated. He made himself look bad on psychological tests as well. He scored so poorly on one test, said Livingston, that she would expect to see a raving, psychotic lunatic, someone totally out of touch with reality in her office, not someone with the superficial charms of Ross Carlson. Razzle-dazzle. She was also sure that Carlson was competent. For starters, Carlson knew he was charged with "two counts of first degree murder" and stood to serve "about forty years" in prison. With that, the week ended.

## Outrage and Horror

Over that weekend in Sunday's *The Denver Post* friends of the Carlsons were reported as outraged at the defense's relentless accusations of abuse. These stories were bogus, they said. Bill Cathey, Rod's "best" friend, said that "all this talk about abuse—I just can't understand it. We wish there were more people out there like Rod and Marilyn Carlson. They were professionals, Christians, honorable, and had good values." Another friend said that "They loved Ross. They would have sold their house—gone anywhere, done anything for Ross." Savitz and Gerash, they said, were scraping the bottom to get stories of abuse.

As these six friends spoke to the reporter, another question surfaced, one which bothered me from the first time I read about the murders. Why did Rod and Marilyn just lie down to die? That was, their friends said, the biggest puzzle. "I wake up in the middle of the night, thinking about them," said one woman, "and see them lying there. And I think of the horror they must have gone through." Why did they just lie down and die?

# ROSS MICHAEL CARLSON HAS DISAPPEARED

Bob Chappell was lucky to have the two psychiatrists he had available to testify. At first, the state hospital provided only one, Dr. Alan Fine. But, in an unusual move Fine asked Chappell to get more help. Shortly before the hearing, Chappell managed to convince Judge Turelli to allow him to add another expert, Dr. Scott Reichlin. This had prompted Gerash's Rip Van Winkle comment about Chappell: "He woke up too late. Rip Van Winkle. He just woke up. He woke up too late . . ."

### Who's On First?

Dr. Reichlin found Carlson "charming" and "overtly cooperative" as he sat with "casual indifference" and a hint of condescension through three interviews. Reichlin saw no switches but Carlson had no trouble instructing Reichlin about his MPD. During their second interview, Carlson told Reichlin that he was a multiple, had "lost time" since childhood, and listed the names of each personality along with their characteristics: Steven, "analytic thinker"; Justin, "charming"; Blue, "helpless"; Gray, "depressed and suicidal"; Norman, "belligerent"; Stacey, "athletic"; Black, "the protector."

Carlson also told Reichlin of a new personality, "I don't know," named by Carlson's response to Fairbairn's question of who he was talking to. "I don't know who you are talking to" became reified; the name for a new personality. This reminded me of the Abbott and Costello bit: "Who's on first?" "No, he is on second." . . . "Well, who's on third?" "No, I don't know is on third." The new alter, "I don't know," would be hilarious if not taken so seriously.

Carlson also said the last thing he remembered was a bite of roast beef at the Canterbury Inn. Then he "lost time." Carlson did not remember any more bites of his meal, nor anything else until he regained his memory as he drank a beer with Ken Cortez after the movie. He went blank, he said, at 7:30 and awoke at 11:45 on that August night.

Reichlin did not find Fairbairn's tape convincing. Carlson's personalities were not distinct; the amnesia between personalities was too variable. He concluded, as did Livingston, that though Carlson had many characteristics of a multiple, he was a fake.

### Reichlin's Debut

Bob Chappell decided to put Reichlin on first and have his assistant, Michael Watanabe, take Reichlin through his testimony. If Chappell and Watanabe thought they would be allowed to present their case in an organized way with Gerash in court, they were wrong. As Watanabe began, Gerash jumped up to interrupt.

GERASH:     Your Honor, at this time we would like to have a chance to chat with Dr. Reichlin before he is examined by the prosecution and before he is examined by us.

DAY:     Would you mind telling me why you're waiting to this late date . . . ?

WATANABE:     Judge, I think counsel have known of Dr. Reichlin's appointment by the court for some time . . . I think they have had ample opportunity to talk with him . . .

As Chappell feared, Eddie Day capitulated. Then Gerash, before Watanabe could even get off the ground, took Reichlin apart, piece by piece.

GERASH:     Dr. Reichlin, you finished your residency in 1982 . . .

REICHLIN:     Yes . . .

GERASH:     So you really have been in practice almost a year . . .

REICHLIN:     Well, in private practice . . .

GERASH:     Let me ask you this question as to your qualifications.

|            |                                                                 |
|------------|-----------------------------------------------------------------|
|            | You have never diagnosed multiple personality disorder, have you? |
| REICHLIN:  | That's correct.                                                 |
| GERASH:    | You've never treated a multiple personality disorder, isn't that correct? |
| REICHLIN:  | Yes.                                                            |
| GERASH:    | You've never seen a multiple personality disorder in Pueblo, have you? |
| REICHLIN:  | That's correct . . .                                            |
| GERASH:    | That's all I have . . .                                         |

Within less than two minutes, Reichlin was wounded badly. The next day, perhaps because of his humiliation on Monday, he decided to strike back, always a big mistake. Gerash must have been delighted.

|            |                                                                 |
|------------|-----------------------------------------------------------------|
| GERASH:    | Did you palpate his head to see what happened to the top of his skull and why Mrs. Carlson was delayed going home for six days? |
| REICHLIN:  | I didn't palpate his head . . .                                 |
| GERASH:    | . . . Why did you take a history from him?                      |
| REICHLIN:  | Why did I take a history from him?                              |
| GERASH:    | Yes, yes . . . Does not Cornelia Wilbur, does not Kluft, does not Putnam, do not all the experts in the field . . . say that child abuse, sexual abuse, is one of the hallmarks of the beginning of disease. |
| REICHLIN:  | You finally said something that is correct.                     |
| GERASH:    | Oh, I see. Only what you say is correct? Everything I uttered here is incorrect . . . ? |
| REICHLIN:  | Well . . . you're talking like a psychiatrist, and some of your information is not accurate. |
| GERASH:    | You are getting very hostile, aren't you?                       |
| REICHLIN:  | No.                                                            |
| GERASH:    | This is your debut in your first murder case, isn't it?         |
| WATANABE:  | Objection, that's irrelevant.                                   |
| DAY:       | Sustained . . .                                                 |

The damage was done; Reichlin was buried. Reichlin's report was well thought-out but his courtroom performance was a failure. A good psychiatrist, he was a bad actor. Through ridicule, Gerash had gotten to him and by so doing Reichlin lost his mantle as "expert."

## Letters of the Accused

Despite Reichlin's showing, Chappell was still confident. For one thing, he still had Alan Fine and for another he planned to introduce thirty-one letters written by Carlson from the hospital and jail between his arrest in September 1983 and June 1984, the time of the hearing.

Carlson was constantly in contact with someone, somewhere, by telephone and by mail. Since his arrest, he wrote letter upon letter to buddies, old girlfriends, and to his maternal grandparents, the Reverend and Mrs. Hill. Carlson chatted about books, the rigors of jail life, religion, old romances, his mistreatment, and his dislike of institutional food. He never admitted—as he did with Fisch and Fine—that he had a clue how his parents died. In fact, he vehemently denied he had anything to do with it at all.

In those letters, Chappell hoped Eddie Day would see, not a dissociated multiple, but someone who was trying to save his skin. They demonstrated, thought Chappell, that between his arrest and hearing, Carlson always knew who he was, what he was charged with, what the consequences of his actions were, and that he could cooperate with his attorneys. Ross Carlson was not amnestic and he was not confused.

When I read them, I found Carlson's spelling atrocious, the remnant of his mild dyslexia. A voracious reader and precocious talker, Carlson just could not spell. *Speek* for *speak*, *artical* for *article* and so forth. But Carlson's spelling did not stop him from turning out letter after letter.

Shortly after being jailed, Carlson told his mother's parents, the Reverend and Mrs. Hill, about his renewed belief in Jesus Christ. He had discarded his "old" notion that "only the week" needed the Bible to "be told what to do . . . Now I feel," he wrote, "that the direction the Bible gives is of great importance." A cynic might have pointed out that Carlson's renewed enthusiasm for Christ reflected an awareness that he needed the Hills' cooperation, too, to shake his parent's money loose for his defense.

Carlson also said he was framed. "I even found out that [a friend] was trying to help the cops pin it on me. It seems the cops want a scape goate." He harangued friends with "you are supposed to be innocent untill proven gilty"; that "an independent investigator feels very strongly that I could not have done the crime I am accused of."

Two days before his interview with Ralph Fisch, Carlson protested his innocence when he wrote to friends: "I am being held unjustly by an unjust system. I have been accused, tried, and in essance been convicted by an over zelous press . . . I can not think of any thing worse than the experiences of loosing what I have lost and being accused of such a action . . . Only the people who know me seem to be assured of my innocence . . . ."

On March 11, 1984, three months after he told Fine and Fisch about the shootings, he wrote to the Reverend and Mrs. Hill again. "We all, especially me, tried to help the police. I did my best and this is what I get. I will never talk to a cop again . . . You are supposed to be innocent until *proven* gilty . . . I appreciate your concern and prayers."

Carlson was aware of his press. "I've been reading my favorite fiction, the *Denver Post* and the *R. M. News*! They . . . haven't gotten any story straight on my case in a number of weeks . . . I suppose it just goes to show you believe 3/4 of what you see, 1/2 of what you here, and 1/4 of what you read." Carlson, it seemed to me, thought a lot about deception.


## Movies

And he thought about illusion. In the fall he wrote to a girlfriend that he had seen ads for a new Richard Gere movie. Carlson was a great fan of Gere's. One of his two favorite movies—the other was *Body Heat*—was *American Gigolo* in which Gere, as Julian, was a slick male prostitute framed for a brutal murder. I wondered how *Body Heat* and *American Gigolo*, both about sex, deception, and murder, influenced Carlson's reality.

In December, Carlson wrote to another girl about illusion. "I am finding," he wrote, "that by spending so much time alone gives one time to think. [This] has been a real blessing for me. It gives me time to think through future movie projects. I think a good romantic comedy would be a real nice change of pace . . . ."

For the most part, Carlson's letters were empty and self-serving. Carlson's new belief in Christ and his love for his fellow man lacked conviction. But, banal or not, Carlson's letters were cohesive. He was smooth and polite to a fault as he referred to "gentlemen" and "ladies"; he always remembered holidays, birthdays, and illnesses. He signed all his letters with a flourish, with either "God Bless," "with love," or "take care." All were signed "Ross"; I did not find a Black, Blue, Gray, Norman, Stacey, or Antichrist among them.

I don't think Chappell wanted Eddie Day to read Carlson's letters because of Carlson's religious conversion or interest in film. He wanted Day to read them because in Chappell's eyes, Carlson's words revealed that he grasped his legal predicament—a central feature of competence.

For example, in the beginning of October, Carlson understood the intricacies of trying to get hold of his inheritance. "It appears that I won't have any access [to the money] for an additional 3 weeks at least. Until I secure these funds getting Walter Gerash to get moving on the case is postponed." On October 17 he wrote that "the judge in essence decided not to make any dissicion. Savitz wanted him to order the trust officer to disperce the funds. And now the trust officer dose not have any clear cut directions."

On November 16 he said he had spoken with "Walter" who was trying to "talk to Truman" about bail. A little later he wrote that "My situation is rather 'precarious' to say the least . . . The events of the next little bit will determine what the cource the rest of my life takes. Not just the next six months, but the next 50 to 60 years . . . my life is at stake." Carlson was right: his life was at stake.

But after Reichlin stepped down, Judge Day refused to accept Carlson's letters as evidence. Instead, he scolded Chappell for "dumping something" on his desk. Day said that he needed an expert to tell him which personality wrote what! At that moment Chappell looked over at the prosecution's table and muttered "holy shit" under his breath. This was the first time, Chappell later told me, that he knew he was in trouble, that Eddie Day had "bit off on MPD."

### The Youngest Gun

Chappell's disappointment came just before his last witness. Alan Fine had done, I thought, the most thorough evaluation of Carlson and had ferreted out details of the murder from Carlson. Fine saw Carlson in Pueblo six times starting right before Christmas and ending January 26. It was Fine who ordered the psychological tests performed by Dr. Livingston. Fine concluded that Carlson was not insane at the time he killed his parents and was competent to stand trial now.

Carlson told Fine about a grim childhood. First the diaper incident and then how at age three he tightened his mouth around a
glass so hard that it shattered. He painted a picture of his parents as
"unavailable"; that he always felt that he "let them down." At six,
he thought of killing himself and told Fine that he was "disci-
plined" by his father with a belt and a wooden spoon.

Just as he told Fisch, Carlson explained that after high school he
experienced "divergent personalities" which were "all good or all
bad." He laid out his three current ones: Ross, Justin Nicholas
Time, and the Antichrist, the three he "revealed" to Fisch just
weeks before. Fine thought it odd that Carlson, if a real multiple,
could remember the three so freely. Furthermore, Fine concluded
when he watched Carlson on tape, he seemed to switch "on demand."

### Details: "Bang! Bang!"

Carlson also provided details of the murders: how he directed his
parents to Cottonwood Road, how he pulled out his gun, how he
ordered his parents to lie facedown on the ground, how his mother
turned around and said "This is hell. I don't want to live. Just go
ahead and shoot me." And finally, how he shot his father first and
then his mother, once each, in quick succession. "It was like this,"
Carlson told Fine, shooting with his right index finger, "Bang!
Bang!" It was, said Carlson, like "things were speeding up, like I
had been shot out of a cannon. My mind was doing two hundred
miles an hour. I seemed to be watching everything that was happening as if it were in a movie." A movie.

But Carlson said he did not remember the .38 Rossi or hiding the
black bag. "To be perfectly honest with you," he told Fine, "I don't
remember ever having a gun at all," despite the memory of shooting
his parents.

### Gerash, Again

As soon as Bob Chappell called Fine to the stand, Gerash was
quickly on his feet.

GERASH:    Just a few questions . . . were you still in your residency
           program when you examined Ross Carlson in 1983?
FINE:      No . . .

GERASH:     You never testified in a murder/insanity case before, have
            you? . . .
FINE:       No . . .
GERASH:     You never treated a multiple personality disorder before?
FINE:       No.
GERASH:     You personally have never diagnosed anybody with a mul-
            tiple personality disorder before, have you?
FINE:       No.
GERASH:     You personally have not seen a multiple personality disor-
            der on the wards in Pueblo?
FINE:       No . . .

Gerash had struck again. That, I thought, was that. Fine's testimony was, like his report, thoughtful, but after this interchange his
thoughtfulness did not seem to matter at all.


## Cuing the Shooter

Chappell led Fine through his testimony. Fine told Eddie Day that
Carlson switched on demand on the tapes; therefore his switching,
if real, was still under his conscious control. Fine also noticed what I
did, that Ralph Fisch unknowingly primed Carlson about "the
double," that "the double" did the shooting. Fisch unwittingly
cued Carlson what to say in other ways as well.

CHAPPELL:   Doctor, can you find the question by Dr. Fisch about
            the face of the parents.
FINE:       (reading from the transcript)
            Fisch: Okay, if you can imagine that scene again, they
            are there and you are going to shoot them . . . as you
            look at them . . . does either one of them . . . seem
            to look like you, or do you seem to look like them?
            Carlson: They seem to look . . . like me, and I look
            like them. Well, I shouldn't phrase it that way. The
            shooter looks like them and the shootee looks like me.
CHAPPELL:   . . . Does Dr. Fisch ask Carlson whether this was the
            first time he had ever related that to a doctor?
FINE:       Yes . . .

Ross Carlson was, in Fine's opinion, "highly suggestible." "I can
easily see how he," Fine explained, "by playing the role of different
personalities, has found a way to explain what he did . . . and . . .

alleviate having to look at what he did and . . . facing the terrible pain that would cause . . ."

As I read, I now understood why Chappell had seemed tentative. He was stuck with two different explanations. Reichlin called Carlson a fake. Fine emphasized that Carlson learned how to act like a multiple; that Carlson might actually believe he suffered from MPD. Though not mutually exclusive theories, Chappell, by having to argue each, diluted their impact. Besides, the notions that Carlson was either a fake or had learned the symptoms of MPD were too subtle for development on the tenth and eleventh day of a hearing. It was getting too late.


### Egg Roll

When Gerash's turn to cross-examine came, he made quick work of Fine.

GERASH:    When you questioned Mr. Carlson he became so angry and violent that you thought your life may be in jeopardy . . . and you terminated the session for fear of your life. Right?

FINE:    I think that's an exaggeration.

GERASH:    Let me use your words. In your report you said that his anger became so intense that "I terminated the interview for safety reasons." Is that right?

FINE:    That is correct . . .

GERASH:    You were isolated and afraid and uncomfortable and afraid that Carlson would strike out. It was very menacing and frightening. That's your words, isn't it?

FINE:    Yes.

GERASH:    You didn't know you were looking at Black then, did you?

FINE:    I am still not convinced of that at all.

GERASH:    And at that time you didn't know what an eye roll was from an egg roll; right?

FINE:    That's correct . . .

The eye roll, egg roll bit made the TV news. So much for Alan Fine.

### The Surprise of Randall Louis Staton

Bob Chappell thought the parade of experts was over and time for closing arguments. He was wrong. It was time, instead, for another Gerash surprise, a witness who Chappell had no idea was coming. Chappell objected to Randall Louis Staton, but in vain. Gerash told Judge Day that Staton had "powerful evidence" about a "dramatic incident" which proved that Carlson was a multiple well before he killed his parents.

A few years before, according to Staton, Ross Carlson, as scheduled, came to the Staton house to mow the lawn which he had been asked to do since Randy's parents were out of town and Randy was in a knee cast. From the house, Randy watched Carlson work. A few hours later, Carlson returned and knocked on the Staton's side door. When Randy opened it, Carlson asked who had cut the lawn. When Randy said that Carlson had already cut it, Carlson accused Randy of trying to gyp him out of five dollars and of having cut the lawn himself. When Staton reassured Carlson that he would be paid, a mollified Carlson left.

This was, the defense said, a clear case of amnesia. Chappell did not mount an effective cross-examination. These five minutes of Randy Staton cinched it.

### Doctor Day

By now, Chappell had little doubt that he had lost. It turned into a nightmare. On Thursday, June 21, Eddie Day read his ruling to his packed Douglas County Courtroom. First, Day said, in his opinion Carlson suffered from multiple personality disorder and that Carlson was inhabited by at least seven different personalities.

"The weight of the evidence favored the diagnosis [made] by those experts who between them have half a century of experience" and not just three years, said Day. Chappell, he suggested, should have produced more experienced experts.

Day said he believed Staton, O'Hagan, Lebel, and Rhoads. Especially Staton. He found Staton's story of Carlson's lawn mowing amnesia compelling, therefore Carlson, said Day, had symptoms of MPD well before the murders. And, Day added, he did not believe that Carlson was cued to act like a multiple by Fisch and Fairbairn. Why? Because of Wilets's blurted out comment the day after the crime that he had missed the diagnosis of MPD. Gerash's repetition of that uncorroborated fact had worked.

Day said he could see with his own eyes that Carlson was sick: he could see his "inattentiveness, lack of concentration, animated talking with his lawyers followed by apparent napping or sleeping." It was, he said, "incredulous and boggles the mind" to think that Carlson—sitting there switching and floating—was a fake. It couldn't, Judge Day said, be done.

As far as Eddie Day was concerned, Ross Carlson was a multiple and a very sick man. Now what about competence? First, Eddie Day said that Carlson was in touch with reality. He knew he was in big trouble. Why else would he hire a lawyer? Carlson also understood the charges and the legal consequences of those charges. The problem, Day said, was amnesia. Day believed Carlson when he said that he could not remember. And because of his amnesia, Carlson could not participate in his own defense. Ergo, Carlson was incompetent. Judge Day had bought memory versus knowledge.

## A Hard Month
As Day read his opinion, Bob Fairbairn, as he did every day, morning, and afternoon, sat at Carlson's side treating him like a hothouse rose. Every day, all day, Carlson did the Spiegel eye roll as he switched from Justin to Steve to whomever and back.

Chappell's logic had been no match for this razzle-dazzle. After court was adjourned, Chappell picked up his large cardboard box filled with his files and stalked from the room. He refused to comment on Day's decision. "It has been a hard month," he told reporters.

## Unprepared, Outmatched, and Outwitted
Chappell told me later he was shattered. Chappell had gone to war without his best troops. He was taken by surprise by Randy Staton and both Reichlin and Fine looked too inexperienced.

Chappell's prosecution also lacked coherence. I thought he tried to sell two theories about Carlson's illness—Carlson planned the multiple defense well before the murders and, therefore, was an out-and-out fake or Carlson learned to be a multiple under the tutelage of Fisch's and Fairbairn's inept questioning. But Gerash had only one theory to sell: that Carlson was very, very sick and Day equated the presence of MPD with incompetence.

In retrospect, Chappell's thinking was clouded by what he knew of Carlson's guilt. Chappell told me he was outraged by Carlson and haunted by Carlson's words to Alan Fine. "It was like this: Bang! Bang!" Carlson said, as he shot his parents in mime, his outstretched finger pointed slightly ahead and to the ground. "Bang! Bang!" And because of his outrage, Chappell lost. Chappell did not believe until the very end, that anyone would buy Carlson's story.

Responses to Day's ruling were quick. Day's criticism of the prosecution was echoed by other observers at the trial. Chappell "didn't seem to have a game plan," said one lawyer who closely followed the case. "It looked to me that they were unprepared, outmatched, and outwitted." Another lawyer who had watched the hearing was unsure why Chappell had picked experts with so little experience. He also felt that Chappell had consistently failed to follow up on key points during cross-examination and so did I. "They really did drop the ball," he said. "I would imagine there is a lot of soul searching going on right now at the District Attorney's office."

But in public, Chappell's boss, Robert Gallagher, said that his assistants had presented their case in a "very, very professional manner. We did not engage in a circus act or in any theatrics . . ." Perhaps they should have but they did not realize, until too late, what they were up against.

Gallagher pointed out that Carlson would eventually have to face an insanity trial. Once all the facts of Carlson's planning were revealed no jury would find him insane, the prosecution still hoped. And when ruled sane, Carlson would stand trial for two counts of murder in the first degree. But when the sanity trial would be was anyone's guess. It had receded far into the distance.

**Bleeding Heart**
While Chappell was still stunned, Savitz and Gerash worked the press. This was the first time in Colorado, they said, that a defense of MPD has been successful in a competency hearing. Savitz was ecstatic. "My heart has bled all along for this young man," he said. "Someone has finally responded to his howlings and to his crying out." This was Carlson as victim; tormented and abused by a sadistic family.

They now began to tell the press that Carlson could not receive adequate treatment for MPD at the Colorado State Hospital at Pueblo. "We are going to make every effort to impress upon the people in Pueblo of the absolute necessity that this young man be treated in a responsible, humane way," Savitz said. "We will be monitoring that very, very closely." He should not, they said, be "warehoused."

Dr. Cornelia Wilbur, who treated the famous multiple, "Sybil," was quoted in the *Post*. Carlson may be "doomed" if sent to Pueblo, she said. "There isn't anyone in the state hospital who knows a damn thing about multiple personality," the seventy-five-year-old Wilbur told a reporter from her office in Lexington, Kentucky. "I'll bet you they find more than seven personalities." Wilbur had never seen Carlson. I bet, I thought, they had sent her the tapes.


### Outrage

Rod and Marilyn's friends were outraged. "All I can say," said Rod's closest friend, "is that the loving, faithful nature of his parents was not brought out by the prosecutors. The defense tore Rod and Marilyn to pieces. The prosecutors did a very, very poor job." Another friend was more direct: "It's a bunch of hogwash. I think the judge ought to be declared incompetent . . . Somebody's responsible for Rod and Marilyn's deaths—somebody did it . . ."

She was right. Antichrist or illusionist, someone had done it. But Day had "bit off" on MPD. As far as Day was concerned, Ross Michael Carlson had long since disappeared. The question was no longer what Carlson did and how he did it. Multiple personality disorder, not murder, was now the issue. Day put multiple personality disorder on center stage and the defense meant to keep it dancing there. Carlson's parents were stone cold dead but why Ross Michael Carlson had killed them was the furthest thing from anyone's mind.

For the second time *The Denver Post* ran another of their box scores of Carlson's personalities:

**Steve:** Age 42. Mature, intelligent, logical but hopelessly boring. Steve is out frequently, especially during the legal proceedings. **Justin Time:** Age 16. Affable, but aloof and superficial. Meticulous and materialistic. A lover of fine clothing and fine dining. Lawyers are unsure about the meaning of the play on words in his name. Justin had been identified by Ross as his twin. **Blue:** Age 6. Weepy and frightened. Emerges during times of stress. Carlson's body seems to shrink when Blue comes out. Believed to have been created when Ross had trouble with his ABCs and dyslexia. **Gray:** Aged 12 to 14. Suicidal, depressed. Often appears when Blue is so anxious and distressed that he contemplates suicide. **Stacey:** Age unknown. The athlete. A weight lifter and karate enthusiast. Likes to drive cars. **Black:** Age unknown. Aggressive and violent. The protector of the other personalities. Carlson said he fears he will be cured and sent to prison where Black will no longer be able to protect him. **Norman:** Probably an adolescent. Verbally obscene and assaultive, aggressive, rude. A "loud-mouthed punk." **Anti-Christ:** Demonic, evil. Possibly a combination of Black and Norman . . . may have been responsible for the slaying of Carlson's parents.

# ·CHAPTER·
## ELEVEN
# THE ICEMAN

.

## Trap

I first faced Ross Carlson four and a half months after he was sent back to the state hospital at Pueblo for restoration of mental competency by Judge Day. Judge Day had told Dr. Haydee Kort—the Argentinean director of the state hospital—that she and her staff had to treat Carlson for an illness none of them believed Carlson had.

Now the state was in a trap. Kort and her doctors couldn't question Carlson's diagnosis without risking being found in contempt of court. But if Kort's doctors treated Carlson for MPD, they also risked turning him loose. If they agreed Carlson was a multiple now, Carlson must have been a multiple then, the night of August 17, 1983.

So Kort had a problem. Her every move was watched by Gerash, Savitz, and Eddie Day. She told me no case had been this complicated and no case had gotten this kind of intense scrutiny by attorneys, a judge, and the press. The energy that she and her staff had to spend on Ross Carlson, she said, brought her hospital to a screeching halt.

## Contempt

This scrutiny—it was like working in a fishbowl—proved to be too much for one of her doctors who, soon after Carlson returned to Pueblo, lost it. A psychologist told Carlson that Walter Gerash was a "scumbag." Gerash, he claimed, would dump Carlson when his money ran out. This outburst gave Gerash and Savitz the ammunition they needed to challenge the state's ability to treat Carlson at all.

They went to the press and to court, again. Savitz, in the newspapers and on television, called Carlson's care "appalling" and "obscene." The attorneys asked Day to find four people at Pueblo—including the diminutive and gracious Kort—in contempt of his ruling because the "doctors there," in Savitz's words, have "warehoused Carlson in a climate of hostility, skepticism, defiance, and neglect."

"The hospital hasn't devised a treatment plan for him," Savitz said on the first day of October. "He is not doing well because he is surrounded by a very hostile environment. The doctors are still questioning his disorder and questioning his sincerity." I thought it had been a mistake to return Carlson to the same ward where he had been evaluated the prior winter by Drs. Fine and Livingston. Livingston was still there and nothing had made her—and the rest of the staff—change. No matter what Eddie Day said, they were angry that Ross Carlson was back and not in jail.

This crisis might have been avoided. First, Chappell had realized too late that Carlson had hired legal and psychiatric heavyweights. Now, Kort and her doctors treated Carlson as if he did not have the same lawyers watching their every move.

Kort barely escaped Eddie Day's censure. "I want to know what is going on down there," Day said on October 19. Though, "at first blush, it appeared there may have been some foot dragging down there," Day decided to postpone a contempt hearing until early December. Kort was lucky but the hospital was on notice, Savitz said. "We want them to know," he told a reporter, "that we will be our client's watchdog."

## Seal of Approval

To defend themselves, Pat Robb, the hospital's in-house lawyer, announced that Kort planned to hire outside experts to help plan and pass judgment on Carlson's treatment. This was a time-honored way: hire consultants. Hire consultants to give advice; hire consultants to cover your back. When this hit the papers, little did I know that I was to be one of them.

One day, Kort called. Because of my work with adult victims of child abuse, she knew I was interested in dissociative disorders—the category of illness into which multiple personality disorder fell. She wanted my opinion on Carlson's treatment—were they doing the right thing? I was dubious about getting involved but I liked her and was curious about Carlson. So I agreed.

I first limited what I would do. I would not be drawn into the debate about Carlson's MPD and I did not want, I told her, to go to court. I knew the formidable forces arrayed against the state and, although she just wanted my advice, everyone connected with Carlson was closely watched. Of course, there was Gerash and Savitz; I wanted no part of them. Carlson must have been abused, I said to Kort before I hung up.


## November 14, 1984

The weather was appropriately ominous when I finally drove the one hundred and five miles to Pueblo. I had put off my visit until the last moment. I pulled my car out of the medical center parking lot and turned south and merged with the noonday traffic on Colorado Boulevard. Past the strip of gas stations, Burger Kings, and tire stores which bisect all western towns, when I got to Interstate 25 I continued south toward Pueblo. As I crossed the outskirts of Denver and Littleton, I passed close to the Canterbury Inn, the Ramada Renaissance, and not far from Cottonwood Road.

Soon I drove past the Douglas County Justice Center which sat, low and brown, off to my left where Eddie Day, five months before, had set in motion the events which had led to my drive. As I drove south, the clouds got darker and the temperature dropped. The weather mirrored my mood. I thought to myself that I had never heard of anyone killing their parents in such a cold, evil way.

In 1984, the current psychiatric rage, MPD, was new to me and so far I had managed to avoid its controversies. I, like many other psychiatrists, thought true MPD was rare. I did not think my patients who suffered from dissociative episodes—who had been badly abused, who thought of themselves in highly disjointed ways

—were multiples. However, to partisans of MPD I was one of the naive, outdated psychiatrists who missed MPD because of ignorance. I was not on the cutting edge.

However, it was not MPD or the legal circus which had made me put off my visit. As I passed Colorado Springs and the fourteen thousand foot Pikes Peak, I understood the real reason I wanted to limit my involvement with Ross Carlson. In my highway reverie, I imagined it happening to me. Instead of his parents, I felt my face in the rough dirt and bullets smashing into the back of my brain. Ross Carlson frightened me.


## Pueblo

The Colorado State Hospital—Pueblo as it is called—was built on the west side of town, facing the Rockies. It is an eclectic collection of red and yellow brick buildings, some very old, spread out over many acres of treeless brown prairie. Maximum security—built, I was told with a snicker, by a paranoid governor—lies behind enormous electrical and steel security.

I parked my car and entered the maze of cages, constructed like an oversized dog run, which led to the steel front door of Max. Once inside, I had to state my purpose, show my driver's license, and then was buzzed through into another room for another once-over.

As I was cleared through these checkpoints, I found myself agreeing with the paranoid governor; the people housed in Maximum Security were the most crazy and violent of the criminally insane. One patient, I was told, murdered a man and then ate his brain. In my opinion, the governor was the realist and the man who snickered at him just did not want to admit how horribly violent some people were.

I did not see Carlson right away. First I met Dr. Gregory Trautt, Ross Carlson's psychologist and therapist. Dr. Trautt had already spent a lot of time with Carlson. I was eager to hear what he had found.

We met in the hall and moved into Trautt's small office. Trautt, who is large, intense, and earnest, wedged himself into his chair. I quickly found the room claustrophobic but I was pleasantly surprised by the level of Trautt's sophistication. He had formulated a sensible plan. He wanted, he told me, to establish "a trusting relationship" with Carlson so that Carlson could begin to talk about the tumultuous events of his past year and, eventually, to face what he had done.

Trautt, more than I, was inclined to accept that Carlson suffered from some form of dissociative disorder, that parts of his amnesia were genuine. But, Trautt told me, until now Carlson had said little in their sessions and was loath to talk about what had happened. "What if," he asked Trautt, "someone pops out and admits to the crime?"

The problem, of course, was that Carlson was frightened that anything he said could also be used in court. Carlson, therefore, refused to "involve" himself in therapy until the charges against him were "resolved." But, I thought, how could those charges be resolved if he did not involve himself in therapy and was not restored to competency?

Carlson had told Trautt some things. For instance, his mind was like a computer with different "files" of stored information, each of which could be accessed with the appropriate password. Each "file" was separate, and each, like his alter personalities, had a unique function. The information contained in one file might at times be "accessed accidentally," but that was rare.

When Trautt asked Carlson whether he knew the passwords for each file, Carlson became upset. He could not, he told Trautt, get into those files. When Trautt said to become "fused" Carlson would have to learn each password through psychotherapy, Carlson became even more upset. So far, Trautt told me, Carlson kept those "files" under wraps.

## Rage

Trautt had also performed a series of psychological tests and found some oddities. During one session, Carlson appeared to switch at least once. At another point, Carlson became confused and forgot the test instructions.

Overall, Carlson had presented himself in a cool, aloof, and highly logical way. Carlson's IQ, though not in the genius range, tested out as bright normal. Also, contradicting Norma Livingston's testimony, Trautt did not think that the test results showed that Carlson tried to "fake bad" or malinger on the test.

Carlson's test results were pretty bad, nonetheless. Overly suspicious, Carlson was in a major identity crisis and was not always clear about who or what he was. Unbelievably, on the inkblot test, thirty-four out of thirty-nine of his responses were *identical* to the test he took with Dr. Livingston in January 1984. This, according to Trautt, showed that Carlson had an incredible memory and, therefore, Carlson had a tendency to store up angry feelings and carry a grudge forever. His hostility, said Trautt, could erupt suddenly and unexpectedly. Now people in the hospital were concerned for Norma Livingston's safety.

Carlson's tests told Trautt something else. Like many murderers Ross Carlson was raised in an emotionally distorted family. His parents, the inkblots showed, had held back the full brunt of their own rage. The family, Trautt speculated, operated with the unwritten rule that they should never express their true feelings. They were, after all, strict Baptists. But Carlson had smashed that rule in a very big way on Cottonwood Road.

Finally, though no test can prove the existence of MPD, Carlson's results, Trautt told me, were compatible with MPD. In other words, Trautt told me, somewhat sheepishly at first, Ross Carlson could be a "real multiple."

### "Ghost Pains"

Carlson had told Trautt and the staff other things. For instance, Carlson said he suffered from "ghost pains" as a child, as if "someone was trying to come out and take over." For years, he also said, he felt "possessed." Carlson recently told his nurse that he was now experiencing "memory surges"; new scenes and experiences, he said, previously unknown to him, were coming into his brain. But he would not tell her much about what he saw.

Carlson also complained that he had experienced "time lapses" and had been "losing time" for years. On the ward he always wore a watch and carried a notebook to make lists, he said, and to keep track of time. But Carlson was vague and evasive when asked about the crime. He would not even provide the same details he gave Alan Fine, in the same hospital, ten months before. "It could be used against me," he said. And if he learned what his other personalities think and have done, "it would drive me over the edge."

Carlson wanted to keep, he said, the protection of his amnesia. "There is," he said, "something inside of me that tells me 'do not talk.' " And outside. I knew that first Gerash's partner, then Craig

Truman, and now probably Savitz and Gerash told Carlson to keep quiet. Finally, Trautt said it was good that Carlson was transferred to a new unit, one which had not been contaminated by the competency hearing. But he admitted that it was tough for him and the ward having every word and deed scrutinized by Savitz and Gerash.

### First Interview

It was now time for me to see Carlson. At three, I was led downstairs, through another maze of halls and into a large room filled with old furniture. It seemed as if the room had not been used in years. As I walked in I was relieved to see that he was not yet there. I noticed that one wall was covered with a one-way mirror. The rest of the room was painted a pale, depressing yellow, the corners in dark shadows. I set up two chairs in the middle of the room, about eight feet apart. The one dirty window was covered by a heavy screen mesh; designed to prevent escape, all the screen did was prevent whatever light was left of the deepening gray November afternoon from coming into the room.

The first thing I noticed when Carlson walked in was that he was bigger than I expected. I am five eight and he was at least a head taller and solid. He had those almost soft, boyish all-American good looks and a hint of a smile as he walked slowly toward me. Carlson's hand was dry but noncommittal. I hoped he did not feel my perspiration.

I motioned him to his chair and then I sat down. Carlson sat across from me, legs apart, hands in his pockets, elbows spread out. He was relaxed, composed, but ready for action. I saw that he kept his hands in his pockets, an indication that he was hiding something but this was not news. Those were the hands of a murderer.

I told the tech that I wanted to be alone with Carlson because I thought, alone, we would have an easier time talking. The tech who brought Carlson in watched, I hoped, from the other side of the mirror. I, for some reason, did not think it was dangerous to be alone in this room with a killer.

If one thing characterized Carlson's entrance, it was his total assurance. His clothes looked freshly pressed. He wore with casual elegance a pink button-down shirt and gray slacks. His hair, which I later learned he spent hours on, was neatly combed, parted on the left. His skin was clear, almost alabaster. As I took him in, Carlson reminded me of a mannequin: almost too perfect. My eyes stayed on his blond hair. Thick, sculpted, brushed, and not real. Like a model—which Carlson was—or a movie star. The only thing which was not seamless was his bull neck and shoulders; the result, I knew, of hours in the weight room. So far, Carlson had not taken his flat blue eyes off of me.

I told Carlson who I was and why I was there and that what he told me was not confidential. I was there, I said, to judge whether his treatment was appropriate. I then paused and thought that I saw a little nod. Still he said nothing. He had yet to look away.

I asked how he was doing. "I'm having," he said in an even voice, "good and bad experiences here." His words hung in the air between us before they fell away, replaced by silence. We sat and looked at each other. It felt as if he dared me to ask him more but I waited; I wanted to see what he said next. His hawklike eyes had not yet moved.

By now both of his hands were out but his palms remained hidden as they lay on each thigh. He said nothing. Was there anything that he wanted to add? I asked finally. No, he said, that was it. Interviews could be like this in the beginning. He wanted to feel me out. Would I be dangerous to him and his cause? Would I help?

"I want to get out of this place," Carlson finally said, as he shifted in his chair. "I am mentally competent. I don't know why I am here." As he talked his mouth moved but his body stayed still, waiting.

Suddenly, for the first time, he looked away. Was it a lie which made him avert his eyes or were murder memories breaking through? As soon as he told me he was fine, he added that his thinking was "disorienting," not exactly a sign of competency. But he was quick to add, "the world seems more cemented." He looked back at me.

Was it in pieces before? What did he mean? Did he feel fragmented? Carlson ignored my attempts to have him explain. He remained stilted and stiff, his answers elliptical, not meant to inform. If I did not know before, by now I knew he was in full control of the conversation. It had become a contest and the first round went to Carlson.

Finally, after a very long pause, he said, the "way I was taught, the world has a price." He then added, "You pay for what you get.

That is what my father always said to me. 'You pay for your thrills.' "

When the word father passed his lips, a shudder went through me but Carlson remained impassive. As I looked into Carlson's face, I wondered what I should say next. Did he kill him? And his mother? Of course he did.

Why did he do it? What was his motive? This last question had been lost in all of the hoopla of the circus. But it was the question which lay at the very center of the case. Why did he shoot them? I wanted to know. I did not know him well enough yet to ask.

My thoughts drifted. I knew he was weaned on the Old and New Testaments. "And parents are the pride of their children . . ." Proverbs 17:6. Was his murderous act some kind of weird, upside-down, inside out version of Abraham and Isaac? Did he, his father's child, because of some crazy God-like demand, set out to sacrifice his father—and mother?

But God did not, as he stopped Abraham, stop Ross Carlson. Was that because his heart was not pure? Was that why he called himself Antichrist, the man of lawlessness, the man doomed to destruction? I knew his grandfather thought so. He thought that his grandson was "possessed by demons as stated in the Bible." Carlson snapped me out of my biblical preoccupation. His eyes seemed to darken when he said: "Whatever you do, you are responsible for it." It was as if he had read my mind.

It. The murders. Bingo.

I took the opening. Responsible? Did he feel responsible for what happened?

I thought I saw his small smile return. Carlson chose each word carefully as if they were nitroglycerin which, if they came out wrong, could have blown off his head. "I don't recall anything." His darkened eyes seemed to relax. To me, Carlson looked as if he did not feel anything. I looked at my watch. We had talked for nearly an hour.

When we parted, Carlson bid me a polite and empty good-bye. "I hope that I have been of some help." I wrote a brief note in his chart: "cooperative but guarded." I said I would return.

As I drove home, I had plenty of time to think about what just happened. Not all state hospitals provide decent care but Trautt was a thoughtful, devoted psychologist. He wanted to help Carlson deal with his "blocked emotions," and "blocked memories," so Carlson's anger could be expressed in less destructive ways. Trautt, I thought, was on the right track. He was also not hung up on the charge of fake; Trautt was willing to give Carlson the benefit of the doubt. But I had gotten nothing from Carlson—so far. He had not switched. He would not or could not remember the murders. I had yet to ask about abuse. I remembered that I still thought Carlson would talk. I would bide my time.


## Number Two

I returned to Pueblo exactly two weeks later. I checked in with Trautt, who still conducted twice weekly sessions with Carlson. He told me that nothing much had changed.

I met Carlson in the same grim room. His button-down oxford was now yellow but he was the same. He was a carbon copy of the last time we met, impeccable and crisp, polite to a fault, but he now seemed to barely tolerate my presence. He sat facing me directly, hands palm down, almost like a challenge, slightly bored and condescending. "How can I help you?"

Did he miss his parents? He deflected me but I sensed no grief, no worry, no remorse. It was like talking to myself, as if no one else were there, eerie and disjointing. For some reason during that second visit, I was more aware that he was mechanical, so cold and so remote. Underneath his immaculate armor I did not have to remind myself that he was capable of great cruelty. I imagined Carlson pumping bullets into his parents' brains.

I wanted to get underneath. I tired of the small talk and asked what he remembered about the shootings. He told me that they had nothing to do with him. Carlson's expression did not change.

"That is being litigated. I cannot talk to you about that." The muscles around his eyes seemed to jump for a moment before he relaxed. The flicker of emotion disappeared and was replaced by silence.

As I thought about his parents' execution, I felt the return of the slight twinge in the back of my head. Bang. Bang. I felt it but could he feel? I had seen something pass over his face and quickly disappear. What was it?

Carlson treated me like a thing, a doorknob. To him, I was just someone to be manipulated, to be turned, pushed, and pulled. Where did he learn to be like this? Where was his warmth, his humanity? How could he have looked into their eyes and know he would kill them in a few hours? Did the flicker mean that he had any doubts?

What did he think it was like for them? As he held the Rossi, did he feel their terror? When he shot them Bang, Bang, did he feel their pain? Or was he, as he was today, an all-American machine? Where was his heart and soul? Did satanic forces take his heart and soul away from him too? Trautt's idea of suppressed rage came back to me. What Carlson did was a rageful act.

I called a halt to our meeting. The shadows had deepened in the room and Carlson was more closed than before. I still had not gotten one scrap of real information; he was all form and no content. But his form was the message and the message was that he was shut down tight.

In 1984, Ross Carlson was twenty and I was forty-two and had practiced psychiatry for twelve years. Yet he had again controlled the interview. In fact, I felt he had spent the whole time interviewing me. I could not get in touch with him at all. I wanted to find some empathy within myself for this young man who so fascinated and evoked tenderness in the defense team. But I was having a hard time. He was a mannequin, a mannequin with a little smile. In my notes I wrote that "if he is a multiple, he is a sociopathic multiple. All of his personalities don't give a damn."

But I would give it another try.


## Number Three

I returned to Pueblo on December 6 for my last visit. I was determined to have some questions answered. I wanted to know, for example, what it was like growing up? How did his parents discipline him? Was he abused? I should not have been surprised when he dropped all pretense of civility.

He spent the time ridiculing his treatment as if from a script. The doctors and nurses, he said, were beneath being able to take care of him. I asked if his lawyers encouraged him not to cooperate? He answered that he was being "warehoused"—Eddie and David's word. Did he know it was their word? Had he been reading the papers? He did not answer.

Besides, he added, Trautt was not bright. I knew he was wrong; he just did not choose to talk to Trautt or to me. Carlson must have thought I was a dope too. On the other hand, Carlson now added, Bob Fairbairn was "intelligent and perceptive."

Here was, I thought, a mutual admiration society. Fairbairn seemed to eat up everything Carlson put on his plate; Trautt was more picky. Was that why he liked Fairbairn and showed him all of his personalities? Silence. Carlson just looked at me. From the first day we met, his confidence had not wavered one bit.

I knew I still had to ask some things. Did he work as an "escort"? Was this how he paid for his fancy suits, ties, and shirts? But he would not tell me. He said, as he always did: "I can't talk about that."

I asked again about the shooting. I have no recollection of the shooting, he said. He was being "attacked on many fronts" and unjustly accused and tried in the papers. It was a setup.

The depressing room was getting darker. We were wasting each other's time. He knew it and so did I. Now Carlson treated me as if I were not there and hardly talked to me at all. He swatted my words like gnats; I and my questions made no impression. Carlson had killed his parents and might have been a multiple. He knew, however, what he did was wrong and he knew what he was doing now. If he were a true multiple, each personality was on the make. A multiple or not, he was an iceman.

But I did not say that. Instead, I said good-bye and was glad to leave Pueblo and Carlson after wishing Trautt and the rest of his team good luck. They were in an awful spot, a spot that I did not want to have anything more to do with.


## Chameleon Man

In our three meetings, Carlson, always cool, did not switch, even when I challenged him. He was never surprised or bewildered and never lost his train of thought. I did not find evidence of MPD; he always looked the same to me.

His experts would say he did not trust me and therefore did not let me in to his private, tortured world. MPD was, after all, a disease of secrecy. The very lack of evidence for MPD in Carlson, they would say, was evidence for that. He kept himself under wraps.

So far, Carlson was what people wanted him to be; an "as if" chameleon man. He had a knack of mirroring perceptions of him. If he sensed admiration—such as Fairbairn's—Carlson reciprocated. If he sensed belief in MPD he would switch. He might even show Black. But if he sensed doubt, the gates were thrown up and he withdrew.

But MPD was not the key. As I drove home I realized that, so far, multiple or not, Carlson lacked coherence. I still could not explain Carlson and his motives and I found this disturbing. An abused victim? An evil psychopath? I knew two things for certain. He had killed in a cold and calculating way, and he had hired two very talented lawyers. That was all. Multiplicity was one question and motive was another. But multiplicity, no matter how real, did not explain the other.


## Capitulation

The next day, I told Haydee that Greg Trautt was a serious and competent psychotherapist who was giving Carlson every chance to talk. The hospital was, I told her, doing the right thing. I wished her good luck; with a laugh, she said she needed it. Then she told me something which I already knew. She had capitulated and filed a retraction with Eddie Day. Because of the threat of contempt citations, Carlson's diagnosis had been changed: it was now MPD.

Ross Carlson had officially become a multiple. Why? It was the threat of Eddie Day, Gerash, and Savitz. The hospital had rolled over. This was not medicine; it was diagnosis by coercion. When asked to comment on this turn of events, Bob Chappell said, "It's not for me to tell anyone what to report to the court." Chappell knew his case was now in even deeper trouble, but I was gone and Chappell's trouble was no business of mine.

# THE JACKSON ROUTE OUT

Carlson now openly demeaned Trautt. "Most of what I say you don't get," he said. He told Trautt that Trautt was lucky to have the opportunity to work with him: "I will be a feather in your cap." Furthermore, the staff, he told them, was not "competent" to treat his "disorder." One week later, Carlson was more specific and grandiose. "If you own a Ferrari, you take it to a specialist for repair, not to just any mechanic."

As I waded through Carlson's file I guessed why Savitz and Gerash relentlessly ridiculed the hospital. The ridicule began *before* Carlson was returned to Pueblo by Eddie Day in part, I thought, because the two attorneys would not want their Carlson to talk to anyone in Pueblo and run the risk of revealing too much. If Carlson could be treated by a private psychiatrist, what Carlson said would be confidential. Though—technically—anything Carlson said about the crime during his incompetency could not be used by Chappell. If Carlson said, "I confess, it was me all along," it would only make things tougher later.

## Quinn

The therapist favored by the defense was Dr. Barry Quinn, a psychologist who ran an outfit based not far from the hospital called "Creative Alternatives." He had "fused" an inmate friend of Carlson's, a felon and purported sufferer of MPD, a patient of psychologist Fig Newton. The felon and Carlson hung out together and spoke daily. This friend bad-mouthed Trautt and told Carlson that Trautt did not really believe in MPD. Trautt, on the other hand, was convinced that the felon interfered with his relationship with Ross.

David Savitz arranged for Carlson to meet with Quinn on December 17, 1984. After the session, Quinn wrote in Carlson's chart, by now many inches thick, that Carlson could experience "mild irritation" without dissociating but that "fear and strong anger" caused splits. Quinn thought that Carlson's "main personality can tolerate very little emotion." Carlson told Quinn that he dissociated five to six times per week, but in Quinn's opinion it was more like three to four times per day.

## Carlson's Third Option

Soon after Quinn's visit, Trautt had enough with Carlson's noncooperation. On January 9, 1985, Trautt confronted Carlson about his total lack of involvement with him, with the ward staff, and with his treatment. Carlson listened to what Trautt told him and then in a very coherent discussion laid out his three options.

He could, he told Trautt, cooperate fully and agree to be open, agree to be hypnotized, and agree to attend all groups. He could, he said, try to get better. The second possibility, he said, was to continue "as is" and attend some treatments but not say much when he did. His final option, Carlson said, was to withdraw entirely. At the end of their brief conversation, Carlson told Trautt that he probably would chose number three. He would, Carlson said, tell Trautt his decision the next day.

True to his word—the same personality must have been out because Carlson remembered his promise—on Thursday, January 10, 1985, Carlson told Trautt that, from then on, he would not attend groups or individual treatment with Trautt and his other ward psychotherapist, nurse Barbara Swerdfinger.

Carlson was open about why he chose the third option. He told Trautt that he wanted Judge Eddie Day to intervene. "I'll force his hand. Eddie Day won't allow this to continue when he learns what is going on down here." What Carlson wanted Judge Day to do was not clear, but from then on Carlson refused to meet with Trautt, saying that he had "better things to do." I could not believe that Carlson was so open about his intentions but, then again, Eddie Day was on his side. On January 17, a new "problem" was added to Carlson's problem list in his chart: "Resistive to treatment." Trautt wrote that it was a well thought-out but irrational decision. I soon would learn that it was not irrational at all.

## Stalemate

On January 28, Quinn returned. In Quinn's opinion, Carlson was "motivated and willing to work toward integration." Quinn recommended that the staff "accept" the diagnosis of MPD. Quinn told the staff that treatment of Carlson's MPD could not take place unless Carlson was taken at face value; otherwise Carlson would feel mistrusted and misunderstood. In this, Dr. Quinn appeared to agree with what Fisch had said seven months before: "Counselor, the patient never lies."

Once again, this was the fallacy of lies only this time not because Ross Carlson looked honest but because he was a multiple. Total acceptance was the "correct" way to treat multiples according to aficionados of the disease. Nothing like this existed in the rest of medicine where diagnoses were always refined and reevaluated. But not with MPD. Finally, someone pointed out that Carlson had stopped all contacts with staff after Dr. Quinn had arrived on the scene. Quinn did not seem to realize that patients charged with murder might lie. Quinn, for the moment, was asked to withdraw.

Quinn's removal had no effect. By spring, Carlson spent most of the time in his room, reading or writing letters, or sitting in the day room watching the soaps. Sometimes he spent hours in bed with the covers over his head. He did talk to some patients but was elusive with staff. He grew a beard and kept it, like everything else about him, meticulous. He showered daily and ate well. He only attended weight training, which he did five hours per week. Again he had no trouble sleeping. It had become a stalemate. Everyone waited for the next move to be made.

Twice each week, Greg Trautt asked Carlson to resume treatment. If in bed, Carlson would just pull up the covers over his head.

"No thank you," he would tell Trautt. Trautt diligently documented his attempts. He knew he would have to account for everything in court. Sometimes nurses noticed Carlson staring into space, shoulders slumped. His eyes would swing back and forth and he would not respond when spoken to. Afterward, he would go about his business. On occasion, Carlson seemed startled by what he was wearing—for example why he put on a tie—or what he was doing.

In April Trautt asked Carlson to meet before they all drove north to Douglas County and to Judge Day for the next treatment review. Surprisingly, Carlson agreed and on Friday, April 19, Carlson entered Trautt's tiny office, sat down, but refused to talk. Instead, he was mute and acknowledged Trautt's questions shaking his head yes or no. Trautt allowed this session in mime to last for six minutes before he called it quits. Mutism was not part of MPD, I thought, as I read this. Carlson obviously expected he could do as he pleased.

## Chappell's Visit

Five days later, Bob Chappell called me. He had seen my name in Carlson's chart and wanted to come and chat for a few minutes. Of course I said yes. I knew that despite my deal with Haydee Kort which I hoped limited my involvement, once I went to Pueblo I was fair game. But I also knew I would say no.

Chappell had a pleasant, open face, and intense gray-blue eyes. I thought he must have decided to grow a mustache to make himself look a little older, despite his neatly combed slightly graying hair. Chappell was dressed in a gray jacket and tan slacks. I remembered this because other lawyers I had met usually favored the dark blue suits of court. He also did not carry a leather briefcase like other lawyers. Instead, he kept his papers in a cardboard folder.

With a smile and a shrug, he came right to the point. "Dr. Weissberg," he said, "I'm having a helluva time finding psychiatrists to help me. People are scared of this case. They are scared of Carlson and they are scared of Gerash." No one, he said, seemed to want to get involved. He needed, Chappell told me, to find someone willing to help him "get this thing back on track."

Chappell was not going to retreat or give up. I remember his frustration that "things had become tied up" and "needlessly confused" and that Carlson was now "squirreled" away in Pueblo. "This was," he said, "the weirdest case" he had ever had. He did say that he had made some mistakes. But, he said, "the defense" had Eddie Day "eating out of the palm of their hands."

I had figured Chappell wanted me to testify, but I hated court and did not have a lot of experience with criminals. Furthermore, once involved in a case, my time was no longer my own. Court dates were always changed; told to appear at a certain time, I would probably not testify for hours or days, or the trial might be put off or continue for months. My schedule would be up in the air; it was very disruptive. And once on the stand, I would not like being badgered.

Furthermore, there was a special flavor to this case. Carlson would not talk and his lawyers had so far criticized anyone from the state who tried to treat him. MPD was a slippery diagnosis. I would have to do weeks of work just to master the literature. Finally, simply put, Carlson still frightened me. I could not think of one reason to say yes.

"Carlson," I finally told Chappell, "is an iceman, the most dangerous person I have ever seen." So I felt bad when I said no. I offered a few lame excuses and Chappell and I shook hands. As Chappell walked out the door, I knew I had chickened out and shirked my civic duty. I thought I was off the hook.


## Bring Back Steven

The next status review hearing was held at the end of April. Savitz and Gerash told Judge Day that the reason Carlson was not getting better was because Carlson "mistrusted" his therapists who still doubted his diagnosis—something they could not do if Carlson were to be treated.

The alternative explanation, Chappell argued, was that Carlson did not cooperate. In court, Trautt conceded that he never had diagnosed a multiple before and that he was not one hundred percent certain that Carlson suffered from the disorder. But, Trautt said, "I'm saying there is evidence to indicate the probability." I knew Trautt had an open mind. But Savitz and Gerash wanted Haydee Kort to invite Quinn to return to Pueblo and, furthermore, to pay his fee.

On May 2, 1985, *The Rocky Mountain News* ran the following story which gave a picture of what the hearing was like:

CASTLE ROCK—Ross Michael Carlson, accused of killing his schoolteacher parents in 1983, has switched personalities several times during District Court hearings this week, Carlson's attorneys said . . . They say that doctors at the Colorado State Hospital in Pueblo . . . do not believe Carlson is suffering from a multiple personality disorder [and] want former state Supreme Court Justice Edward C. Day . . . to order the hospital to allow outside therapist Barry L. Quinn to treat Carlson.

Defense attorneys David Savitz and Walter Gerash said Carlson became agitated during the proceedings and "split" into different personalities. "At one point, he was whining, complaining of a headache, really moaning and groaning," Savitz said. "He could not sit still." Savitz said that personality was "Gray," an irritable adolescent.

"I reached over and rubbed his back and neck to calm him down," Savitz said. "And I suggested that he bring Steven back." 'Steven', Savitz said, is the most intellectual of Carlson's personalities. "So he closed his eyes and hypnotized himself and brought Steven back," Savitz said . . .

Gerash has maintained that Carlson cannot establish a rapport with therapists nor be restored to competency because he is being treated in a "doubting environment." . . .

## "Do Not Try to Change My Mind"

A new tension surfaced during the hearing. This time, it was not differences about Carlson's diagnosis which caused Day to unload on Chappell, as he did when Chappell tried to introduce Carlson's thirty-one letters into evidence in 1984. Day was angry that Chappell had continued to investigate Carlson.

"Why?" Day asked Chappell. "Are you trying to change the Court's mind? If you are trying to change my mind with new records or information, you won't . . . I sat here for eleven days and heard all the testimony from your young state doctors, and I was convinced that Mr. Carlson suffered from MPD . . . the testimony from the defense doctors was overwhelming . . ."

## Hill, Staton, and Mettille

What riled Day was that after his ruling, Chappell continued to fashion his case since he one day hoped to be able to take Carlson to trial.

For instance, on July 30, 1984, Brian Bevis interviewed Eldon Hill, the Ford salesman. Carlson had come to the showroom, given Hill a business card, and then spent ninety minutes looking at Thunderbirds, Broncos, and LTD Crown Victorias. Hill noticed that Carlson tried to avoid Susan Rhoads after she spoke with him. In retrospect, Hill thought Carlson knew what he was doing and was trying to put one over on him.

Then Bevis tracked down Randy Staton, whose lawn cutting testimony blew Chappell out of the water. But what Staton told Bevis had a different twist than what he implied in court. The first time Carlson came to cut Staton's lawn he came with his lawn mower but the second time he did not. The first time he cut the grass and left. The second time, he walked up to the house—which Staton thought Carlson might believe was empty—and rang the doorbell. When Staton answered, Carlson accused him of cutting the grass even though Staton's leg was in a cast and he had crutches.

In other words, Carlson likely thought the house was empty since the Statons were out of town. Bevis theorized that Carlson planned to rob what he thought was the empty Staton house. It was attempted robbery, not lawn mowing amnesia, which prompted Carlson to say he had forgotten he had been there before. Staton also told Bevis, when Staton came to testify on June 20, 1984, that David Savitz told him to sit downstairs in the coffee shop and not speak to anyone. Presumably, the defense wanted to take Chappell by complete surprise.

It took until February 1985 for Cheri Mettille, one of Carlson's girlfriends, to talk to Bevis. Cheri, an attractive, brown-haired, fourteen-year-old girl, dated Carlson from October 1982 until the murders. It was Cheri, Michelle O'Hagan had testified, who was stood up by Ross who "had forgotten" the date. This was, according to Gerash, another example of Carlson's amnesia.

When they first met at Skate City, Carlson gave Cheri his ROSS ENTERPRISES card. They spent their first date drinking champagne, parked in a deserted field. Later, Carlson told Cheri about "the mob"—that he knew men who smuggled dope and murdered for hire. Ross always had, according to Cheri, some get-rich-quick scheme on his mind. Once, Ross said that he would not kill for money—that was why, he said, he was not rich. One month before the murders, Carlson drove Mettille around the area of Cottonwood Road to "see what was out there."

Mettille told Bevis that Ross was intensely interested in the movies, wanted to be a producer, and told her that his favorite was *Body Heat*. Cheri also said that Ross carried with him in a black briefcase pictures of outfits from *Gentleman's Quarterly* and a "portfolio" of dresses he had drawn.

Cheri said Ross was always tender and loving, always answered to "Ross," never had memory problems, and never forgot her name or any plans they had made. Finally, Cheri told Bevis, she had no recollection of ever being stood up by Ross and told her friend, Michelle O'Hagan, that she must have been mistaken.

But Judge Day did not want to know about any of this—about Hill's version of Susan Rhoads's story, about Randy Staton and Cheri Mettille. Judge Day promised to rule on Dr. Quinn in twenty days and Carlson was sent back to Pueblo.


**Quinn's Return**
On July 18, Judge Day ruled that the hospital had to allow Quinn back. Carlson, according to the judge, had a right to a therapist he could trust who had no doubts about the diagnosis of MPD. "The hospital," Day said, "has no one on its staff who can treat the defendant." Carlson, Judge Day went on to say, "will never be restored to competency under the circumstances now existing." Exactly who would pay Quinn's bill was not clear.

Quinn—who had told Day that it would take him three to six hours a week for many years to treat Carlson—saw Ross on August 5, their session lasting from 9:45 to 12:40. He saw him again on the seventh. I was struck by the fact that in typical practice sessions are forty-five or fifty minutes, but Quinn's was almost three hours. But with multiples, it was rarely business as usual and not uncommon for therapists to do things they would not dream of doing with other patients.

Some therapists become enthralled with their patient's productions; this fascination is one effect that multiples produce. One friend of mine allowed "her" multiple to run up a bill of twenty-five thousand dollars before she called it quits and discharged the man.

Another acquaintance, otherwise a competent therapist, did not charge "his" multiple at all although he saw her four times per week. Multiples become very special patients—the more personalities they bring out, the longer their therapists stay with them and the less some are charged. This lack of therapeutic structure is not good for people who lack structure of their own. But this is what often happens.


### Even Experts Fail

Quinn saw Carlson again, this time for three and a half hours. In his note he wrote that they discussed "losing another therapist if payment is not arranged" and "early memories of father: i.e., being tied up, testis pulled . . . is concerned about ability to stay logical when he becomes emotional." I did not understand this reference to Carlson's testicle. Perhaps he was talking about the operation he had during adolescence for his one undescended testicle and the prosthesis which was implanted. Who would pay Quinn was still being litigated.

On August 21, Quinn and the defense decided to halt Quinn's visits because payment had still not been arranged. The defense did not want Quinn paid from Carlson's trust—seventy-five dollars per hour or two hundred twenty-five to four hundred fifty dollars per week—the same pot which provided for his legal defense. Carlson's trustees, representatives of the United Bank of Denver, agreed.

In September, the trustees told Day that it would be wrong for Carlson to use his inheritance for this treatment because if Carlson were eventually found guilty, the money would no longer be his. This got to Day who said from the bench that the "next step may be to sue you people . . . I don't think the bank can just sit by . . ." Judge Day then suggested Savitz sue the trust, but Savitz declined—it was a conflict of interest he said—since, if the court ruled that Carlson's treatment had to be paid from the inheritance, there would be no money left for Savitz and Gerash.

This legal wrangling took months. Finally, on the last day of 1985, Eddie Day ordered Haydee Kort to seek a special appropriation from the state legislature to pay Barry Quinn. By now, Ross Carlson had been refusing treatment for a year. The state appealed.

That is how it went. Months of noncompliance in Pueblo with spurts of legal maneuvering eighty miles to the north. Along with

Quinn, 1985 came and went. Carlson lifted weights and talked to staff about books, television, or things that he needed in a clear, coherent manner, but not about himself. But a sense of what he thought leaked through. In May 1986, Carlson was again asked to explain, as part of an evaluation, what "even monkeys fall from trees" meant. This time he said: "Even experts occasionally fail." Which experts did he mean? Those who thought he was a fraud or those who thought he was real? Or, did he mock the experts on both sides?

### The Reversal of Judge Day

On July 14, 1986, the judges of the Colorado Supreme Court finally reversed their old colleague. Day had gone, they said, too far. The hospital did not have to pay for outside therapists and Day could not appoint one. Judges, his colleagues said, were not well suited to determine psychiatric treatment and should not do so. "The extensive treatment recommendations" in Day's original commitment order were "unwarranted."

Day was stung. "As far as I know," he responded, "they're just warehousing him down there. Far as I know, he will be there for the rest of his life." But this was not what the defense had in mind.

### Theon Jackson

Initially, I thought that the defense castigated the state hospital— and wanted to convince Eddie Day that Carlson would never get better there—so their therapist, Quinn, could treat Carlson. Just as with Fig Newton's mild-mannered rapist, Carlson would be fused, sent back for a sanity trial, and if he won—a big if—he would shortly be set free. I was wrong.

Once, Gerash silently pointed to the case of Theon Jackson in an open book which lay in front of Chappell. Without a word, Gerash then walked away. From then on Chappell knew the defense would try to fashion another ticket out for Carlson and the ticket's name was Jackson. This route would skip the sanity trial altogether, the sanity trial which, because of Chappell's facts, would be so hard for Carlson to win.

During the 1970s, an Indiana native, Theon Jackson, a twenty-seven-year-old deaf mute with the mind of a child, was arrested after he stole two handbags. Brought into court, Jackson was ruled incompetent to proceed to trial because his mental state did not allow him to participate in his own defense. Jackson was sent, like Carlson, to a state hospital to be "restored" to competency.

Of course, Jackson could not be "restored." Doctors could not teach Jackson to talk or to hear, and they could not raise his IQ. Since he would never be found competent, Jackson would never get out of the hospital. Jackson was given, in essence, a life sentence for a nine dollar crime. Four years later, the United States Supreme Court ruled that Jackson's punishment was both cruel and unusual. If someone was found to be *permanently* incompetent, that is to say, unable to be treated and restored, then the charges may be dropped and the defendant, no longer a defendant, may be freed.

The defense planned to shape Carlson in Jackson's image and this, I guessed, was the real reason why they ripped the state. If Day was convinced that the state could not treat Carlson's MPD, Day could find Carlson permanently incompetent. Then the two counts of first degree murder charges would be dropped; Carlson would be "Jacksoned" and set free.

The key was to prove that Ross Carlson refused treatment because the treatment was bad. Nice strategy if it worked. Savitz and Gerash always had plan one, the insanity plea, if Jackson failed. If any judge in Colorado would go for the Jackson defense, I thought, Eddie Day was their man.


## The Appearance of Cooperation

On November 5, 1986, Ross Carlson started to meet with Trautt again ninety-four weeks after he had stopped. But though their meetings resumed, all Carlson spoke about was his mistreatment. The hospital was, he said, a "psychiatric prison"; Chappell had "fabricated evidence" against him. This was not cooperation at all, but the appearance of cooperation.

Why did Carlson resume his meetings? "I've been starved into submission," Carlson claimed. His psychiatrist had withheld Carlson's evening snack to encourage him to attend therapy. I did not think, however, lack of food brought Carlson back. I guessed Carlson met with Trautt so the Jackson defense could be used; he did not want to be accused of noncooperation.

Two days after he resumed meeting with Trautt, Carlson demanded to be placed on a pork-free diet. The reasons for Carlson's demand were obscure, but his wish was granted.

Once, Carlson's rage broke through and Trautt felt unsafe—Carlson was incensed over the lack of hot water. "I'll stick my finger up your fucking nose, if I want to," he told Trautt. Mostly, Carlson was remote. On another occasion, Carlson, as if in a trance, poured a glass of ice water over his head and, on January 8, 1987, he sat through an entire session, eyes closed, mute. Carlson was back, but did not talk. "I'll force his hand. Eddie Day won't allow this to continue when he learns what is going on down here."

### The Arrival of Theon Jackson

With the addition of Jackson, I realized that the stalemate was not a stalemate at all, but revealed its logic. Chappell waited for Jackson, certain that he would arrive. The day finally came. On February 13, 1987, Chappell learned that the defense planned to play their Jackson card and ask Eddie Day to dismiss all charges.

On February 10, Savitz wrote to Eddie Day: ". . . we will be requesting during the restoration hearing the termination of the criminal proceedings . . ." Savitz sent a copy of the letter to Ross Carlson who, I now realized, had known for a long time that it paid not to get better.

### Ex Parte Eddie

This was a dangerous moment for Chappell, who decided to strike first. The seventy-eight-year-old Day vacationed in Palm Springs when Chappell acted. Chappell had removed Turelli and now he would try to get rid of Eddie Day and filed a motion asking him to disqualify himself from the case. Day, said Chappell, had acted improperly by having a number of private—ex parte—communications with David Savitz. Chappell said that these communications—letters, conversations—had gone on between Savitz and Day for a full three years. Day had these contacts, Chappell said, before making key rulings in the case.

Day had provided Chappell with ammunition. He had not lent Carlson his maroon Cadillac DeVille, but at the October 1984 hearing—when Day severely chastised the hospital for "foot dragging" —Brian Bevis saw Eddie come to court with David Savitz in

Savitz's car. Eddie Day left with Savitz, too, this time in full view of everyone. Ex parte contact between the defense and the judge, Chappell's motion read, was improper.

Chappell's motion papers claimed there were hints of other contacts. During a conference call on December 13, 1985, soon before Carlson withdrew completely from treatment, Judge Day indicated, according to Chappell's motion papers, that Savitz had taken Day's wife shopping. The conference call line, controlled by Savitz, suddenly went dead. It was, Chappell said, improper for there to be contact between Day and Savitz especially since Savitz and Gerash had also become witnesses in June 1984.

Day, Chappell said, was not an impartial fact finder; his comments were full of bias. For example Day said on August 13, 1985: "Now it is obvious they can't treat this man down there. They haven't got the people to do this. They haven't got the facility to do it. They don't believe anything about what other people have said. They've stonewalled on this from the beginning."

Day, maybe because of his seventy-eight years, or maybe because he was Eddie Day, had apparently also lost it a few times in court. According to a statement filed by Chappell, he told Assistant Attorney General Caroline Lievers, "shut up and sit down," and another time called her "that black girl." Dr. Kathy Morall, a black psychiatrist hired by Haydee Kort, had already testified in the case and would do so in the future. Day, Chappell concluded, was "biased," an "advocate" of MPD. Carlson called Chappell's motion "full of lies." Judge Day said it would take a few months for him to decide what he would do.

### "Cure of the Ages . . ."

On June 9, 1987, *The Denver Post* ran the following story under the headline JUDGE DENIES BIAS, THEN QUITS CASE.

> CASTLE ROCK—A special district court judge Monday rejected a motion that he remove himself from a controversial murder case because of bias, then stepped down from the case for another reason. The departure of . . . Justice Edward Day means another judge must be appointed to preside over the complex court proceedings for Ross Carlson . . .
>
> Day said he decided to remove himself from the case when

state officials notified him . . . that they believe Carlson is now competent to stand trial, even though the suspect has had no treatment at the hospital . . . He said [this] information "flies in the face" of all the expert testimony the court heard during Carlson's competency hearing and falls in the category of a "psychiatric cure of the ages. Well," he said, "some other judge is going to hear that testimony . . ."

Day said he decided to withdraw before Chappell tried to get rid of him. During a television interview, he reiterated that he could not tolerate another state doctor claim that Carlson was "cured." He admitted that he rode to court with Savitz because his car was broken but that his wife never went shopping with the attorney. "In my forty-one years as a judge I've never, never had any lawyer impugn my integrity on the bench, and I am not going to stand for it now." With that, he dismissed court and stepped down from Carlson for the last time. Eddie Day had broken the stalemate, but instead of Carlson out via Jackson, Day was gone.

A reporter observed that throughout the hearing, a somber Ross Carlson sat with his neatly trimmed beard, hands on his lap. Savitz told the reporter that this was the "older, intelligent, very matter-of-fact ego state in charge of the academia involved in this case." It must have been, I thought, forty-two-year-old Steve.

# THE EDUCATION OF JUDGE ROBERT KINGSLEY

Judge Day was replaced by another retired judge—the kind of no-nonsense jurist Chappell had hoped would replace Turelli in 1984. But former Chief Denver District Court Judge Robert Kingsley complicated things for Bob Chappell. Chappell had clerked for the seventy-five-year-old Kingsley and Chappell wondered if he still saw him as a "young pup." Clearly, Chappell thought of Kingsley as a father. Their history was a new wrinkle in a case now full of wrinkles.

## Carlson Two, Fall 1987

The first I learned that Carlson had given birth to a brand-new personality was when I read Walter Gerash's opening remarks for his second competency hearing. At the end of September, Chappell and Dr. Kort were ready to try their luck with Kingsley and have Carlson restored so he could move on to the sanity trial. By now, Carlson had been in Pueblo for three years.

As the hearing opened, the new defense refrain was: Ross Carlson · was abused by the hospital, was worse, and would not get better. Carlson had developed a new personality named Holden to deal with his "barbaric" treatment. "Holden," said Gerash, "has no knowledge of anything that happened before 1985 . . ." We are, Gerash said, going to ask the court to dismiss the case.

Since Ross Carlson was legally incompetent, the burden was Bob Chappell's to prove otherwise and Greg Trautt was his lead-off witness. When Trautt took the stand—he spent two days testifying—he did not claim that Carlson was "fused" or "cured" as Day predicted he would, only that Carlson could cooperate with Savitz and Gerash.

When questioned by Savitz, Trautt said he may have talked to Holden, but that Holden recalled things which occurred before 1985. Savitz disagreed. Anything Holden remembered was "knowledge" not "memory" and came from Carlson's copious notes which he now kept on his new word processor—paid for by his trust. Carlson, Savitz went on, might switch under the stress of a murder trial and not be able to keep track of what was going on. Carlson was, therefore, incompetent. In return, Trautt did not agree.

Judge Kingsley—as Day did before—tried to understand the logic of MPD. Had Trautt discussed "Holden" with Carlson? he wanted to know. "I tried," said Trautt, "but he would not talk about him."

"So, Carlson only talks to you about what he wants to talk about?"

"Correct," said Trautt.

"He has talked to everyone, except to who he should talk to," mused Kingsley, as he noted Carlson "had talked about the murders—how he held the gun, the things his mother said to him before he pulled the trigger—to everyone except his therapists." At the end of the first day, Kingsley called a halt to the session sounding fed up. "Okay, I've had enough." This was Kingsley's introduction to MPD. There was more to come.

**Asleep in Court**

As before, Carlson did his thing in front of Kingsley's face. The defense needed to educate Kingsley the way they had educated Eddie Day. The reporter for the *News* filed the following story on September 29:

CARLSON'S STATE WORRIES ATTORNEY

CASTLE ROCK—Attorneys for accused killer Ross Carlson, who appeared to doze behind tinted glasses several times during a hearing in Douglas County District Court, fear he may be lapsing into a trance . . .

Defense attorney David Savitz had a psychologist step down from the witness stand and examine Carlson several times yesterday as Carlson sat upright in his chair with his eyes closed and hands folded in his lap . . .

Yesterday morning, at Savitz's request, Dr. Gregory Trautt approached the defense table and peered at Carlson, who seemed asleep. Trautt shook him gently by the shoulder, but Carlson did not respond. "I can't determine what state of consciousness he's in without [a test] to measure his brain waves. I have no way of judging whether he is asleep or in a trance," said Trautt . . .

"As Ross Carlson is now, how is he able to assist us today in court?" Savitz asked yesterday, pointing at the seemingly unconscious defendant.

"If he is asleep," Trautt said, "he can assist you by your waking him up . . ."

Prosecutor Bob Chappell said yesterday he had no opinion about Carlson's dozing. But Judge Robert Kingsley indicated impatience with Carlson's behavior, saying "The defendant is trying to control the proceedings."

This was pretty funny. "Even monkeys fall from trees and experts will fail"; Carlson, I thought, mocked the world. But I did not laugh long. Instead of Greg Trautt hopping on and off the stand—like a monkey—when I had to testify it might soon be me.

After Trautt, Chappell put on the rest: nurses, doctors, techs who had watched Carlson since 1984. They had only seen one personality, they said. Carlson may not be cured of his MPD but he was capable of standing trial. Dr. Kathy Morall was struck by Carlson's coldness. When she asked Carlson if he ever felt sad about his parents' deaths, "he simply said no" and called his parents "two fine teachers who are no longer here." He did not, she said, have MPD.

## The Defense Refrain

The defense now tried to counteract any damage inflicted by Chappell's witnesses. By now, Bob Fairbairn was the defense psychiatrist who had spent the most time with Carlson. Gerash put Fairbairn on the stand on Friday, October 9.

In Fairbairn's first moments—usually a routine part of the examination—as Gerash led him through his qualifications—medical school in Vancouver, residency in Vancouver and Colorado—I saw that Chappell had taken a page from Gerash's book. Chappell jumped in just as Gerash had done with Fine and Reichlin in 1984.

Do you, Chappell asked, have your boards in psychiatry? No, was Fairbairn's response. Well, Gerash interjected, you have qualified for the boards, haven't you? No, was the damaging reply. Having one's boards is no guarantee of excellence but Chappell had made his point. Fairbairn looked like the quintessential "expert," but his diplomas did not back him up. Chappell, I saw, was well prepared. Gerash changed the subject.

Fairbairn then began the refrain: Carlson was worse, not better and the hospital was to blame. During a visit to Pueblo, Fairbairn was shocked. "He looked like a back ward patient . . . had lost weight, had a stubble beard, and did not know me." Cool and unfriendly, Carlson looked wasted. "He used to have a vital, alive, intense appearance . . . [and was] a virile young man [and now] he had a wimpy look. . . .

"I was aware," Fairbairn continued, "that yet again another personality had been formed and the new personality did not know me." I had an alternative explanation for Fairbairn's poor reception. Fairbairn had hardly seen Ross since 1984; Carlson, one might assume, felt deserted. When Fairbairn asked who he was talking to Carlson answered "Holden" or "Holding." Carlson would not clarify what he said, so Fairbairn decided on the name "Holden."

## The Bevis Report

Gerash also made a big deal of Brian Bevis's investigation of Carlson. Bevis interviewed many people who knew the Carlsons both in Colorado and Minnesota, and could not confirm any instances of childhood abuse. When Chappell delivered this report to the hospital in February 1985, this lack of evidence for abuse increased suspicions about Carlson. Carlson, said Fairbairn, could not be treated in such an atmosphere of mistrust.

I was surprised to see Judge Kingsley step in.

KINGSLEY:    What is [Carlson's] goal?

FAIRBAIRN:   His goal is a terribly shallow thing, to be declared competent . . .

KINGSLEY:    Do you think he ever lied to you in any of his personalities?

FAIRBAIRN:   I really don't. No. This split, shattered, mentally ill young man has been scrupulously honest with me. I've never caught him in a lie.

KINGSLEY:    Well, if he is evasive, how could you catch him? . . .

FAIRBAIRN:   . . . I have never had that sensation from Ross Carlson or the alters that present to me.

Fairbairn took Carlson on faith. Carlson was "scrupulously honest"; Fairbairn said he "never had the sensation" that Ross Carlson or any of his alters lied. Like Ralph Fisch, Susan Rhoads, and Eddie Day, Fairbairn believed Carlson. Why? Because he appeared to be honest.

### The Great Snack Debate

An example of Carlson's mistreatment, according to Fairbairn, was Carlson's evening snack, or lack of it. Carlson complained that a Dr. Lori Greene stopped his snack, that he was being starved, and had already lost eleven pounds. Fairbairn, outraged, approached Dr. Greene about reinstating the food but it was, Fairbairn reported, "like talking to a brick wall . . . I was appalled . . . this was unprofessional and inhumane and barbaric . . ."

"What do you mean by 'the barbarities,' doctor?" Kingsley interrupted. "Doctor, I don't know that there is any evidence that any doctor at the hospital has abused or brow-beaten this defendant, except perhaps [one earlier incident], and that happened in July 1984." Fairbairn tried to get a word in edgewise but Kingsley went on. "There is no evidence," finished the judge, "that any doctor has abused him since then." Fairbairn repeated what he said. "I think to withhold food from a mentally ill person is barbaric."

**Cross**

Now it was Chappell's turn to examine Fairbairn. Had Chappell learned, I wanted to know, to counterpunch? From his opening shot about Fairbairn's qualifications, I thought he had.

CHAPPELL:   Dr. Fairbairn, you state your belief that taking away the milk and cereal snack at bedtime is barbaric . . . ?

FAIRBAIRN:   Yes . . .

CHAPPELL:   You don't know what was eliminated from his diet, do you?

FAIRBAIRN:   That is correct . . .

CHAPPELL:   If the record showed that he did not lose all eleven pounds during that time, would that indicate to you, perhaps for the first time in this case, an instance where the defendant has not told you the truth?

GERASH:   We object, because we don't believe all those records.

KINGSLEY:   Overruled . . .

FAIRBAIRN:   It is improbable he would lie . . . What I saw with my own eyes was consistent with what he was telling me.

Fairbairn must have seemed naive to the experienced Kingsley. Now Chappell zeroed in.

CHAPPELL:   [In 1985] did you give [Carlson] a gift?

FAIRBAIRN:   . . . I gave him an electric razor.

CHAPPELL:   The year before, when the defendant had his twentieth birthday . . . did you give him a gift?

FAIRBAIRN:   Yes . . . a book . . .

CHAPPELL:   How many other subjects of forensic criminal case evaluations have you given gifts to?

FAIRBAIRN:   None.

Gifts; a diagnosis; complete belief. Fairbairn admitted that his major source of information about Carlson's "barbaric" treatment was Carlson himself. At that moment, I wondered if Fairbairn ever thought that he might be a monkey too: that he was dancing on Carlson's string.

CHAPPELL:   Do you remember reading an interview where Mr. Bevis talked to Ross Carlson's athletic idol? His name was Stacey . . . ?

FAIRBAIRN:   No . . .

The athletic personality, Stacey.

CHAPPELL:   Do you remember reading about one of Marilyn Carlson's kindergarten students who visited the Carlsons by the name of Blue?

FAIRBAIRN:   No.

Small, weepy, Blue.

CHAPPELL:   . . . Did Mr. Gerash give you the report of an interview with a Mr. Kachel who told Mr. Bevis that in the fall of 1982, he discussed with Carlson setting up an insanity defense based on different personalities?

Gerash had enough and objected. Interesting, I thought. Gerash said he had not shown that report to Dr. Fairbairn because, he told Kingsley, he had just gotten it. But, of course, Gerash could have shown it to Fairbairn. However, even if he read it, Fairbairn probably would not have changed his mind.


**"David Will Ask for the Charges to Be Dropped . . ."**

Chappell had hurt Bob Fairbairn. Now he was ready to bury him.

CHAPPELL:   At [a November 1986 meeting with Savitz and Gerash] was there a discussion of utilizing a provision in the statute to have the criminal case terminated?

Gerash immediately saw where Chappell was going.

GERASH:   Wait. I'm going to object . . .

KINGSLEY:   [Mr. Gerash], you don't have to make faces or look at them. Look at me.

GERASH:   I'll look at you . . . you look like Clarence Darrow, quite frankly. You do . . .

Gerash's diversion did not work. Kingsley wanted to hear the answer to Chappell's question: how early was Theon Jackson discussed? Gerash objected correctly. What happened at a meeting with Carlson's lawyers was privileged but Chappell could get at Jackson another way.

KINGSLEY:   I think the objection is good to the form of the question. [Mr. Chappell], you can get it in a different way . . .

CHAPPELL:   Dr. Fairbairn, have you ever discussed with Carlson the provision in the statute or termination of a case because he cannot be restored to competency and proceed to trial?

FAIRBAIRN:   Yes . . .

CHAPPELL:   . . . Can you see where I've highlighted a portion of

your notes [of your June 21, 1987, meeting with Carl-
son]? . . . what does that say?

FAIRBAIRN: . . . David will ask for the criminal charges to be
dropped.

CHAPPELL: Who made that statement?

FAIRBAIRN: Ross Carlson . . .

Kingsley wanted to be certain what he had heard. On June 21,
1987, Carlson told Fairbairn that "David will ask for the criminal
charges to be dropped." That meant to me that the tactic of having
the charges dropped was discussed with Carlson before June 21,
1987.

KINGSLEY: The defendant told you that in June 1987, that "David
will ask for the criminal charges to be dropped"?

FAIRBAIRN: Yes . . .

KINGSLEY: You did not tell him that?

FAIRBAIRN: That is correct. He told me . . .

Chappell then tried to find out how early Theon Jackson was
mentioned. Was Carlson's entire hospitalization from 1984 designed
to point toward the Jackson defense?

CHAPPELL: Okay. Now directing your attention to this page . . .
Can you tell us whether the highlighted portion was a
notation from your meeting with the defendant on September 26, 1986? . . .

FAIRBAIRN: I would be almost certain that it is . . .

CHAPPELL: [What does the notation say?]

FAIRBAIRN: "There is a provision that could negate all the
charges."

CHAPPELL: And who made that statement?

FAIRBAIRN: Ross Carlson.

CHAPPELL: So, in September 1986 when you met with him, he told
you there was a provision that could negate all his
charges?

FAIRBAIRN: Yes.

CHAPPELL: And again in June 1987 he told you that David will ask
for the criminal charges to be dropped?

FAIRBAIRN: Yes . . .

I could not believe that Fairbairn wrote these damning things in
his notes and that Chappell had the good fortune to find them.
Carlson knew about Theon Jackson *before* September 1986. How
much earlier, I wondered? As early as January 10, 1985, when he

stopped attending all of his treatment sessions? As early as 1984? I did not know if I could ever find that out.

I heard from a number of people who were in the courtroom during Fairbairn's testimony, that Fairbairn was not as crisp in the fall of 1987 as he was in June 1984. Savitz and Gerash did not use Fairbairn in court again.

## Sybil

Kingsley did not allow Savitz and Gerash to testify as broadly as Eddie Day had let them in 1984. "The diagnosis looked pretty phony in the beginning," said Gerash. "But I am convinced of it now." How had Gerash educated himself about MPD? He read a number of "professional" publications and rented the video of *Sybil*.

Savitz used a chart—a cardboard cutout of a man with all of Carlson's personalities depicted as heads on a pinwheel. To make his points concretely and dramatically, Savitz flipped ten different heads onto the body—the "original" personality Ross who had been replaced by Justin; Steve, the forty-two-year-old; Michael, the boisterous one; Stacey, the athlete; Blue, the child; Gray, the older adolescent child; Norman, the punk; Black, the protector; and Holden —each to sit on the shoulders of Carlson's body.

Savitz's pinwheel was meant to impress Kingsley that Carlson was different people. Proponents of MPD often thought that way and pointed to "proof," such as different psychological test results or brain wave tracings for each personality. But actors who faked different personalities showed greater brain wave differences than true multiples. So much for proof.

## Non Sequitur

If I had not known the outcome of Carlson Two, I would have been shocked. Despite Judge Kingsley's obvious discomfort with the accusations of barbarism in Pueblo, all through Carlson Two—it dragged on for close to a month—Bob Chappell told me he had picked up bad vibes from Kingsley. He was right. On October 23, 1987, Judge Kingsley backed up his colleague, Judge Eddie Day. Chappell's attack on Carlson's MPD and Fairbairn's weak testimony had not swayed "the old man."

Like Day, Kingsley made multiple personality disorder synonymous with incompetence. Ross Carlson was a multiple, Kingsley wrote, and, therefore, incompetent. This was the non sequitur which plagued the case. It was not Carlson was mentally ill *and* incompetent; it had become, Ross Carlson had MPD and therefore must be incompetent. Of course, Carlson's MPD was hotly debated; and even if real, mental illness per se is not tantamount to incompetence.

Noting that Judge Day warned against "warehousing" Carlson, Kingsley said that "I find that this is exactly what happened." Carlson, Kingsley said, was entitled to "meaningful" treatment by "competent professionals." Finally, he ordered the state to "consult" Carlson's doctors—Fisch, Fairbairn, Newton—and to use hypnosis to treat Carlson.

Kingsley also told Dr. Haydee Kort to find the money to hire experts such as Barry Quinn, among others, to treat Carlson and "instruct" the staff of the hospital. He then added an ominous warning. He would step in and "exercise" his "remedial powers" if she did not seek "outside expert advice."

Kingsley left his ex-clerk one slim ray of hope. Though Carlson had been at Pueblo for almost three and one half years Kingsley, for the moment, rejected the Jackson argument. For now, he refused to turn Carlson loose.

### Shambles

When Kingsley finished, Chappell stalked out of the courthouse the same way he had over three years before. Afterward, he told reporters that defendants often can't remember—or even understand all the details of their crimes—yet are tried every day. The American system, Chappell said, dictated that a defendant get a "fair trial, not a perfect trial." Carlson, he later told me, had no right to a perfect trial yet that was the standard which was being used.

Of course, Gerash was relieved. At the end of the hearing, Gerash turned to a television reporter and asked "How can you punish an innocent boy for what only one of his eight personalities did?" Ross Carlson was innocent; only Antichrist was guilty. Or maybe, according to Gerash's reasoning, Carlson was only one eighth to blame.

## Betrayed

When he returned to Pueblo, Ross Carlson, or Holden, would not talk to the staff—he would only nod yes or no—but he did regularly talk to his attorneys on the phone. Carlson also began to wear very dark sunglasses, whether inside or out. Carlson remained for most of the day in his room with his computer or reading and writing, only coming out for snacks, meals, showers, and telephone calls. On occasion he would come out to watch television or play pool. He, as always, had no trouble sleeping.

He did, however, exhibit something new. Carlson seemed edgy and preoccupied with being betrayed by people he trusted. I expected Carlson to dump on his treatment, the hospital staff, and the courts, but he now began to ridicule his attorneys. He was competent, he said; he had an excellent understanding of the legal system. His attorneys were wrong. In the past, when Carlson claimed to be fine, he then would act crazy. Carlson always protested too much. But why was he openly critical of Savitz and Gerash?

Because, I thought, Carlson expected to take the Theon Jackson route out and now had been blocked. Was he worried that his case had gone on too long, cost too much, had gotten out of hand and taken on a life of its own? Carlson had just learned that the state would bill his trust two hundred and fifty thousand dollars for his hospital stay. They might not collect, he knew, but was Carlson tired of being a cash cow, worried that he was being milked dry?

## Olive Branch?

On November 24, 1987, Bob Fairbairn wrote to Dr. Kort, "in the spirit of offering an olive branch," and told her that he was available to help according to Kingsley's instructions. He could arrange to visit the hospital two days per month to teach, treat, and supervise. "Ross Carlson," he wrote, "is a very bright young man with an important and fascinating disorder who is eminently treatable with the proper care." Fairbairn was still the advocate.

At the same time, Fairbairn filed a complaint with the Colorado Psychiatric Society's ethics committee against the "barbaric" Dr. Lori Greene, the young psychiatrist who had withheld Carlson's snack. If this was an olive branch, it was an olive branch with thorns. Greene, who told me about the complaint, could have lost her medical license. Now, in Carlson's chart, I found the letter which confirmed the investigation. Greene was easily exonerated but the message was clear: If you went against Carlson, you could be torn to shreds. I would have to watch my step. The circus was not over and the circus was not benign.

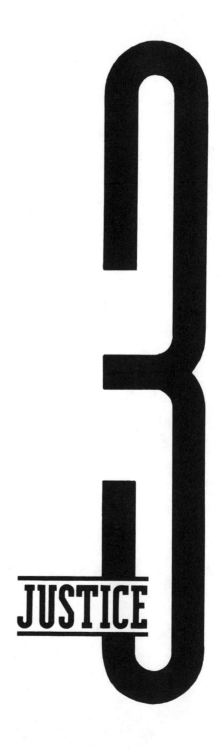

JUSTICE

# A FURTIVE SCHEME

By the end of 1987, the state's case was still paralyzed and Bob Chappell thoroughly demoralized. Four years had passed since the murders but Ross Carlson was still in Pueblo and still ran the show. He did what he wanted, when he wanted. Every move made by the hospital was challenged in court. The state's doctors were on thin ice; they couldn't turn around without Walter or David saying boo. Kingsley's order kept it that way.

## Call Haydee

Sometime in mid-November my chairman at the medical school, Dr. Jim Shore, called me down to his office. Our meeting lasted only minutes. "The state hospital needs help, Mike," he said. "I want you to head up a panel of experts to sort out the Carlson case. Call Haydee and find out the details." That was it.

I did not like what I heard. I realized Jim knew that I was not a forensic psychiatrist and that I did not routinely deal with courts, criminals, lawyers, judges, or murderers. But Jim knew I had experience with perpetrators and victims of violence. Court, however, was not my favorite place and this was not my favorite case. But while I could say no to Bob Chappell in 1985, I could not say no to my boss now. This time I had to agree.

It was clear the hospital needed protection and the panel would provide this kind of shield. But why had they picked me? Were they —Bob Chappell, Haydee Kort, or Jim Shore—so sure what I thought of Carlson? Were they certain that I doubted his multiplicity? I had not written anything of substance in his chart in 1984. Were they assuming that I, like my colleagues, was dubious about Carlson or was this the beginning of my forensic paranoia?

I walked slowly back to my office; it was three years since I had driven down to Pueblo to start my three sessions with Carlson. I thought I had left him behind; now I knew that I would have to see him again.


## Pry Open the Back Door

I wanted to edge into it slowly and make sure there would be no misunderstandings, no surprises. That afternoon I called Haydee. She was delighted that I had agreed. I told her that I had no choice. We knew that this would not be a short consultation like before; this could go on for years.

We then talked money. I told her that this would be expensive. From the news reports I knew that, dollar for dollar, the defense's experts had gone largely unchallenged. It would cost to match their experience and I did not want to go into court without at least one big gun. She knew that already. "Anyone you get will be expensive," she said. "I'll get the money from somewhere."

I also told Haydee that I would make recommendations about Carlson's treatment only after I examined Carlson and reached my own diagnosis. This was against both court orders, but I told Haydee that I could not, in good conscience, make recommendations without doing this first. It would be like prescribing an appendectomy to someone without knowing if they had appendicitis. It made no sense and was bad medicine. What went unspoken was that I would pry open the back door on Carlson's MPD. Though it was against all orders since 1984, Haydee agreed. "Michael," Haydee left me with, "if you find that he is a multiple, so be it."

That night I told Susan that our life had just changed. After dinner I pulled down a standard psychiatric text and read about the Spiegel eye roll. I knew all about egg rolls: I had heard Gerash's devastating put-down quote on television. Alan Fine had been humiliated in 1984; I did not want to find myself in the same situation. In the next weeks I meant to immerse myself in the literature on multiplicity. I planned to learn it backward and forward; I needed to get a handle on MPD and I did not want to look like a fool in court.

### Routine Medical Practice

Ten days later, I met with the medical director of the state hospital, Dr. Mark Pecevich. I wanted my role to be crystal clear, and in writing—more forensic paranoia. My task, as I saw it, was to consult to the hospital—the hospital, not I, was responsible for Carlson's care. And, of course, as part of my consultation my panel and I would do our own diagnostic assessment of Ross Carlson. That was, I told Mark, just "routine medical practice."

Mark sent me the letter on December 22. First provide a diagnostic assessment, then recommend treatment. With this letter in my file, I hoped I was protected. Mark also sent me the first reams of Carlson's state hospital chart. I called Mark and asked for all the transcripts, videos, and police file as well. In a couple of days, Brian Bevis brought them by.

### Christmas 1987

I spent Christmas 1987 wading through Carlson. As Christ's birth was celebrated, I read about Antichrist. I began with what Bevis called Fairbairn's April 6, 1984, "show-and-tell" tape, Fisch's interview, and the transcripts of the 1984 hearing in Eddie Day's court. I read about Carlson's admission to our hospital and his charts, papers, reports, newspaper articles, everything I could get my hands on including my notes I found in Carlson's 1984 record.

As I immersed myself, the question I had when I first heard of the shootings was the same one I had now. But because of the battle, no one else seemed interested, not the defense and not the prosecution. It was simply this: why did Carlson do it? Someplace, I thought, lay the answer. Perhaps, I would find out when I met him again. But other things would have to come first. Carlson was still in Pueblo, incompetent. The question of motive had to go to the back of the line.

**Big Gun**

The next review in front of Kingsley was scheduled for April 1988, in four months. Before then, I had to hire and coordinate my panel. I wanted two or three more psychiatrists, preferably one big gun from outside of Colorado and then one or two more locals. I could not use my first choice—John Macdonald—or Sy Sundell, the two muzzled experts who examined Carlson within weeks of the murder. I did not want MPD "enthusiasts" who saw MPD at the hint of forgetfulness. I needed scientists, not advocates. Personally, I planned to stay in the background.

I knew Haydee wanted me to hire Martin Orne because Orne had so effectively debunked the Hillside Strangler's MPD defense. Orne already knew all about Carlson since he had helped Bob Chappell—long-distance—since 1984. But he had not seen Carlson, and Kathy Morall had visited his lab in Philadelphia to prepare for her failed testimony.

Before I left my chairman's office, I also had thought of Orne. He had all but proved that the Hillside Strangler, Kenneth Bianchi's claim to be a multiple was bogus; that Bianchi had learned the ins and outs of the multiple role from cues provided by the very experts hired to examine him. Bianchi was taught to be a multiple, just as I thought Carlson might have been. I did not want to call Martin Orne without investigating if he were the man for the job and did not want to be called Chappell's or Kort's stooge.

He checked out well. Everyone I called spoke highly of Orne. When I talked with a lawyer in Ohio, she told me about Ohio's famous multiple, the rapist Billy Milligan and his plea of insanity due to MPD. She also suggested Orne. He would be the most "scientific" she said; some of the other experts would be too likely to see MPD even if it were not there.


**"Hire Orne"**

I then met with the forensic psychiatrist I trusted the most, John Macdonald. When we spoke I could not resist and again asked Mac whether he thought Carlson was a fake. He gave me his deadpan look as he had done twice before. Though Mac remained silent, he answered me nonetheless.

"Hire Orne," Macdonald said. I understood the code. "Haydee should not have been so cheap," he told me. "She should have gotten more experienced people involved years ago," he said, his voice clipped with his New Zealand accent. In case I did not get the point, he also told me to buy a book on lying. Orne and a book on lies; how many clues did I need to tell me what Macdonald thought of Carlson?

In late January, I reached Orne at his University of Pennsylvania lab. He told me that Haydee Kort had contacted him in 1984. At that time, Orne did not want to come out to Colorado to testify but now he agreed. Throughout our conversation, Orne used only Carlson's last name—but in a way that indicated that he knew him well.

Orne had been through these inquiring telephone calls many times. "I will send you my *Frontline* tape," he said. I had to think for a moment. "My *Frontline* tape"? Then I realized *Frontline* had done a program on the Hillside Strangler and Orne played a starring role. "And I will send you my résumé." I wanted to tell Orne that he did not have to sell himself—I was already sold—but when he told me how much he charged I realized why he had. Martin Orne was expensive. This was the big time. I told Orne that I would have to check with Dr. Kort first. We then talked about Carlson.

The two keys, Orne said, were secondary gain—that is to say, what did Carlson stand to win or lose by his behavior? The other one was to find—or not find—unequivocal evidence for what Orne called "Carlson's prehomicidal alters." If Carlson were clearly a multiple *before* he killed his parents, he was a multiple now. It was the Rhoads, Staton, O'Hagan stories all over again. Only this time they would have to be more convincing to reach the level of "unequivocal evidence." Orne ended our half hour conversation the way Haydee ended hers: "We may find that he is a multiple and we may not."

The next day, Orne's packet arrived Federal Express. He only used Federal Express for important documents, never the U.S. mail. It was my personal copy of *Frontline* along with Orne's impressive résumé—at that time Orne had 139 scholarly publications—and some articles relevant to Carlson, one which Orne had written about Bianchi, the Hillside Strangler. That night on *Frontline* I watched with interest as Orne tricked Kenneth Bianchi into developing a third personality. I wondered how he would trick Ross Carlson.

He also sent me an article written by another expert who at first diagnosed MPD in Bianchi and then recanted when faced with the facts. Working with criminals, he said, was the big difference and something he had not taken into account. He had made the mistake of not evaluating the context in which Bianchi's MPD first arose. Criminals, he said, often lie.

Two days later Haydee agreed to Orne's fee without missing a beat. What else could she do? Macdonald was right; by skimping early, Ross Carlson had already cost her a bundle. Because of the expense, we decided that I would head a "panel" of only two; me and Orne. My fee for legal work was at that time half of Orne's, but after she asked I agreed to charge Haydee even less. Finally, I told Haydee that Orne would be available in the spring. That gave me February and March, plenty of time to master the file and learn more about multiplicity.

## The Spirit of Cooperation

My honeymoon with the case was short and unpleasantly interrupted. The defense somehow got wind of me. On the morning of March 15, I got a call from David Savitz. I was surprised by his call; we had, as far as I knew, nothing to talk about and I did not even know the man. I decided to wait until the next day to return his call.

When we talked, Savitz said that he called in the "spirit of cooperation" of Judge Kingsley's orders of October 23. I listened as he began to feel me out.

Savitz asked what my plans were. When I told him that I was asked to form a panel of experts, he said that he did not think that was necessary. Carlson's diagnosis, he reminded me, was not in question. I should, he said, just work with the experts who were already available and use Fisch, Fairbairn, and Newton for my panel. I mumbled something.

Savitz seemed most interested in who I was going to bring in and how much it would cost. I did not want to mention Orne; I thought that he and Gerash would do something to try to block us. I told Savitz, instead, that it was not yet clear who would come—actually, the final arrangements with Orne had not yet been made. Besides, it really was not his business who I hired. Savitz was polite but insistent. I told him nothing.

Two days later I got a letter from him summarizing our call, almost word for word. Savitz wanted me to make corrections or agree that his letter was a factual representation of the substance of our conversation. "If I have misstated any of our reported conversation,

please advise . . ." he wrote. It was like a contract. Was he ready-
ing a dossier? Was this how it would be, each conversation recorded?

I did not answer Savitz but sent the letter to Mark Pecevich
since, in my mind, I was consulting to Haydee Kort, Mark, and the
hospital staff. By sending me this letter Savitz let me know that he
would watch me the way he, Gerash, and Carlson watched everyone. The message was clear, don't make a misstep. If his call and
letter meant to make me nervous, to intimidate me, he succeeded.
But it did not end there.

### April Fools'

On April 1, Pueblo's attorney, Pat Robb, responded to Savitz's letter. Three days later, Gerash got into the act. In a letter to Robb
with a copy to me and Chappell, he opened with "I noticed [your]
letter was written on April Fools' Day. I wondered if the letter
constituted a vitriolic joke. In order to orient you to reality,"—he
went on to Pat Robb, a nice grandmotherly woman—"I am enclos-
ing the latest judgment of the court." And Gerash went on: *His
diagnosis is multiple personality disorder, determined by two court proceedings in the last four years.*" And don't you forget it.

That was the tone. "I dare say that you and Mr. Chappell have
gotten together for this 'new diagnosis' to set up additional experts
to get ready for another competency hearing, entitled 'Carlson
III,' " Gerash wrote. We will, he warned Robb, go into court to
block Dr. Weissberg's new panel. But Gerash was wrong. Neither
Pat Robb nor Bob Chappell had reopened the can of worms of
Carlson's diagnosis. I had, and these two letters introduced me to
the realities of the case.

First, unknown to me, Savitz made notes of our conversation and
now Gerash threatened legal action. They wanted to neutralize me;
they had constructed a high tension wire around their client and
they meant to scare me off. I wondered if it was such a good idea for
me to have said yes after all. The only thing that made me feel
better was that, for some reason, Gerash and Savitz seemed scared
of me and what I might do.

### A Mockery, a Furtive Scheme

Then on April 7, before I had even seen Carlson, they tried to head me off. The defense filed a motion for a full-blown status review. It was yet, again, another court hearing. Savitz and Gerash seemed to continually file motions and go to court. The attorneys wanted Haydee to show what she had done so far to implement Kingsley's orders. In their motion, the defense told Kingsley that the hospital doctors were "arbitrary and dogmatic" in their approach and were making a "mockery" of his orders.

Then they got to me. The hospital, they wrote, was "pursuing a furtive scheme" to find experts who would support the "disbelief" of Mr. Carlson's "illness." This would allow the state to "amass more experts for future hearings and trials in this case."

So that was it. They did not want any more experts who could testify, not only about Carlson's competency but about his sanity as well. Savitz and Gerash had neutralized all of the state's experts since 1983. They were not scared of Fine, Reichlin, Morall, Trautt. Macdonald and Sundell were out. But they would not have wanted new doctors spoiling their strategy of decimating the opposition experts.

Savitz and Gerash demanded that Judge Kingsley "order" Haydee Kort to "withdraw" her request that I conduct an "independent" evaluation and assessment of Carlson. They wanted me gone, but Kingsley did not grant the defense motion and allowed me to proceed. He scheduled a status review for later in the spring. That still gave me time.

# STONEWALLED

Frightened of another stunt, I wanted Carlson to learn of our visit only hours before we arrived. Orne had other cases in New Jersey and L.A., so I arranged for him to fly to Denver on Friday evening April 15, 1988, and leave Monday morning. Orne only flew first class, he told me, since a man of his size—six feet four inches, and over two hundred and sixty pounds—could not be expected to sit in coach. Orne was easy for me to spot at the airport but hard to fit into my small car. He wore glasses and had a round face which, like many heavy men, looked younger than his years. The drive to Pueblo was cramped but interesting.

## Abuse

First, I talked about abuse. What Carlson did was very, very cruel and abused children are often full of rage. Therefore, abuse was a key. From the moment I heard of the murders, I told Orne, I thought Carlson had been abused. Only, so far, there was no evidence for it. Bevis found none and I had found none. Still, I was suspicious. Subtle emotional abuse was hard to detect.

Too many things were called abuse, Orne replied; normal child rearing practices now were looked at as pathological. Orne wanted clear definitions and clear evidence, certainly, before reaching a conclusion about Carlson. I agreed. Besides, even if Carlson were abused, it did not mean he was a multiple. Furthermore, even if abused and a multiple, Carlson could still be competent and sane.

As we drove south, I pointed in the directions of the important places in Carlson's life: his home in Littleton, east toward Cottonwood Road in northern Douglas County, Castle Rock, and the low brown courthouse and jail. It was dark when we pulled into the motel parking lot.

We checked in to the Holiday Inn which Haydee's secretary promised was the best in town. Thirty miles north of Pueblo, we had begun talking about dinner. With Orne, finding a good restaurant was always one of the first orders of business. Surprisingly, we found one in the motel. So when we arrived, we ate and talked more about Carlson over platefuls of langostino. The last thing that Orne said before saying good night was that he hoped that Carlson would talk.


**Saturday**
It was a bright and sunny Saturday and I was up, showered, and dressed quickly. After a large breakfast and another food discussion —this time about soft boiled eggs, I think—we drove to the hospital in under ten minutes. When we showed up at the 1960s style brick and glass administration building, Mark Pecevich took us to the large conference room on the second floor and then went to get Carlson.

I was familiar with this room since I had given talks here before. On one end, fifty seats were set up theater style; in front was a long conference table. The room was quiet and empty. I set up our video recorder—Orne wanted everything taped—and arranged three chairs at one end of the table. We sat and waited for Carlson to be brought over from his ward.

When Carlson walked in I was struck by how he had changed since 1984. Adversity sometimes ennobles a person; not Carlson. His college boy good looks had soured. His thick blond hair was now close-cropped. Almost black glasses covered his scalding blue eyes; his new blond beard hid the rest of his face. Carlson looked older, tougher, meaner, hardened. He had been transformed into the part of prisoner and murderer. Like Dorian Gray, Carlson's pretty-boy looks had been overwhelmed, not by age, but by himself. He looked evil.

This was, according to the defense, Holden. We introduced ourselves and told him why we were here, but Carlson did nothing to acknowledge us. We did not shake hands. Instead, he sat at the end of the long table, black glasses on, head down, mute. From the side, I saw that his eyes were open but he kept them fixed on his lap. At least he was awake. I took notes; Orne wanted a record of everything before we turned on the tape.

Carlson kept on his gray polar fleece jacket, collar up. His glasses were so dark I could only see the sides of his eyes. As I looked at his plaid shirt and jeans, I wondered if this were the murder outfit or only a copy: red plaid shirt, jacket, and jeans. The only things missing were his brown work boots and surgical gloves.

The first thing Orne told Carlson was that the video was not on, but that if he did not answer we would assume it was all right to tape. In response, Carlson clutched his yellow notebook which lay in his lap and was silent. Finally, after eight minutes, I signaled Mark to turn on the tape. As if in response, Carlson slowly raised his head so that it was three-quarters erect. That was an improvement, but by looking around his glasses I could see that he now had closed his eyes. Carlson clearly knew we were there. My heart sank when I realized that he meant to outwait us.

Orne tried to coax him to talk. "You must be at least as curious as I am," said Orne, but there was no response. Nothing. In the background, I heard the hospital operator page a doctor over the speaker system. Carlson did not move a muscle. With his beard covering the lower half of his face and his black aviator glasses covering his eyes, he was in his bunker. After fifteen more minutes Carlson's head was at full staff, totally erect. He had done it so slowly that I only noticed that he had done it when he was finished.

I looked over at Orne who finally motioned me out of the room but not before he signaled Mark to leave the camera on in a clumsy attempt to trick Carlson, in case, while we were gone, Carlson decided to get up and do a soft-shoe rendition of "I Shot the Sheriff." The three of us, Mark, Orne, and I then left; the two techs who brought Carlson over remained behind.

In Haydee's office, Orne was distressed by Carlson's silence but not surprised. We wondered what to do next. Later, I saw that Carlson remained motionless for the whole time we were gone.

When we returned, Orne told Carlson that he would benefit from "allowing us" to talk with him. "You are choosing not to talk," he said, an understatement. As Orne spoke, Carlson did not move a muscle. I was amazed by Carlson's perseverance. Talking to Carlson was like talking at a brick wall, an angry brick wall. But, Orne, I was learning, could be immovable too.

Orne then tried to make contact and moved to pick up Carlson's right hand. As skin touched skin, Carlson suddenly pulled his head to one side and mumbled incoherently. To me, he looked as if he was silently weeping but I saw no tears. "Are you frightened now," Orne asked in his deep, steady voice. "Do you get this way often?" Carlson did not answer.

With his right hand, Orne again slowly reached for Carlson's right hand. "I want to see if you can relax your hand." By now, I was slightly somnolent. Suddenly, the voice of the hospital operator punctured my reverie: "Your attention please, this is a drill, code zero, surgical ward, room C49, this is a drill." Hospitals use codes: code 99, code zero, code blue, when someone is dying and needs immediate resuscitation. But this was a drill; no one was dying in room C49.

I remembered the Catholic hospital where I did a rotation as a medical student. Code 99 was always followed by "calling Father McCarthy, calling Father McCarthy." Father McCarthy was so quick, he often arrived ahead of the doctors. Last rites were important in case resuscitation did not work and the patient could not be brought back. I thought of the last rites Carlson administered to his parents: Bang. Bang.

I watched Orne; he seemed to take forever to reach Carlson. I expected fireworks when they touched. But the only thing that happened was that Carlson raised his head a little more. His eyes were still shut. Even with eyes closed he was menacing.

Somewhere down the hall, a door slammed. I jumped but Carlson did not change. If possible, he was even more still. Orne let Carlson's hand drop and we broke for lunch at 12:10.

Bob Gonzales, who sat through the entire hour with us, now asked Ross to get up. For at least three minutes, Gonzales and the other tech stood on either side of Carlson but Ross did not move. The two men looked uncomfortable; they had an audience and they were on tape. The other tech finally touched Ross. "Do you want to go back to the ward?" Carlson remained as if in a stupor. Finally, Gonzales gently pulled Ross to his feet.

At that, like a burned cat, Ross leapt to his left, batting away the arms that tried to pull him to his feet. As he moved, I saw a white spot on the top of his head flash before my eyes. It was the ugly scar, the mark of his birth, quarter-size, on top of his head. I only saw it for a moment before he slammed to the floor. I then heard Carlson shriek something unintelligible as he cowered, knees drawn to his chest, in the corner.

"They are eating my brain." That was all I understood. "They are eating my brain." He then lay crumpled, shackles on his feet, silent. Gonzales bent down and put Carlson's loafers on him which had come off in the struggle and then gently patted Carlson's knee. "Get up, Ross." Pecevich, who worked the camera came over to help Carlson to his feet. Even while upright, Carlson hung there limp, like a rag doll. A moment later, he shook his head and looked around, eyes unseeing, as if just awakened from a deep sleep or a trance. Then, clutching his book, he shuffled out with the two men. It was 12:32 when I switched off the camera. "Some performance," Orne said, as we walked from the room.

## Saturday Afternoon

When Orne, Mark, and I returned from lunch, we learned something interesting. As soon as Carlson returned to the ward he asked to call "David," undoubtedly Savitz. Carlson then went to the telephone and dialed the number himself. Weeping, he told "David" that "they want to kidnap me" and "they are eating my brain." According to a nurse, Carlson talked to "David" for twenty minutes.

What Savitz told his client we did not know. But this made a deep impression on me; Carlson was capable of talking to us but had clearly chosen not to do so. Instead, he acted crazy. Why he had not spoken, and whose idea this was, we did not know.

At 2:35 we began again. I rearranged the chairs which had been disturbed in the struggle. Pecevich busied himself with the video camera; I noticed the red light as he switched it on. Orne was not easily swayed and meant to outwait Carlson.

As soon as Carlson came in he sat and slumped over. As far as he was concerned, we were not there. He looked as if he was trying to sleep, despite the lights, camera, and five men in the room.

No one, Orne repeated, will hurt him, he told Carlson. "Are you frightened?" There was no response. "Did anyone tell you that we would hurt you?" Again, no response. "You were told we were going to see you, weren't you?" No response. "Would you mind telling me how old you are now?" No response. With that, Carlson appeared to go to sleep.

So far, Orne had been polite. He sat impassively, as if he had all the time in the world. But Carlson, by not talking, did not provide Orne a handhold; no conversation, no hypnosis, no diagnosis, no chance for a trick like Kenneth Bianchi's third personality. For all of Orne's experience, Carlson remained incommunicado.

The afternoon wore on. "I am here to help find out what will help you. I find it strange that you don't talk." By now, I was deeply impressed with Orne's patience though I still waited for the Orne magic. We again took a break and let the camera run; Carlson slept while we talked. We returned in twenty minutes.

Finally, Orne turned up the heat. He asked—actually told—Carlson to take off his sunglasses so we could see his face which, until now, was hidden. Of course, Carlson did not respond but appeared to be listening.

"I will have to have someone take them off if you won't do it yourself. You are not asleep. You can hear me loud and clear. Please take off your glasses." Orne's patience had, at least for the moment, disappeared.

Finally, Orne signaled for one of the attendants to approach. Right before he made contact, as if suddenly scalded again, Carlson jumped to his left. I was amazed how quick he was. Fairbairn thought he was thin and starved but he looked plenty strong to me.

This time Carlson huddled in the corner, and covered his face with his book and squeezed his legs together like a girl. Was he worried we would steal his genitals? I remembered he was born with an undescended testicle and had a pingpong ball prosthesis put in many years ago.

"Clearly you understand me," Orne said, standing up.

After a moment, I heard high-pitched, otherworldly sounds coming from Carlson. "The cyborg, the man . . . cyborg, you eat my brain."

Orne did not understand. "What are you saying?"

I told Orne that Carlson said "cyborg." At least Carlson now talked, even though he was talking crazy. Maybe a conversation would develop, no matter how bizarre.

"Are you serious about that? How could I possibly eat your brain. Is it a book? A television program? Where did you get that thought? I know you understand what I am saying. Talk to me. No one is going to hurt you."

Carlson still huddled; as I watched, the scene in front of the fifty theater style seats had a false, theatrical flair. I had never seen a bona fide patient act this way. We knew there were schizophrenics on Carlson's ward; at lunch, Orne guessed that Carlson was trying to imitate one.

"I came two thousand five hundred miles to see you . . . we have to talk." It was four years since Fairbairn's tape, I thought. Then, he switched on demand; today, he acted insane. Finally, Orne spoke what was on both of our minds. "Tell me what grade did you get in acting when you were studying acting?" We knew he got *A* pluses.

After ten minutes, the attendants lifted Carlson back onto his seat and we stopped a few minutes later. As he walked out, Carlson looked for all the world like someone playing a Forty-second Street bum. I then had to remind myself that just as I could not tell if someone were truthful because they appeared honest, I could not be certain they were a fake because they appeared to lie.

As we drove back to the motel, Orne was upset but I felt surprisingly good. Carlson, I thought, had given us an opening. But Orne's professional pride was hurt because he had not been able to coax a conversation out of Carlson. In a way I was glad because what Carlson revealed was that, while he was mute with us, he talked to "David." While reaching a diagnosis without Carlson's cooperation would be difficult, Carlson's mutism alternating with his ability to use the telephone had nothing to do with MPD; his mutism had to do with Ross Carlson.

That night, Savitz called the hospital and told Bob Gonzales that he did not want his client "questioned." Of course, Savitz had nothing to do with who could or could not talk with Carlson. Whether Savitz had something to do with Carlson talking back I did not know.

**Sunday**
We began at 10:30. This time, Carlson came in without his glasses—
Orne insisted that he not bring them. He wore, however, the same
outfit as yesterday; red plaid shirt, jeans, polar fleece gray jacket,
only this time he had on white sneakers instead of black loafers.
Maybe he wanted better traction. Glassless, Carlson still acted
weird. He squinted and tilted his head to the left while he mumbled, sniffed, and breathed heavily. "You made them lock my
hands, and now you are going to try to get into my soul and eat my
brain." It was a child's voice. Was it Gray? Blue? "You lie. You make
them rip them away." As he sat there, the Forty-second Street bum
had become a crazy person on the subway. He suddenly stopped
and sat silently.

"I can see that you have put yourself into a trance state. You
apparently have learned to put yourself into a trance state," said
Orne.

"At this point you can choose to open your eyes. Did your lawyer
tell you to behave this way? Or did he tell you to cooperate? Do you
enjoy being in the hospital? Would you like to continue to stay
here?" Orne was certain Carlson was terrified of the penitentiary at
Canon City, of being sodomized and being made someone's wife.
Fear of rape in the pen was one reason why, Orne guessed, Carlson
refused to get better. Carlson wanted to wait it out in the safe
confines of Pueblo.

Time passed slowly. It was late morning; I was now sure Carlson
would outlast us or at least me since I had to return to Denver that
night. Carlson had hunkered down since 1984 and we had been at it
for only one day. This round, I thought, he would win.

But then like a hypno-judo expert, Orne tried to use Carlson's
own trance power against him and push Carlson into an even deeper
state. "You find yourself floating . . ." Orne instructed Carlson,
"the arm might get heavy, your eyes are heavy, and your shoulders
relax." As I kept my eyes on Carlson, I wondered if this would be
the moment Orne would get the upper hand? Was Carlson's trance
deepening, was this the long-awaited Orne trick? The flurry of excitement did not last; not much happened and at the end of the
morning Carlson shook his head again as if to wake up. Dazed, he
again theatrically shuffled out the door.

## Sunday Afternoon

As soon as we returned from lunch, I called the ward hoping to learn that Carlson found his voice after he left us. Sure enough, he had. As soon as he arrived on the ward, he placed another call.

We resumed a little before two. Still without his black sunglasses, Carlson sat, this time with his left hand covering his eyes. He then shifted hands and brought his right hand to his face as he strained not to see. In two days, he had not looked at us for more than ten seconds. But he must have known we had a large screen television and VCR set up next to the table across from where he sat.

"I have had a chance to see a number of tapes, the one with Fairbairn, the one with Newton. In those tapes you cooperated nicely," Orne began. At lunch, we discussed showing Carlson one of the 1984 tapes to see if he could engage him. But he gave no response.

"I will ask you to look at one of the tapes. Mr. Carlson, you may want to look to see what you looked like at the time." With that, Orne switched on the VCR. The screen was filled with Carlson's June 1984 face, the weekend before his competency hearing. This was a tape Fairbairn made with Fig Newton. Carlson was breezy, ingratiating, impeccable, smooth, not at all like today. Orne turned up the volume.

I heard Fairbairn tell Carlson "you have been heroically patient with me . . ." and apologizing for "exposing" Carlson to another interviewer. Carlson smiled his boyish, charming smile as he looked intently at Fairbairn. This was Bernauer "Fig" Newton's first chance to examine Carlson.

Orne shut off the VCR. He wanted Carlson to lower his hand and watch but Carlson did not and Orne restarted the machine. On screen, Carlson told Fairbairn that he "appreciates" that he was "taking the time" with him. Graciously, Carlson's 1984 version told Fairbairn and Newton that "the least I can do for people is be cooperative."

Cooperative? I looked over at Carlson. In case we missed the point, he now had both hands over his eyes, one hand for each eye. He did not want anything to come through.

On screen, Fairbairn asked about Carlson's twentieth birthday, May 28th, 1984. "There was ice cream, cake, you and Walter and David came," Ross said. "I appreciated that." That was the birthday Fairbairn gave Carlson a book.

"You sent me two thank-you notes. What do you remember about that?" asked Fairbairn. Carlson could not explain it; one must have been sent by Justin the other by Steve.

Orne's voice drowned out the soundtrack. "You were very cooperative when this tape was made. Who told you to behave this way with us? This is certainly not the way you behaved with Fairbairn."

Orne turned toward the screen. "I found that mental health is very painful . . . you adapt to things, you have survival skills," Carlson went on. He may not, he said, want to get better or to change.

"You have no trouble talking to others. Why are you not talking to us?" Orne looked at me with raised eyebrows. "You can wake up any time you want to. You can do it."

This was a one-way conversation. An hour had passed and Carlson still sat, eyes covered. On screen, Carlson almost happily described Black. "He gets you out of things without physical damage . . ." It was ironic, I thought, as I sat watching. *Body Heat. American Gigolo.* Carlson always wanted to be in the movies.

A sigh came from Orne. "You are just not helping." Suddenly, Orne reached over with his right hand and touched Carlson. This time there were sparks. As if jolted, Carlson sat ramrod straight, made a fist, and threatened to hit Orne in the face. Orne drew back. "Ah, you know who I am. I want to know who you are." But Carlson put down his head and closed his eyes. The moment passed. He shut down again.

On screen, Carlson, glib and smooth, continued to talk about Black. "There is a gentleman, you might say, and he is an acquaintance of mine. He takes over when he senses danger. His name is Black." Carlson then spelled each personality out, one by one. Just like his phone call and collage to Fisch, he was patient in his education of Fig Newton. Only Newton did not seem to notice that he was in school.

"I don't talk to the other personalities . . . There is telecommunication; like a party line. I can tell they were here by a metallic taste in my mouth." But, Carlson said, he could not tell friends that he has lost time. His friends would think he was crazy. At the end of our table, Carlson appeared to slide into another trance. He was a sharp-featured Tom Cruise on the screen; clean shaven, blond hair beautifully combed, pink button-down oxford with an open collar. Today, we faced a thug.

Carlson suddenly glared at Orne, daring him to interfere, and put his head on the table. He now showed only the top of his closely cropped head; the angry scar again drew my attention. On screen, the conversation was lively. "Would you be willing to talk with me about the incident where your mother and father were killed?" Newton asked. Incident, I thought; that was an antiseptic word. It was a massacre.

"I suppose," Carlson said, "I don't see why not. But I am confused about what I have been told, what I think, and what I think I remember," Carlson went on in his monotone. "I can try." A sob suddenly arose from the end of the table. Carlson was not watching but I knew he listened.

"I know that my folks were . . . ah . . . I have been told that my folks have been shot." I could not hear the tape because Carlson's sobs drowned out the sound. But the sobs were eerie, false. "I was told that they were shot . . .

"I recall that morning, supposedly on the day in question. I got up late and read the newspaper," Carlson went on. "I usually only read the entertainment section." The sobs distracted me. "It was like any day, a shower, and a pizza . . .

"I ran some errands." I again looked at Carlson; he had stopped. It was disjointing. Now, in front of us, he was mute. On screen I watched and heard his story of the day of the murders. Carlson in a time warp; was any of this real?

"I don't remember where I went. I made a phone call. I remember I had a bag of quarters. Rarely do I carry change. I think it is a waste of time. I recall discussing with a gentleman I know going out for the evening to have a bite. He was making the reservations for dinner. I remember," said Carlson, "I think I ate prime rib, as I recall. I remember meeting somebody but I am not sure . . . I remember the act of getting dressed quite well, and I remember leaving the theater . . . I mean I remember leaving the restaurant and going to the theater."

Interesting slip; Carlson left the theater—and Ken Cortez—to shoot his parents. But Carlson caught his stumble. "I remember leaving the theater and going to Tenneco and I recall going to sleep . . . and hanging my suit up in my closet." But the time of the murder was blank, a black hole.

I looked at Carlson who now slept, was faking sleep, or was in a trance. For a moment I heard tap, tap. Then, imperceptibly at first, and then faster and faster, Carlson's chair rocked and banged against the wall. Bang. Bang. Like the shots. Bang. Bang. Then I heard deep breaths, gasps almost, match the rhythm of the chair. Bang. Bang. Gasp. Gasp. Was this one of his autohypnotic techniques? By now the chair was smashing against the wall. Bang. Bang. It was mesmerizing as we sat and watched. "You seem to have been troubled when the issue of the killing of your parents came up," Orne finally spoke up. Nothing. "You really should look at what you looked like. You were quite a handsome man. Considerable charm. It was strange to see you discuss killing your parents with such lack of feeling."

Bang. Bang. Lack of feeling is a hallmark of a psychopath. No feeling for others, no ability to walk in someone else's shoes.

On screen, Bernauer "Fig" Newton now asked to hypnotize Carlson so he could recover more of Carlson's memories of Cottonwood Road. Carlson agreed. I will let you, Carlson said, because "you seem to be an astute person." This was Carlson at his polite best.

"If at any time you want to stop we can." Newton looked to be in his mid-sixties, his hair combed like a Julius Caesar. But his tone, calm, did not vary. He expertly put Carlson into a trance. Carlson stared at a spot and took deep breaths. "Have the tight feeling flow away . . . with each breath you will feel the tight feeling flow away." Carlson was beautifully hypnotizable and if he did not know much about trance induction before he met Newton, he knew a lot about it now. Especially the breathing.

In the room, the chair stopped and the deep breaths subsided. Carlson's head slumped and rested full force on his chest. Orne reached over and lifted Carlson's hand. There were no fireworks; Carlson was limp. Newton had put Carlson into a trance both on screen and in the room. Newton was good; I started to feel tired too. Then, Newton got to the point. "What do you know about what happened to your mother and father?"

"They were killed . . ." In our room, Carlson's face grimaced. "Do you remember anything about it?" asked Newton.

"No." Hypnotized or not, Carlson was closed. He did not even divulge to Newton the details he told Fisch and Fine. Newton pushed. "I want to talk to someone who has some memory of what happened to your mother and father."

"Okay," said Carlson. There was a long pause followed by what must have been the emergence of another personality. "I remember seeing things from behind . . . from behind me."

"What did you see?"

"I see a man in blue . . . I see his back . . . I see legs, his hair, I see his arm . . ."

I took a long look at Carlson. On screen, he was mechanical, cold as he told Newton about the shooting. But he was wound tight as he sat with us. It was taking enormous energy to remain motionless, eyes shut, jaw thrust forward. I knew he listened to every word.

Back on screen. "It seems frozen in time," Carlson said. "All I can see is this one frame." Ross Carlson was in the movies again. "I see an arm . . . the arm of the man . . . I see a weapon . . . I see a black gun, handgun . . . I see me on the ground . . ."

"What are you doing on the ground?"

"I am lying next to me. I can't see the two very well. I am too far away. I see a road."

"I don't understand," said Newton.

"I see the man in blue discharge the gun . . ."

"Who is the man in blue?"

"I don't know . . . There is something really wrong . . . But it won't matter. When he killed us we would be gone and nothing will matter. I keep seeing the gun discharge, I keep seeing the gun discharge," Carlson repeated, as if no one pulled the trigger.

"Who was hit?" Newton's excitement overwhelmed his struggle to remain neutral. "Who was hit?"

Orne shut off the tape and broke the spell. "Have you cried for your parents? Ever?" Carlson moved his head away as if he found Orne's words toxic. Orne repeated himself. "No matter what else there was, you must miss them." Nothing.

Orne put the tape back on. "I see a blue car. I see him picking up something and walking to the car . . ." Carlson stopped. Carlson was now as silent on the screen as he was with us. He did not answer Orne or Newton. In response, Newton deepened Carlson's trance.

"What did the man in blue pick up?" Carlson was still. The fluorescent lights flickered slightly.

"Will you talk with me?" Newton now began the plea that everyone eventually pleaded with Carlson. "Will you talk with me?" Carlson took Newton to the brink but no further; Ross Carlson talked to no one.

Orne interrupted. "Even with Newton you did not answer questions that you did not want to answer. You stonewalled him too." That was an apt phrase. Carlson was an angry stonewall.

Deep breathing came from the VCR and from Carlson now. These two Carlsons, four years apart, did the same thing. With each breath, each Carlson, then and now, blew everyone off.

"Do you feel like talking?" Newton begged Carlson. But Carlson was silent. Even to his own experts he did not really say anything other than he was a multiple. He gladly told them about lost time, Black, Blue, and Antichrist, but little about the crime even when hypnotized by someone as expert in MPD as Newton.

I heard Carlson say: "I seem to hurt. I feel like something in my heart just dropped out . . . my hand hurts and my heart." Newton must have thought Carlson was finally letting a memory out and quickly put Carlson into a deeper trance. Newton asked whoever caused his hand to hurt to come out at the count of three. One. Two. Three. Carlson breathed deeply. I could not believe it, but on screen Carlson started to snore. They remained like this for what seemed a long time. The doctor from L.A. and the snoring Carlson.

Finally, Carlson said softly, "Flowers . . . pretty flowers." I laughed to myself. Carlson had shut Newton out with flowers while here he shut us out with crazy behavior. "It is white and pink. Like an orchid." Newton asked about death and Carlson gave him flowers; flowers were a long way from murder and Cottonwood Road. People, I told myself, could fake hypnosis even with very experienced hypnotists and lie when genuinely hypnotized. As Carlson said, experts can fail; even monkeys fall from trees.

Orne shut off the tape and we sat in silence. I looked at my watch; it was a quarter to five. We had sat here for three hours and I had to go back to Denver. Orne would spend another hour with Carlson in the morning and meet with the hospital staff and talk to them about MPD as per Kingsley's orders, but now I had to leave.

Bob Gonzales and another attendant tried to help Carlson to his feet. This time there were no cyborgs. "Let's go," Gonzales finally said, "C'mon, let's go." Carlson did nothing, not even shuffle out of the room. The two men, supporting him under each arm, started to pull the limp Carlson out. Carlson's knees dragged on the floor as his legs splayed out behind him. The last I saw of Carlson were the pale, rippled soles of his sneakers as he was pulled around the corner like a man who had a stroke or was dead.

*Left:* Ross Carlson at six months. His mother carried this photograph with her in her wallet the night he murdered her. *(Courtesy of the Arapahoe County, Colorado, District Attorney's Office)*

*Above:* Carlson at eighteen months—one month before he was severely burned on the wrist. Mrs. Carlson also carried this photograph the night of her murder. *(ACDA's Office)*

*Above:* Carlson during high school, also in mother's wallet. *(ACDA's Office)*

*Right:* Carlson's 1982 high school yearbook picture found in mother's wallet. *(ACDA's Office)*

*Left:* Marilyn Carlson during the summer of 1983, just weeks before Ross shot her. *(ACDA's Office)*

*Above:* Rod Carlson less than two years before his death. *(ACDA's Office)*

*Top:* The Carlsons' Littleton, Colorado, home on August 18, 1983, the morning Rod and Marilyn were found dead. *(Courtesy of the Douglas County, Colorado, Sheriff's Office)*

*Bottom:* Aerial view of the bodies on desolate Cottonwood Road, the morning of August 18, 1983. *(DCS's Office)*

Search of the crime scene, August 18, 1983. *(Steve Groer/*Rocky Mountain News*)*

*Top:* The Carlson case was Investigator (now Lieutenant) Robinson's first homicide investigation—photographed in front of Douglas County court and jail.

*Bottom:* "It seemed to be a dinner out, an evening at the movies." Movie ticket (top) and receipt for prime-rib dinner. *(ACDA's Office/Mark Groth)*

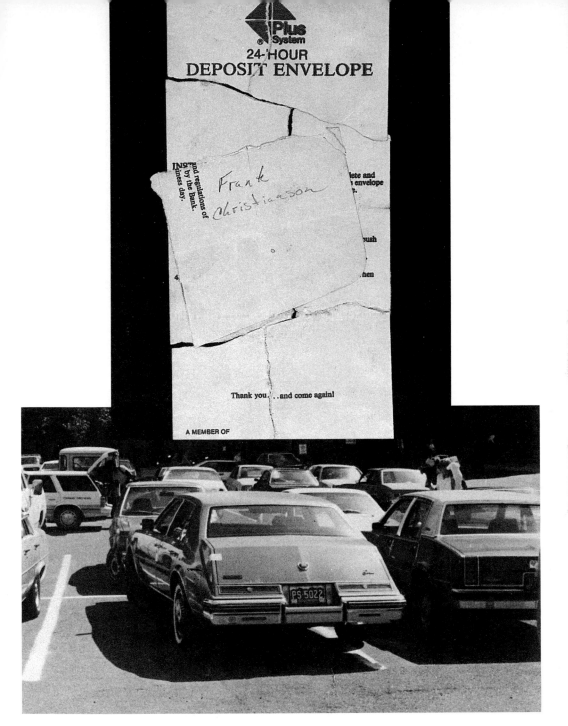

*Top:* "Only open this if I don't return," Carlson told his friend. No one named Christianson has ever come forward. *(ACDA's Office/Mark Groth)*

*Bottom:* When Carlson parked his parents' Cadillac, he left the window down and the keys in the ignition. *(DCS's Office)*

*Top:* Because of an errant kick of a football, David Trigg stumbled upon Carlson's black bag hidden in the trees on the far right of this picture. *(DCS's Office)*

*Bottom:* When Investigator Robinson opened the black bag he found Marilyn's purse, Carlson's phony driver's license, surgical gloves, and Carlson's clothes. The .38 Rossi was in one of the boots. *(DCS's Office)*

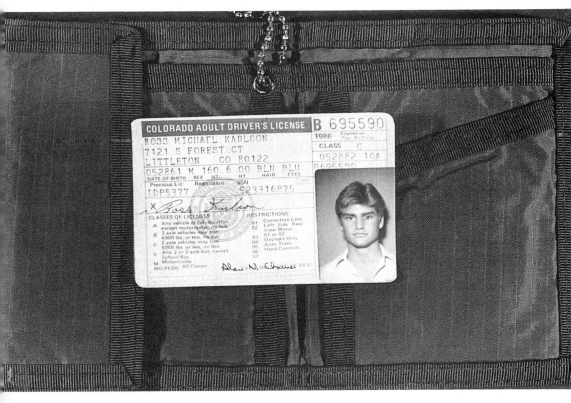

Carlson's wallet and phony license found in the black bag.
*(ACDA's Office/Mark Groth)*

*Top:* Chief Deputy District Attorney Robert Chappell in the fall of 1991. Chappell was on the Carlson case from the beginning.

*Bottom:* The prosecution believed that Carlson planned to use Walter Gerash, one of Denver's best-known defense attorneys, if he was caught. *(Dave Buresh/*The Denver Post*)*

Carlson and attorney David Savitz in court June 6, 1984, during his first competency hearing. *(Lyn Alweis/*The Denver Post*)*

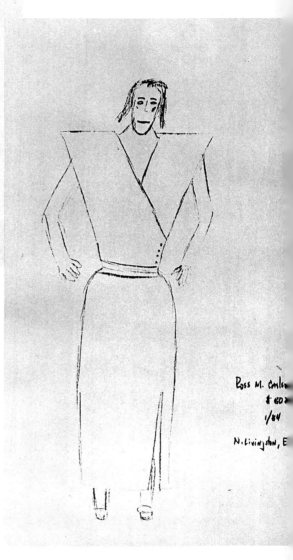

As part of his psychological evaluation by the state, in the winter of 1983–1984, Carlson was asked to draw pictures of a man and a woman. The man is small; both drawings suggest hostility. Asked to give three wishes for them, Carlson replied "an evening out, a rose for the woman, and a theatrical performance for both."

Ross M. Carlso

# 60

1/84

N. Livingston, E

Ralph Fisch thought that Carlson's collage, which Fisch received on February 25, 1984, "confirmed" the diagnosis of MPD. The defense found hints of satanic ritual abuse here; note the devil in upper left-hand corner and the bound wrists in the upper right. *(Courtesy of David Savitz)*

*Top:* Carlson said he did not recall shaving off his eyebrows in 1984. "I woke up and they were gone." *(DCS's Office)*

*Bottom:* Carlson's "Holden," April 23, 1988, five days after our "stonewall" interviews. According to the defense, Holden emerged to combat the "brutality" of the state hospital and could remember nothing before 1985. *(DCS's Office)*

Judge Robert Kingsley, who replaced Judge Eddie Day after Day was forced to step down. "What did I learn from Carlson? Never believe anything you hear. Or see."

*Top:* Ross Carlson at the state hospital in September 1989, right before his last competency hearing. *(Chuck Bigger)*

*Bottom:* "Ross Carlson asked to be buried next to his mother. His wish was granted." *(Sunset Memorial Park, Minneapolis, Minn.)*

## Tactical Error

So this was it. I just spent a chunk of the state's money to fly Martin Orne out and this is what we got; Carlson in a dead swoon. Sometimes Carlson acted crazy; sometimes he was mute. But whatever he did, he did not talk. We did not know if this had been his idea or if he followed instructions. Maybe he figured that if he did not talk we could not trip him up.

Orne was unhappy because he could not hypnotize Carlson and try to uncover his fraud. I, however, thought we gained something. I wondered if Carlson made an error because mutism was not a symptom of MPD, it was just Carlson with his mouth shut. Furthermore, noncooperation was not grounds for incompetence. The defense, I guessed, would say Carlson was silent because he was frightened. But if Ross Carlson had spoken, our visit might not have been as effective at all. Like David Trigg kicking his football next to the little black bag, Carlson's stonewall might become, I hoped, another one of Chappell's lucky breaks.

# GESTAPO

Unsettled April weather greeted us as we walked out of the building. It had already started to spit rain and the winds were kicking up. After some small talk, Orne said we had one more thing to do; call Newton. The world of hypnosis was small and Newton and Orne knew each other well. A call, Orne thought, would help fulfill Kingsley's order that the hospital "cooperate" with the defense. I wondered if I heard a tinge of sarcasm in his voice when he said "cooperate."

I was puzzled when Orne wanted to find a Radio Shack, which we did moments before it closed. It turned out that Orne wanted to buy a device which, when attached to the phone, allowed me to listen in and take notes of his conversation. He knew exactly what to look for and exactly how to wire it up. It was raining heavily by the time we arrived at the Holiday Inn. After he attached the microphone to his phone, I checked it out. Orne then called Newton. I listened as the telephone rang in L.A. I was disappointed when no one answered.

While waiting, I flipped through more reports and learned Carlson told a friend that he made money as a "gigolo"; that he "stole almost everything" he had and bragged about "servicing" older women. Carlson must have been a big hit in his fundamentalist

Christian home. Someone else told an investigator that, during the spring of 1983 Ross wrote a letter to *The Denver Post* about "how someone young and attractive would survive in prison." Carlson wrote this as an English exercise at college but the informant was not sure Ross mailed it. This was more evidence that Carlson feared attacks in prison.

### The Fat Was in the Fire

Orne redialed and, this time, Newton answered with the same calm voice I had just heard on the tape. I looked at my watch; it was 5:20. Newton was surprised but understood immediately why Orne was in Colorado. As they spoke, I started to scribble.

After the usual niceties, Orne told Newton how Judge Kingsley ordered the state "to confer" with Carlson's experts. This sounded like a good idea to Newton who immediately said that he did not think that Fairbairn "knows much." Fairbairn "was, unfortunately, well into it before I got there . . . The fat was in the fire when I arrived. I would have handled [Carlson] differently if I had been there first."

The fat was in the fire. I wondered what Newton thought of Ralph Fisch's leading questions. As if he read my mind, Orne now said that "Carlson had a lot of training before you saw him." Newton agreed. But burning fat did not stop Newton from diagnosing MPD. When told of our experiences of the last two days, Newton was surprised. "Carlson talked to Fisch, Fairbairn, and me," he said. "Why would he not talk to you?" But, I thought, when you asked about murder he told you about flowers.

Gerash and Savitz, I heard Newton say, wanted Carlson to go to trial. Newton was certain that "David" was reasonable and wanted Carlson to cooperate. David had told Newton as much. Orne and I looked at each other. "I don't know why," Newton went on, "Ross is stonewalling." I wondered if Newton was ignorant of Theon Jackson? Did he not know of Carlson's fear of being raped in the pen?

Orne laid out his concerns. The key, Orne said, was secondary gain. Carlson needed to appear ill to keep his money and to avoid prison. First, Orne told Newton, Carlson was frightened of "rapists" in jail. And if found guilty, he would lose his financial windfall. Newton was noncommittal. Orne brought up Jackson. Gerash and

Savitz, Orne said, might be trying to have Carlson found permanently incompetent so the charges might be dropped. "If I were a defense attorney," Orne said, "I would not want Carlson on trial."

At the suggestion that either Savitz or Gerash might have encouraged Carlson's noncooperation, Newton drew in his breath. "David would not do that," Newton finally said. His voice was lower, less certain. "He wants Carlson to get better. He would not lie to me," Newton repeated. "I am very friendly with David . . . I do not believe that is what he did."

Orne persisted, "Carlson will not get better unless these sources of benefit to Carlson are removed." The money, avoiding the pen, Theon Jackson; Carlson only lost if restored to competency. Carlson, Orne said, was not treatable now. Newton did not agree.

The battle lines had long been drawn but maybe we were swaying him. Maybe Newton would recant, just like Bianchi's expert did. When Orne suggested that Newton fly in sometime during the next weeks and see Carlson together with Orne, he quickly agreed. "What you have been telling me," said Newton, "disturbs me."

The conversation over, I packed my notes and said good-bye to Orne. As I drove home I hoped I was right that these two days of noninterviews might be a turning point in the trajectory of Carlson's story. The manipulation of the last two days was so blatant. I could not believe that he would get away with it. Then again, I wondered, how naive was I?

That night, Gerash got Judge Kingsley on the phone along with Bob Chappell. He wanted Kingsley to issue an injunction to prevent us from talking to Carlson. I knew they would try something; but this time Gerash was way too late. Besides, Kingsley refused. On Monday, I called Carlson's ward to find out what he did after he was dragged out. Carlson had left us dead but when he returned to the ward he made more telephone calls.


### Carlsonology

Orne flew back to Philadelphia. I spent the next weeks reviewing our tapes and writing up our findings. I was so preoccupied with the report and the expected defense counterattack, that my friends began to call me a "Carlsonologist"—it was a new specialty in Denver. In a way, they were right. This case consumed all who got involved. I do not remember how many drafts—all Federal Express—went back and forth between Denver and Philadelphia. I recall that Orne was definite about what he wanted in the report and early advised me to soften my initially outraged tone.

"Michael," he said, "you must give something to Kingsley which he can accept. It is a mistake to back him into a corner." I was still angry about Carlson's performance and the attitude of the defense but Orne's advice was good and I followed it.

I also reexamined page after page of the investigative records, the cold facts about Carlson and the murder which Chappell had so long hoped would sink Carlson and which had insulted Eddie Day. I included all the facts I could in my report—facts which had not yet been presented to Kingsley because of the detour into incompetence and MPD. I hoped Kingsley would read it.

### Carlson's Record

With Carlson, corroboration was the key. Without Bevis's investigative reports, and all the rest, I would have been blind and subject to the fallacy of lies. But with this information—this was more detective work than psychiatry—I could begin to paint a picture of Ross Carlson.

Before the crime, Carlson was a persuasive and skillful thespian. During high school, Carlson did well in speech and acting. Only an average student—he graduated 240 in a class of 544—during his senior year, 1981–82, Carlson received an *A* in Public Speaking and another *A* in Costume and Makeup. He also got top marks in Law and Personal Finance.

Carlson was also unbelievably sure of himself. "This guy is evil, pure and simple," was what Chappell told me when he handed me Carlson's Metropolitan State College transcript. I had to agree. Carlson had registered for a full course load for the 1983 fall semester, which was to begin twelve days after he killed his parents. No way did Carlson expect to go to jail.

The reason for Chappell's comment was the course, "Probate, Estates, Wills, Trusts," Carlson planned to take. He thought the money was in the bag. What confidence; Carlson wanted to learn how to make the best use of his inheritance while his parents still were alive.

## David Kachel

At college, Carlson continued his exceptional performance in speech and received the second highest grade in his class.

During the fall of 1982, after the dynamite episode, Carlson took a speech class at Metro. According to his teacher, Melody Hufman, Carlson was a "real worker, a real performer, a model student." Sometimes Hufman found Carlson a bit flirtatious and he was always, she told Bevis, "very warm." He was an excellent student; Hufman still used one of Carlson's speeches as an example of a speech well done.

Carlson faithfully attended class twice a week for sixteen weeks. Someone named David Kachel was in the same class. Chappell had asked Fairbairn about Kachel during the 1987 hearing. But Gerash had not shown the report to his witnesses. When I read the Kachel report, I could see why he wouldn't want to. Incredibly, Chappell almost did not hear about David Kachel himself because Kachel's story was lost for three years.

During the 1984 hearing David Kachel, like Randy Staton, read about the trial and saw clips of it on TV. Unlike Staton, who called Gerash, Kachel called the D.A.'s office five different times. But Kachel was placed on "hold" a few times and eventually hung up. Twice he left messages but received no answer. After Carlson was declared incompetent, Kachel stopped because—confusing incompetency with insanity—he thought Carlson could not be retried. Coincidentally, when Kachel happened to be reporting an unrelated theft to a deputy, he asked about Carlson and he was incorrectly told that Carlson could not be retried. Kachel called again when he learned that another hearing was scheduled for the fall of 1987.

This time, Bevis returned the call. What did Kachel have to say? That Carlson had talked about using the multiple personality defense as early as 1982.

## John Hinckley

Kachel and Carlson graduated from high school in 1982 and, in fact, had dated some of the same girls. Kachel remembered that Carlson described his parents as "strict and religious." Kachel also told Bevis that Ross was "spoiled rotten" and that he always seemed to be "the same guy, that there was no evidence for MPD." Both young men, after graduation, enrolled at Metro and soon found themselves in Hufman's class.

At that time, John Hinckley's trial—once again Hinckley impinged on Carlson—was a big topic among the students. One day while sitting on the grass at school, Kachel and Carlson joked about what Hinckley should have done "to get off." This was before Hinckley was, indeed, found insane. They talked about how they would "get off" if they were to kill the president and how to use the insanity defense.

It was simple. The killer should arrange to have friends know the killer as another "personality" such as an "altar boy" or a "motorcycle gang member" or a "violent type who beat up other people." Kachel recalled Carlson felt that someone who was going to kill should set up personalities in advance and that Hinckley was "stupid" not to have done so. Finally, Kachel told Bevis, Carlson planned to give a speech on the insanity defense but later decided that it would take too much work and gave a speech on karate instead. Of course, he got an *A*.

## MPD and Hypnosis

Although, when Carlson first revealed he was a multiple, his symptoms were rudimentary, I still wanted to find out how Carlson might have learned about MPD. After all, he was invited to join the national honor society for psychology and at Metro, he received a *B* in psychology. At the college bookstore I read through the text assigned for that course and I found a thorough section on multiple personality disorder and hypnosis. That section was assigned and, I assumed, read by Carlson. I knew that Carlson had not been naive about hypnosis before being hypnotized by Ralph Fisch. Carlson had mentioned Anton Mesmer, the father of hypnosis, and asked Fisch which induction technique he would use, "swinging ball? Spinning circles?"

Bevis checked the public and school libraries but our reading habits are protected by law; the libraries could not reveal which books Carlson had checked out. I knew, however, that Carlson received the 1976 edition of the World Book Encyclopedia from his parents and found that edition in the Denver Public Library. In it was a four page article about hypnosis, which contained the following: "Some persons are able to hypnotize themselves. Doctors call this ability autohypnosis. This is potentially dangerous, because it may be used at times without the person's conscious control." Many experts thought abuse of self-hypnosis was the central mechanism of MPD. I wanted Kingsley to understand that self-hypnosis could be under Carlson's control, so whether or not Carlson actually read this section of his encyclopedia, I put it in our report.

Carlson also brought one self-relaxation audiotape to our hospital at the time of his first admission. This was not proof that he faked or induced his trances but it certainly was suggestive. I told Kingsley about the tape too. But when I looked for other ways Carlson educated himself about MPD or hypnosis, I found nothing.

What confirmed Carlson's premeditation for me, however, was that Carlson tried to buy untraceable or "hot" pistols four different times from four different people during 1982 and 1983, and had gotten hold of the Rossi on his last try. Carlson's interest in "Saturday night specials" was clearly not due to his love of target practice. Hinckley, the gun, the alibi. Carlson had planned to kill his parents for a very long time.


## Why?

We also had to give Judge Kingsley a motive. I was certain that Carlson planned to kill his parents for at least a year. But, with all the planning and forethought, why had he done it? Two things were going on at the time of their death. His parents wanted him to go away to college, and just days before the murder Carlson's parents discovered that Ross had started his "escort service"; Carlson had already confessed to friends that he made his money "servicing" old ladies. His parents dragged Ross back to see Dr. Wilets. Rod accused his all-American boy of being a gigolo, just like the character played by Richard Gere; a few days later, Rod and Marilyn were dead.

Their lurid discovery might have been the proximate reason why Rod and Marilyn Carlson died. But their son's planning had gone on too long for the revelation that he was a whore to result in their death. There must have been, I thought, more. Bevis more than Chappell thought that money played a key role. Carlson had told friends he wanted to be a millionaire by the time he was twenty-one. We told Kingsley that he did it for the money. Money and greed are always possibilities but I did not know for sure.

## Prehomicidal Alters

Carlson's file was important for what I did not find as well. Orne encouraged me to make a big point about what he called "prehomicidal alters." If Carlson was a true multiple, he must have been one before August 17, 1983. MPD revealed during a criminal investigation was highly suspect for obvious reasons. But no unequivocal evidence existed that Ross Carlson had multiple personality disorder before he shot his parents.

Brian Bevis had interviewed schoolmates, relatives, friends, and pediatricians in Colorado and Minnesota. He had not found corroboration of the switches, periods of lost time, amnesias, and other things associated with MPD. Bevis also did not find the bruises, bumps, and contusions which would be evidence for the sadistic and persistent child abuse commonly found in the past histories of people with MPD. Carlson may have been abused but there was no evidence for it.

One grandfather had another explanation for Ross's behavior: Ross was, he said, "possessed by demons as stated in the Bible." Brian Bevis, perhaps, had uncovered the devil but he found nothing about multiples or abuse.


## Counterattack

Savitz and Gerash could not allow Orne and me to go unchallenged. Even before we went to Pueblo they filed a motion for a "status" review and asked Kingsley to order Haydee to fire me. Then they tried to interrupt our evaluation when they asked for the injunction. Those two attempts had already failed.

Now they precipitated a hearing in front of Kingsley with the intent of destroying our credibility, our findings, and our report. On April 19—just days after our stonewall interviews were completed— I was subpoenaed by David Savitz and told to bring all my "tapes, records, notes, telephone messages" about Carlson to court. To get a subpoena was not a pleasant thing. Once subpoenaed you must go when you are told.

The hearing was scheduled for April 25, which would have given me no time to prepare and would not have allowed Orne to return to Colorado. Chappell and Pat Robb went to Judge Kingsley and asked for a postponement so I could finish our report. I was grateful when Kingsley pushed the hearing back into May.

Savitz did not waste a moment. He told reporters that he had been "prepared to argue for dismissal . . . since the hospital has not followed the judge's orders of October 1987 in terms of working with us on a treatment plan for Ross . . ." He cut Orne down as only a "hired gun" brought in by the prosecution to debunk MPD. That afternoon, April 25, David Savitz called me for copies of our tapes. I told him to call Pat Robb; the tapes, I said, were made for the hospital and not for him.

The flavor of the antagonisms was well reported on April 26th, in *The Rocky Mountain News:*

CASTLE ROCK—Attorneys for Ross Carlson, angered by what they contend is mistreatment of his multiple personality disorder, said yesterday they will "vigorously pursue" dismissal of murder charges against him.

. . . Kingsley ordered the state to supply Carlson's lawyers with videotapes of a disputed examination . . .

[Carlson's] lawyers accused the Colorado State Hospital of ignoring Kingsley's order [and] said they will pursue dismissal of the charges because the state is allowing Carlson to "languish."

Pat Robb, attorney for the state hospital, and deputy district attorney Bob Chappell say the hospital is complying with the court order. But the hospital's recent attempt to fulfill Kingsley's order to consult outside expert advice on multiple personality disorder infuriated Carlson's attorneys.

They tried unsuccessfully to halt an examination a week ago by Dr. Martin Orne, a Philadelphia specialist who testified in the Hillside Strangler case . . . Savitz said Carlson called him April 16 and spoke "in an infantile, weeping, sobbing voice.

"He said there were cyborgs coming in with mallets to crush his brain and steal the secrets," Savitz said . . .

Court files show increasingly acrimonious correspondence by attorneys. In a March 17 letter to Robb, Savitz accused the hospital of stalling and said a hospital staff member told him there was no treatment plan for Carlson. "Stop dillydallying and let's get this young man treated," Savitz wrote.

In a reply April 1, Robb wrote, "Dillydallying had been defined as to waste time or to delay, which is exactly what Ross

Carlson has done since he was committed . . . presumably with your encouragement and approval."

Pat Robb might be a grandmotherly type, but she was a tough grandmother. Of course Carlson worried that we wanted to "steal" his "secrets." I wanted to know how far back he had planned the whole thing.

## May 3: Spitz and Freud

I had one more thing to do before finishing but had put it off because I thought it would be a waste of time. Kingsley ordered the state "to cooperate" with the defense. We had called Newton. Now I called Fisch, Fairbairn, and Richard Rewey, another defense psychiatrist, and invited them to meet with me to talk about Carlson. This was necessary in light of Kingsley's order and, I thought, I would ask about any new evidence for abuse.

The day before the meeting, I learned of another Carlson tidbit: eleven days before he killed his parents, Carlson had also gone to Radio Shack and bought crystals which, when put into his police scanner, would have allowed him to listen in on his local police. Did he, I wondered, plan to listen for the discovery of his parents' bodies?

I had this in mind when we met on May 3 in our departmental library under, appropriately, the bust of René Spitz and the gaze of Sigmund Freud. Spitz was one of the first to point out that parental neglect could kill children. Of course, one of Freud's great contributions was that past experience had everything to do with present behavior. It was reasonable that we talked about the question of abuse in Carlson's childhood with these two great men looking down on the proceedings.

When Bob Fairbairn walked in, he looked ill. His silvery good looks, like Carlson's, had also decayed. His eyes were streaked with red. Ralph Fisch was unable to come and Richard Rewey, well tanned, did not say much the whole time he was there.

Fairbairn said he had spent a total of three hundred to four hundred and fifty hours with Carlson. A lot of time for MPD training, I thought, and a lot of money. Carlson's "noncooperation," he said, "stemmed from Carlson's distrust of the system" that had "so badly mistreated him." Fairbairn repeated that the state was "incapable" of treating Carlson; the same story that Savitz told the press when Carlson was first sent to Pueblo by Eddie Day in 1984. Rewey sat back and agreed.

What about abuse, I asked? Was there any new evidence? No. "Everything is explained by Ross Carlson's amnesia," Fairbairn said. He is "amnestic" for his "abuse." Fairbairn was certain that he was abused because he was a multiple. Rewey agreed. I did not point out their circular reasoning.

And, I asked, who killed his parents? His "satanic" personality, was the solemn reply. Antichrist. It was not Ross Carlson at all—it was the devil. Was it the devil, I thought, who spoke with Kachel, who bought the gun, who planned to monitor the police, who signed up for a class on wills and trusts? I did not ask about satanic ritual abuse.

My two colleagues sidestepped the question of Theon Jackson and permanent incompetency; they knew that this was an issue before the court. They were surprised that I wondered if Carlson's noncooperation might be a legal tactic to set him free. In short, nothing changed despite the presence of Spitz and Freud. I stopped our meeting after about one hour.


**Audience**
So this was Ross Carlson's audience. Ross Carlson—and his MPD—could not exist without them: Newton, Fairbairn, Fisch, Rewey, Savitz, Gerash, and of course, Eddie Day. Multiples always had an audience, and I was surprised at how willingly Carlson's audience accepted self-serving behavior as truth. In our culture, slick hype is valued. Anyone who grabs attention, no matter how, is held in high esteem. And the more outrageous the better. Look at Madonna. Was the ready acceptance of MPD a symptom of our society in decay; had MPD become the MTV of psychiatry and Ross Carlson the Madonna of Pueblo?

A few days later I got a bill from Bob Fairbairn for two hundred dollars, his fee for the "consultation with Michael Weissberg." "Dear Mike," he wrote, "would you be good enough to acknowledge this consultation and forward my bill to Pueblo for payment. Thank you. Bob." I sent it to Haydee. "Dear Haydee," I wrote, "I met with Fairbairn and Rewey last Tuesday as per the judge's ruling. Fairbairn sent this bill which seems high for a one hour meeting. Do what you will." I do not know if she paid it. But at two hundred dollars per hour, if Carlson were paying, Fairbairn's four hundred and fifty hours might have cost Carlson's trust up to ninety thousand dollars. Adoring or not, Carlson's audience was handsomely paid.

### Diagnosis

I put as many of the facts of Carlson's case into my thirty-one page report to Dr. Kort as I could pack in, including a reference to the Fisch interview. Fisch was, I said, the first to suggest unwittingly to Carlson that he had a "double," in December 1983. We also pointed out the obvious. Carlson was not a normal "patient" who came for symptom relief; he was accused of murder. Everything he said had to be taken in that light.

As to diagnosis, Orne told me to give Kingsley a choice. "Give him," Orne said, "something he can buy. Don't force him to have to pick one side or the other." I outlined the possibilities. Clearly, Carlson was not normal. Matricide and patricide have been heinous crimes since time immemorial. It was our impression Carlson suffered from either a personality disorder with antisocial features or MPD. That was Kingsley's choice. The defense tapes demonstrated MPD: divergent personalities, lost time, the eye roll, switching. Or, Carlson could be a psychopath. Virtually all the data about this case, I wrote, could be explained by either diagnosis.

Since, however, compelling evidence for preexisting alter personalities was absent, the diagnosis of MPD was suspect. MPD might have been present for years and only recently uncovered, but this was unlikely. In any case, the key, I wrote, was Carlson's purposeful noncooperation, no matter what his diagnosis. Ross Carlson stood the most to gain by remaining incompetent, and the most to lose if he got well.

When we made our treatment recommendations, we could not resist tweaking the defense. I asked the state to bill the Carlson trust for the costs of his hospitalization. This had already been tried and we thought it ought to be tried again. Carlson's hospital bill was now close to three hundred thousand dollars. Whatever money went to the hospital would be that much less for Savitz and Gerash.

I also wanted Carlson's relationship with Bob Fairbairn "clarified" since I suspected that Fairbairn's admiration for Carlson and his disdain for the state hospital contributed to Carlson's noncooperation. I hoped Kingsley would read it. I mailed the report on May 20 and waited for the other shoe to drop.

A few days later, I returned from work and Susan told me that Pat Robb had called. Pat told Susan that our report was "the best and most complete" she had ever seen. I was gratified. But it had taken so much energy that I could not understand how people did this for a living. But I had changed. What started as a reluctant "yes" to my chairman to coordinate the panel had become something akin to enthusiasm.


### Gestapo

Savitz and Gerash had their experts review our tapes. Fairbairn was particularly "enraged" that we used one of his tapes "on Ross." Orne was "brutal," he said, and dismissed our interviews as "sadistic and Gestapo-like." Was this a threat that he would file another ethics complaint? Finally, Fairbairn said that Orne had missed "subtle changes" in Carlson and was "unable to make the diagnosis of multiple personality disorder." In his opinion, Orne had overlooked a "Spiegel eye roll." Just like Alan Fine.

I found the shadow of Theon Jackson in Fairbairn's ridicule. Savitz and Gerash still pushed for the Jackson defense and now their experts solidly lined up in support. Fairbairn said Carlson would never get better. Ditto for Rewey who called our interviews "needlessly traumatic." He said there was no "reasonable likelihood" that Carlson would be restored to competency. Ditto for Quinn and Fisch. A few days later, I heard that Newton decided not to meet with us after all.

# REVERSAL OF FORTUNE

The defense subpoenaed almost everyone connected with Carlson into Kingsley's court for the May status hearing. Because of their shotgun approach, the state hospital came to a screeching halt. Six month judicial reviews were routine in most cases but not with Carlson.

This was the first time I would be in court on Carlson and only the second or third time in my entire, by then, sixteen year psychiatric career. I had done other legal evaluations but they had mostly settled before trial. I had only once or twice been in the witness box, in front of a judge, and examined by unfriendly lawyers.

### "Bang! Bang!"

Chappell also worried, especially about his relationship with Kingsley. He thought he had put on a good case in 1987 but was knocked silly and was worried he would be knocked silly now. Chappell started to repeat, at odd moments, what Carlson told Alan Fine four years before. "It was like this, Bang! Bang!" Chappell said, imitating Carlson shooting his parents. "Bang! Bang!" It was "Bang! Bang!" when we talked on the phone, and it was "Bang! Bang!" when we met. Carlson's confession; those six words covered Carlson with guilt and it was his guilt, Chappell prayed, that would carry the day. "Bang! Bang!"

I was more optimistic than Chappell about the eventual outcome, but then again I was new to the case. Carlson planned the murders, carried them out, acted crazy, and refused to cooperate. Judge Kingsley would have to see through this. In 1987, Kingsley was new. Both he and Day were retired judges of the same generation, and he could not reverse his colleague and turn one hundred eighty degrees just like that. I guessed he had to ease into it; now, seven months later, he could take the next step. And I had in living, videotaped color, seven and one half hours of Carlson's stonewalled noncooperation to show him. But when I tried to reassure Bob, he would give a little smile. I think he thought I was naive.

### Run-up

On Wednesday, May 25, Martin Orne returned to Denver. By now I had bought a bigger car, but Brian Bevis had the duty to chauffeur Orne around the city. That evening all of us, Chappell, Bevis, Pat Robb, and I met with Orne. He emphasized his views on MPD. We all dissociate to some degree, he said; we all forget. But some people do this to its extreme.

Do not forget, he said, that MPD starts as a disorder of memory in highly hypnotizable people. I laughed at his unintentional joke. There were three factors in the formation of a multiple, Orne said. A person must have the capacity to forget, a reason to forget, and then this amnesia reinforced by unwitting therapists. I thought of Carlson's audience; if Carlson were a multiple now, I thought, this sequence would fit him like a glove.

### Schoolboy

The next morning, Chappell set up a makeshift command post in the Douglas County D.A.'s second floor office, across the dusty parking lot and road from the county court house and jail. He had been here many times before. This was my first time. The room was small, paneled with cheap imitation walnut. The table left space for little else and was already strewn with notebooks, yellow pads, and coffee cups. If the case continued much longer there would be no room for us to sit. We would be squeezed out by the boxes of evidence and transcripts that now lined the walls; the ever growing history of Ross Carlson since 1983.

The night before, I had been so excited that I had difficulty sleeping. So it was a letdown when the first thing that happened when I got to court was that Walter Gerash objected to my presence. He did not want me to hear Orne's testimony and hear how Orne handled their interrogation. I had to wait on the hard wooden bench outside.

Gerash had subpoenaed me for the morning and now I had to wait. Did he want me to feel like a little schoolboy?

As I sat in the hall, I watched grim-faced juveniles troop in and out of the courtroom next to Kingsley's with grimmer parents, along with attorneys, police, witnesses, and D.A.s. I wondered if any of them ever tried to buy dynamite? At the end of four hours of cooling my heels, Gerash told me to come back the next day at noon.

## Ex Parte Pizza

I arrived a little after eleven. I had hoped to hear how things had gone with Orne, but at the noon recess Chappell wanted to talk to Orne about his testimony so I continued the second day of my debut in solitude. I exited the one story courthouse, turned left across the dirt parking lot, and crossed the street to a small shopping mall. Once there, I had a typical Colorado choice. Pizza Hut, Pizza Parlor, or 7-Eleven. I picked the parlor.

As I entered the dimly lit room and smelled the pizza, I recalled that pizza was Carlson's favorite food; he was eating it for breakfast when the deputies arrived to tell him that his parents were dead. I then remembered that tomorrow was Carlson's twenty-fourth birthday. He killed his parents when he was nineteen, almost five years ago.

My eyes, pinpoints from the bright Colorado sun, had not yet accommodated to the dim light. I sat down at the nearest red-checkered table, one of five or six set up along the right-hand wall. My heart leaped when I glanced at the table to my left. It was Kingsley.

I nodded and he acknowledged my greeting but I did not know if he recognized me as the witness who he told to wait outside. I sat there for a moment. Should I leave? Should I ignore him? Should I talk to him? I couldn't resist the opportunity and introduced myself. I could see why Chappell liked Kingsley; I instinctively liked him too. He had pleasant but sharp features and intelligent eyes. I then decided to talk. I was surprised how fast the words came out of my mouth. I did not know how much of my report Judge Kingsley had read and I could not be sure he knew anything of the police investigation, the facts of the crime. So I started to give him a summary of my findings.

Ross Carlson, I said, might be sick—he must be crazy to have killed his parents—but he was crazy like a fox. He had, I told Kingsley, planned the murder in exquisite detail as I outlined in my report. In my opinion, he was legally sane at the time of the murder and knew what he was doing now. Carlson was not incompetent, I told Kingsley, he was stonewalling us. It was in his best interests to stonewall because that way he would avoid jail, keep his money, and possibly go free.

I spoke only one minute at the most. Kingsley did not say anything one way or the other. When I finished, he then returned to his plate. We ate the rest of our lunch without as much as exchanging a glance and Kingsley left before I was finished.

Seeing Kingsley at lunch was an accident. But from then on, I felt I had a special relationship with Kingsley. I don't know if this was really true but this thought gave me a boost and more confidence in court. I did not tell anyone, including Chappell, about lunch and what just had happened.

At two Gerash told me he would "try to get to" me today. I cooled my heels some more that afternoon on the hard bench outside the courtroom doors and began to notice, through the glass, what went on inside. As they argued whether I could sit in court or not, I thought I heard Gerash call me an "apple polisher," whatever that meant.

By four o'clock, it was clear that I would have to wait until the next week. I had spent the better part of two days and still had not testified. But I felt a new optimism. Kingsley seemed to be a regular guy. I did not think he would tolerate this BS for much longer.


### Destroy Orne

Chappell later told me that on Thursday and Friday the defense's tactic had stayed the same: they wanted to emasculate Orne—and later me—the same way they did Fine and Reichlin. They tried to nail Orne every way they could: on money, experience, and bias. Through the glass courtroom doors, I saw Orne was an imposing figure—all two hundred and sixty pounds of him—an old courtroom hand. Despite the defense's intent, Chappell said he made an excellent witness and acquitted himself well.

I watched as David Savitz examined Orne. Savitz was a sharper dresser than Gerash's more casual theater and Chappell's slacks and blazers. Savitz showed two inches of cuff; monogrammed with three initials. His gold cuff links went with his rings. Eyebrows perpetually arched, I soon learned that Savitz worked with a knifelike intensity. Chappell told me that he was always prepared. When I met him during a recess he seemed to have, like his clothes, an edge.

Savitz, I later learned, accused Orne of not being "independent"; he pointed out that Orne had half a dozen calls with Chappell in 1984 and had "secretly" advised Kathy Morall before the October 1987 hearing. He had earned eight thousand five hundred dollars just for that work and, Savitz said, Orne returned to Colorado for the money. Orne admitted that his trips to Colorado cost in the neighborhood of sixteen thousand dollars. Why, asked Savitz, was the state willing to pay that bill and not pay Barry Quinn to treat Carlson's MPD?

By now, Newton had given information to his "friend" David with which to nail his "friend" Martin. Newton told Savitz that he had known Orne for twenty-five years and that Orne did not have much experience with MPD. Orne admitted that he had not treated a case of MPD from start to finish since he left Boston twenty years ago and that the last time he made the diagnosis was in 1961. But he said that was because spontaneous MPD was rare—of course he had not seen as many cases as, for example, Fisch who diagnosed MPD much more frequently. MPD, Orne said, was often encouraged by the very doctors who then set out to treat it.

Furthermore, Carlson should not be treated as a special case. "I would not want to take his computer away from him. But I would make [his use of it] contingent upon cooperating with the staff." Of course Carlson would not cooperate, said Orne; that would mean he would have to stand trial. Orne was clear: quit pampering Carlson and recognize, a multiple or not, Carlson did not cooperate because it was in his best interests not to cooperate. Carlson wanted to keep his money and he did not want to go to jail.

When Orne finished, he flew back to Philadelphia. After Mark Pecevich testified I would be on next, and despite my newfound courage I, again, could hardly sleep the night before.

### "Jesus, Walter"

Court was closed on Monday. On Tuesday, Ross Carlson shuffled into court, bearded with his black glasses on, and sat at the defense table with Savitz at his side. He seemed asleep or "comatose" according to some witnesses. To me, he looked like the thug I had seen in April.

I nodded to Kingsley as I walked to the stand and I thought he gave me a small smile of recognition in return. After I was sworn in, Walter Gerash took me. Unlike Chappell, who seemed tethered to the lectern by a one-foot rope, Gerash strode all over the courtroom, often glancing at the audience as he spoke.

Repeating what he had done with Reichlin and Fine, he tried to rattle me. You have no experience with MPD, do you? You have never seen a case of MPD, have you? You really are not an independent panel, are you? This was a setup to get Orne, isn't it? I said that I had treated many patients who could have been induced to act the MPD role if I had hypnotized them and then talked to them in the language of MPD. I could have asked: "Can I talk to whoever is inside?" or "is anyone inside listening?" Then I told Gerash about all the calls I made before I decided to hire Orne.

I sat drinking from a paper cup, my mouth dry. I watched BJ Moody, the court reporter, trying to keep up and follow my rapid speech. Once I was told to stop nodding my head and to clearly state yes or no. Soon I felt demeaned. I took Gerash's attacks personally and had forgotten that while the stakes were high, this was a game. Then I argued. Of course, that was exactly what Gerash wanted.

### Relax

After I was done for the day, Chappell pulled me aside. Gerash, he told me, would get disorganized if I did not argue. He was too used to arguing but was at a loss if the witness did not respond in kind. Relax, sit back, Chappell said. Let Gerash hang himself.

Chappell was right. The next morning was different. Gerash got tangled and repetitious. I could see he was not really questioning me; instead he wanted to make his own points. I picked my spots and found I could say pretty much what I wanted. I explained why I thought Carlson manipulated the system. I also said that forgetfulness should not be equated with MPD. Most murderers report some degree of forgetfulness; amnesia can occur in psychopaths too.

Also, it was hard to prove—or disprove—whether someone was a true multiple. There were no blood tests, X rays, or any tests at all specific for multiple personality disorder. You had to take it all on faith—in this case, on faith from a murderer. There was, I told Kingsley, little evidence in Carlson's story for prehomicidal alters. And contrary to some opinions, mental illness was easy to fake. When Kingsley was not looking, Gerash seemed to be making faces at me. I must be scoring some points, I thought. Soon Kingsley tired of Gerash. I could hear Kingsley muttering "Jesus, Walter" but Gerash could not.

I then began reading parts of Fisch's interview into the record so Kingsley could hear how bizarre it was; Carlson touching his parents' brains, guts, genitals; how Fisch had unknowingly taught Carlson to act. I interspersed this with "of course Dr. Fisch did not mean to coach Carlson" or "of course these were unwitting cues." Gerash tried to get me to stop. At one point he, as I recall, told me to shut up. But Kingsley let me do it; as I read, people came into the courtroom to listen.


**Shut Down Gerash**
On Tuesday, Carlson had been at the table with his usual black-sunglassed-look, asleep or in a trance. When I began on Wednesday, Carlson seemed more alert and sat with his fingertips pressed to his forehead as if in pain. At times he leaned over and whispered to Savitz. He spent the morning that way as I wended through my time on the stand. But after the noon recess, Carlson was gone. All I knew was that Carlson had pulled, in Chappell's words, some kind of "stunt."

That afternoon, Gerash hammered at me but seemed distracted and I sensed his heart was not in it and I slipped in a few more things. Once I asked Gerash whether he or Savitz had instructed Carlson not to talk to us. Was it his idea to undercut Carlson's treatment for the past four years? Gerash fumbled; for once he was speechless. Then he told me to stop asking questions. I looked over at Kingsley and hoped that I had made my point.

Gerash countered with the Staton lawn-cutting episode. "Clearly MPD," said Gerash. I said other explanations were possible such as robbery. Mainly Gerash argued that MPD was a disease of secrecy; multiples did not go around telling everyone that they had it. In fact, the lack of evidence for prehomicidal alters was a characteristic of true MPD. Convenient. After the mid-afternoon recess, it was Chappell's turn.

### Treating a Stonewall

Chappell was a workmanlike courtroom operator. When he began a sentence, he sometimes looked as if he would not get his words out. For a split second he appeared tongue-tied. But it did not last; he just didn't use a lot of words. After reading thousands of pages of testimony and now in court, I saw Chappell used many fewer words than the defense.

Earlier that day while at lunch, I had a moment of panic when Chappell told me he would ask me about treatment. I had not given treatment much thought since Carlson would not talk, so I hurriedly scribbled an outline of a behavior modification program on an envelope, a program to get Carlson to talk.

When Chappell asked, I said that all treatment would fail if Carlson would not talk. "The court," I said looking at Kingsley, "should tell Ross that he must talk to the people who have been trying for years to take care of him. Every effort should be made to get him to speak before the issue of therapy can be addressed." No talk, no therapy.

I told Kingsley hypnosis would only confuse matters more; that memories retrieved with hypnosis were more vulnerable to distortion and confabulation than memories retrieved by normal conversation. Hypnosis, contrary to popular belief, distorted true memories and could create false ones. In fact, descriptions of crimes recovered via hypnosis were highly suspect and not accepted by many courts of law. Hypnosis, I said, was out.

By late afternoon, it was clear that my testimony would drag on into yet another day. It was now one week after I had been told to appear. I had to go home and once again rearrange my patients. No wonder doctors hated court. That night, after calling my patients, I read up on behavior modification.

In the morning, I learned what happened during lunch the day before. The defense had spent a bizarre lunch recess downstairs. I read the *News* report:

In a series of questions, Gerash asked Weissberg if he knew Carlson was born out of wedlock or that he suffered from learning disabilities at age five. Gerash also asked Weissberg about "alleged acts of child abuse," Savitz said. As Gerash spoke, Carlson . . . began muttering to Savitz.

The discussion continued in a jail cell during a noon recess, where Carlson removed his sport coat, shirt, and tie and faced his attorneys wearing a tank top. Repeatedly shaking his fist in Savitz's face, Carlson repeated his demand to "shut down" Gerash . . . When Gerash left the room, Carlson sat and sobbed while calling psychiatrist Robert Fairbairn and Dr. Martin Orne . . . "machines." Later he refused to be examined by Fairbairn . . . and called him a "cyborg." . . . Savitz said he was worried that one of Carlson's personalities capable of murder could put them in danger . . .

Savitz did not miss a trick. He blamed Carlson's outburst on MPD and on Carlson's child abuse, both of which had yet to be proved. But MPD and abuse were the spins the defense put on everything. They never considered Carlson's baser motives. For example, Carlson could have been angry at how his defense was going. It was three and a half years since Carlson had replaced Craig Truman with Gerash. Gerash would be his savior, Gerash would get him out. Now Carlson faced new experts, more experienced than the earlier state witnesses. I knew we were doing well; Carlson probably thought we were doing well too. No wonder Gerash seemed distracted. As I drove toward Castle Rock I did not know what to expect. I was surprised to see Carlson sitting in court as if nothing were wrong.

On the stand, I fleshed out my plan. The aim of treatment was to get Carlson to talk; speech was the goal, mutism the symptom. Carlson had to learn there were consequences to his behavior. So far, there had been none. So far, he could do whatever he wanted, when he wanted. As I spoke, I looked over at Carlson who whispered occasionally to Savitz. Then I was done.

As I walked toward my seat, I knew things had gone well. I was, however, uncomfortable as I passed within six feet of Carlson who did not look up. I had gotten through the last three days by reminding myself that this was a game. But it really wasn't. Ross Carlson was a murderer and I just strongly suggested he was a fraud.

**"You Were Wonderful, Sweetheart."**
That night we all met for drinks at the Hyatt Regency not too far from Cottonwood Road. We were exhausted from the pressure of being "on" for so long. Brian Bevis sat with his suit jacket off, his service revolver in sight. Pat Robb was upbeat. "You were wonderful, sweetheart," she said and gave me a big kiss as I walked in. "That guy," she said, "has tied up our hospital for five years. Now I think it is about to change."

Our optimism was tempered by Chappell. He had, after all, been through this before. "It has been a long haul," Chappell said, "but it is far from over. I don't even want to think about what is down the road." At that, it sunk in that even if Kingsley accepted our arguments and did not dismiss the charges, we still faced a competency hearing and, hopefully, a sanity trial and a murder trial after that. A lot could happen. All through the evening I wanted to blurt out about my one-minute encounter with Kingsley, but I did not.

The next morning, just as I now did every day, I bought a copy of Denver's two newspapers. Chappell told me to read the papers to gauge the effectiveness of our testimony and to get a sense of how the trial was going. Like Judge Kingsley, court reporters had seen a lot of trials, experts, and defendants too. The *Post* described my last day on the stand this way:

CASTLE ROCK—Accused murderer, Ross Carlson, should be ordered by the court to at least talk to state hospital staffers . . . "The court should tell Ross that he needs to talk to the people who are taking care of him," said Dr. Michael Weissberg of the University of Colorado . . . Weissberg suggested Thursday that in addition to ordering Carlson to speak, he should be forced to learn that his behavior has consequences. "Perhaps a behavioral program can be set up using his computer or stereo system," he said. "He speaks to his therapist or he does not get to use his computer or sound system."

Dr. Ralph Fisch, a psychiatrist [*sic*] hired by the defense, testified that Weissberg and Orne are "neophytes" when it comes to multiple personality disorder and their interviewing techniques along with their treatment recommendations are all wrong . . .

**Alice in Wonderland**
The defense then put on their men. Ralph Fisch's testimony, which followed mine, did not surprise me, but Bernauer Newton's did. What I heard disturbed me.

During his conversation with Orne, Newton said he did not know of Theon Jackson and the tactic of permanent incompetency. But after Newton flew in from L.A. he testified that the only way Carlson would be "cured" of his MPD was to have the charges dropped. He thus became the fifth and last defense expert to endorse the Jackson plan. His reasoning was tortuous. "As I understand it," Newton said, "as long as the criminal charges are in effect he must remain at the state hospital. I believe that the only way treatment can be carried out is to get him out of the state hospital, which means dropping the charges."

"Trust" and "confidence" in one's therapist was the key for treating MPD and Carlson did not trust anyone in Pueblo. The therapists at Pueblo would always fail, said Newton, since they are serving "two masters. One is the hospital the other is Ross Carlson."

But Carlson spoke to no one. Following Newton's reasoning, all patients in forensic settings should be set free since none of them would "trust" doctors who worked for the state. This was the naive, Alice in Wonderland thinking which infected this case. Carlson was special, MPD was special: Carlson was victimized by the system and had to run the show if he was to get better.

"He has to feel confidence," Newton continued, "that what he says will not be revealed elsewhere . . . That is what we do in our office with our private patients." This really got Kingsley's attention who suddenly interjected, "Yes, Doctor Newton, but your clients are not charged with murder, are they?"

In closing, Savitz took a unique tack and said Carlson had not stonewalled at all. Carlson was not uncooperative because "there cannot be a refusal of treatment if no treatment has been offered." Again, reality was on its head. Carlson had served "the approximate equivalent of a ten year sentence"; the state hospital had waged "a campaign to wear down" Carlson. Savitz urged Kingsley to drop the murder charges and commit Carlson to a civil hospital like a non-criminal patient. This was the old plan; get Carlson Jacksoned and then get him out.

In response, Chappell took my hastily drawn up treatment plan and presented it to Kingsley. Carlson must learn to cooperate, he said. He must understand actions have consequences. On June 6, Kingsley had both sides draw up orders. He would let us know in two weeks which he had chosen.

### Reversal of Fortune

At the end of June, Kingsley finally made up his mind. Chappell called me at home with the news. In his laconic way he said, "We have finally gotten to first base, Mike." He told me that Kingsley put Carlson's treatment where "it should have been all along": back in the hospital, not in the court. Four years after Eddie Day, Kingsley removed the court from the diagnostic quagmire. Carlson may have MPD or, then again, he may not, wrote Kingsley. Orne had been right. By not forcing Kingsley to choose, Kingsley began to give up on MPD.

Kingsley bought our contention that our consultation had been stymied by "the defendant's willful refusal to cooperate." Carlson's silence looked planned and intentional. He ordered Carlson to cooperate. I had hoped that Carlson's decision not to talk to us would turn out to be one of his biggest mistakes.

Kingsley then rejected the motion to dismiss the two counts of murder. Theon Jackson was about to go out the window. But that was not all. In a shocker, he ordered me to oversee Carlson's treatment. "The Colorado State Hospital," Chappell read, "shall request the consulting panel chaired by Michael Weissberg, M.D., to review the defendant's treatment and progress, and to report the panel's findings to the Court anytime prior to the next review."

I had mixed feelings. My new pipeline to Kingsley would be, I saw, a great advantage. I could use it anytime I chose. Kingsley trusted me. Nevertheless, Kingsley had thrust me deeper into the fray. For years, I wanted nothing to do with Carlson. Then I agreed to head the panel but planned to keep my job organizational, peripheral to the legal battle. Orne, I hoped, would carry the burden. Now Orne was back in Philadelphia and here I was, in the middle. Whether I liked it or not it was done, and for the first time the defense had a significant problem. Bob and I congratulated each other and then we hung up.

# THE FOOT OF THE COLOSSUS

Kingsley was on the fence. He had backed out of MPD but would he also reverse Eddie Day on competency? Within a year, Bob and I decided, we would have the third, and I hoped last, competency hearing. Since I had never thought he was incompetent, not much would change with Carlson, but we had to wait a decent interval before going back to court.

## Sham

From the moment of Kingsley's ruling, I felt responsible for Carlson's treatment though, in fact, I was not. First, I sent a packet of articles about MPD to Mark Pecevich to distribute to his staff. I thought they should become more sophisticated about MPD because they would be questioned about it in court. I also had many conversations with Mark about Carlson's new and, I thought, sham treatment plan, the one designed to get him to talk. It was a sham because Carlson would talk when ready.

In general, I stayed out of the hospital's way. They had, I reminded myself, treated many patients who were incompetent. But Carlson was not a normal patient. In retrospect, I should not have taken such a hands-off approach. At the end of July, I approved a plan which was finally outlined to Carlson on August 11. But by then, as I knew he could, Carlson had already talked. Soon after Kingsley released his order—while we worked on the plan—Carlson began to speak. Until now, Carlson had communicated with the staff only by gestures. But on July 7, 1988, Ross Carlson broke six months of almost total silence. Incredibly, the first thing he did was to demand treatment. Referring to his notebook, Carlson said he was frustrated with how things had been going. He wanted progress. "Am I going to be treated here?" Carlson asked. Within days, Carlson completely reversed his pattern of uncooperative behavior. He spoke in a normal voice. He went to ward meetings. He went to the competency training program. He also met with his therapist. And he did it all before his plan was in place.

### Opening the Pipeline
I had decided to write to Kingsley whenever the opportunity presented itself. I wrote my first letter on October 11: "Something not unexpected happened following your June 22 orders. Mr. Carlson stopped acting in a disturbed, 'psychoticlike' fashion . . . [and] now walks and talks 'normally.' I can reach only one conclusion about Mr. Carlson's sudden and dramatic improvement: Mr. Carlson's behavior is under his conscious control. Mr. Carlson's past episodes of 'psychotic thinking, general noncooperation, and mutism' which alternated with his ability to speak with his attorneys was *volitional*, that is to say, staged and thought out . . ."

### Alibis
One October afternoon Brian Bevis called me, clearly excited and suppressing his mirth. Did I know that Carlson tried to construct an alibi for his alibi? First there was Kachel with his Hinckley story and now David Bassler. Bassler, who had known Carlson since junior high school, just emerged from five years of silence.

Bassler rode the same bus with Ross for three years to Heritage High, most consistently during their senior year. At that time, Ross was a typical eighteen-year-old, according to Bassler, who acted as if "he had the world by the ass." Carlson bragged about his own landscaping business and about making "good" money.

After he read about the murders, Bassler wanted to talk to the law, but he said he was discouraged from getting involved by his parents. Nevertheless, since 1983, what he had to say continued to eat at him. He was older now and moved out of his parents' home, and five years after it happened Bassler finally decided to speak. Bassler told Bevis that Carlson planned a violent "psychology experiment" for the night of August 17, 1983.

Carlson approached Bassler with the "experiment" during a call in the summer of 1983. Carlson told Bassler he was interested in how far the average person could be "corrupted." The plan was for Carlson and Bassler to fake a drug-for-money exchange and to use two black bags doing it. Bassler was to double-cross Carlson and run off with both bags, the drugs, and the money. Carlson had planned it in perfect detail.

The point of the double-cross, Carlson said, was to see if a third student—one who did not know this was a setup—could be talked into shooting Bassler as he ran. Carlson told Bassler that the third student had already been convinced to cheat on a test and to shoplift. Carlson reassured Bassler that the gun would be loaded with blanks. Carlson would pay Bassler fifty dollars for his trouble. The site of the experiment was a remote, dead-end street close to Cottonwood Road.

Carlson, Bevis theorized, planned a second alibi for his movie alibi, a cover for his cover. Carlson's experiment, I realized, was the drug rip-off he told Kenny Cortez about; this would be where Carlson would go when he left the theater. The site of the experiment put Carlson close to the spot where he would murder his parents. He would only have a short distance to go to the scene of the crime.

But at 4:00 P.M., the day of the shootings, Carlson telephoned Bassler and hurriedly called "the experiment" off. Bevis did not know why he finally ditched the idea, but to me Carlson's plan did not come from the mind of a dissociated, innocent son. This was cold cunning at work. Ross Carlson was his own psychology experiment; Carlson had personal experience in how far he could be "corrupted."

Bevis, who by now thoroughly loathed Carlson—he had been tracking him from the beginning—was delighted with his new piece of news. More facts to hang Carlson with if we ever got to the sanity trial. I wondered what else we would learn as we waited for the next hearing.

**December 8: Stop That Car**
By law, every six months the state hospital had to file a progress report with Judge Kingsley. Review and report; as the new year approached, I knew that I would have to interview Carlson again.

The drive was two hours each way so each trip to Pueblo took me a minimum of six hours and usually seven, essentially a whole day. I kept on putting it off, not only because of the time. This would be the first time I would see Carlson since his defeat. I finally arranged my schedule to do it on December 8, 1988. I left Denver at 10:30 and arrived in Pueblo two hours later. Ten minutes after I left, another act of the circus opened behind me.

At 10:40 Walter Gerash called. He wanted, he told my secretary Imogene Tursick, to "save" me a trip and to tell me that Carlson "would not talk today." Tell Dr. Weissberg, he said, not to make the four hour round-trip to the hospital. "There is no need," he told Mrs. Tursick, "for Doctor Weissberg to go to Pueblo."

He then persuaded Mrs. Tursick, who is extremely gracious and always eager to please, to "call the Colorado State Patrol and have his car intercepted." He told her that my day should not be "wasted" and that the skies threatened snow. She complied. I am sure I was low priority; luckily, the patrol did not find me.

As soon as I arrived at the hospital I stopped in to see Pat Robb, who I was becoming very fond of, to chat and to empty her licorice jar. After a short talk—I recall that she was in an optimistic mood and told me that she had planned to retire from the hospital after "that creep" was in jail—I walked over to Carlson's ward to meet with Carlson's treatment team to talk about his progress.

**Uneasy**
This was the first time I would meet anyone who had treated Carlson since I met Greg Trautt exactly four years before. Since Carlson had been transferred to another ward, Trautt was no longer involved. The psych tech, Bob Gonzales, was there, as well as the new psychologist who had done the majority of the work on the behavioral program we had designed.

They told me that Carlson, as he always did, had a good grasp of his legal situation and seemed eager to be found competent. He attended competency training groups and his therapy sessions with

Bob Gonzales but really talked little about anything of a personal nature. He only spoke, as he did with Newton, about "flowers."

In short, though the staff thought Carlson was competent, his lawyers maintained that he was not; they were unsure how to proceed and waited for me to provide guidance. Since he was talking but not saying much, I suggested that they raise their expectations for Carlson's participation in his individual sessions and competency training activities. I told them to discuss the details of the murders with Ross to the extent he could tolerate it.

Begin with Carlson's memories and feelings and his resistances to discussing them. When Carlson blew someone off, ask him why he felt he had to do that and what he thought he had just avoided. Pay attention to how he processed, experienced, understood, and expressed emotion. It was, I told them, routine psychotherapy. Normal treatment practices were required. I also gave them more articles on MPD.

I then walked over to another building to interview Carlson. As I did, I felt uneasy; something bothered me about what just happened. On the surface, the meeting went well. But the staff seemed passive. My advice was nothing fancy; why had they waited for me to say the obvious? And, I wondered, why was Bob Gonzales, who I personally liked but was the least trained in the bunch, assigned to Carlson? Were they still so shell-shocked from the last four years that now, when the chains had been lifted, they did not know what to do?

## Thirteen Minute Tape

Carlson hobbled into the room wearing leg manacles and accompanied by two burly attendants. As he seated himself at the head of the table, he demanded that his leg shackles be removed. One of the attendants complied.

For all the show, this was not a game at all. I was three feet away from someone who killed his parents, and killed them with a calculation I could not imagine. And he knew that I thought he was a psychopath, a fraud. I then faced a disturbing idea. Sometime, somewhere, Carlson might be let go. How would I feel if Carlson got out? I already knew. I then did what I always did and pushed that idea far into the back of my head.

His hobbles gone, Carlson looked in my direction. His glasses were light enough so I could see his eyes, which looked right into mine. I asked if he had been told I was coming but he remained mute. In his lap was his ever present notebook, and on top of that a piece of paper. What was that? I asked. I was surprised when he looked down at it and began to talk, the first time he had talked to me since December 1984.

He read as if from a prepared statement. "I would be more than happy to talk to you when I have my attorneys and my doctor present and the court is apprised of what you are doing." The court knew, I said. He repeated himself. Who is your doctor? I asked. Dr. Fairbairn.

He said more, his voice soft and quavering slightly from anxiety, or was it anger? He would not talk to me unless I gave him one week's notice. "My schedule is very flexible. I am usually available seven days a week. Call me a week ahead of time." I told him he was alerted to my visit six days ago. He ignored me and added that he was "available to meet almost all day long, between eight in the morning and seven at night."

I laughed to myself. He was "available" for interviews like a movie star. Where was his press agent? But Ross Carlson was not joking. This was another imperious demand of a twisted mind. I was still shocked that he talked, even if about not talking. But I tried to keep him going. I pointed to the page he just read. Had he worked on this statement with David or Walter? He would not say. He would only talk when his conditions were fulfilled. I asked to look at the paper but he would not show it to me.

I then pulled out Kingsley's order. "The defendant's silence," I read to Carlson, "is the result of intentional noncooperation rather than an inability to speak or communicate resulting from a mental disease or defect . . ." I read "the defendant is ordered to cooperate with the Colorado State Hospital . . ." When I finished, my eyes again met his but I could not read his face. I handed him the order and he spent a few moments looking at it though I knew he was familiar with it. He then handed it back.

He was clearly disobeying Kingsley. I wondered if he had been encouraged not to talk by his lawyers. By now, I was playing to Kingsley—the videotape machine was on—and I wanted to see how long I could keep Carlson going. "You are in a real bind," I said. You either cooperate with me, as Kingsley has told you to do, or you follow your lawyers' advice and demonstrate that you can cooperate with your attorneys and are competent. "If you listen to your attorneys," I added, "you are disobeying Judge Kingsley's court order. But if you obey the court order, you are disobeying your attorneys. It is a real pickle to be in." I felt a perverse pleasure turning the tables this way, of pointing out the trap he put himself in.

My cleverness did not faze Carlson. Kingsley's order was the work of people who were "against" him. Then he stopped. He had finally caught on that I was drawing him out and would say nothing more. After a few moments, I terminated the interview. I looked at my watch. It had taken all of thirteen minutes.

These thirteen minutes distilled the case for me. Carlson knew who I was, why I was there, and what his legal options were. He was able to cooperate with his attorneys as he read from his statement. I again thought that Carlson's stonewalling was a mistake. To my way of thinking, if he were working with his attorney this way, it would show that Carlson was competent to stand trial. I hoped Kingsley would agree. The next time I saw Walter Gerash in court he called me "Doctor Pickle." Clearly, he had seen the tape.

On December 19, I sent Kingsley letter number two, a three page report, and a copy of the thirteen minute tape. I told Kingsley that the tape would show purposeful noncooperation with me but that Carlson could cooperate with his attorneys. This was the main point of this letter; that I "suspected" his attorneys were encouraging him not to talk. I also told Kingsley of Gerash's attempt to have me stopped by the State Patrol.

## January 1989

There was worry in Chappell's voice when he called. Well before my thirteen minute noninterview with Carlson, Savitz and Gerash had prepared new motions asking Kingsley to dismiss the charges. It was the same story, chapter, and verse. They attacked Orne, they attacked my independence, they attacked our "surreptitious interrogation." Carlson, they said, had been deprived of "liberty without due process of law." They also wanted to limit outside experts—me and Orne—who could examine Carlson and what we could do.

Chappell wanted to be cautious. Kingsley trusted me, he said, and if Kingsley could see the light at the end of the tunnel he would likely dismiss their motions. Could you send him a letter, Chappell asked, and tell him when the next competency hearing, Carlson

Three, should be held? So on January 9, I used my pipeline for the third time.

Carlson would be, I wrote, ready for his competency hearing by early spring, 1989. I did not add that I thought that Carlson had been competent from the very start. I made the two points I wanted to get across to Kingsley. One, Carlson's lack of cooperation should not block restoration since noncooperation was not legal grounds for incompetency. And two, I wanted to add something about his alleged "amnesia," so I told Kingsley that "forty to seventy percent of murderers also claim to have memory problems." The truthfulness of Carlson's amnesia—"I don't remember killing my parents" —would have to be judged within the context of the case. I then wished Judge Kingsley a Merry Christmas and a Happy New Year.

### Merry Christmas!

My third letter apparently drove Walter Gerash mad. I should not, he wrote on January 11, tell Kingsley of my "ex parte" opinions. "You are a very recent newcomer to this case . . . I suggest you do not give legal opinions on competency before there is a hearing. Your . . . suggestions concerning memory loss are . . . off the wall . . . and . . . should not be discussed" with Kingsley. "We will," he said, "object to you imperiously discussing the case ex parte with the court or in a sub-rosa manner, amassing experts in an adversary manner so they may . . . testify against my client."

In case I did not know he was furious, Gerash then wished me "a Merry Christmas and a Happy New Year" and sent copies to Kingsley, Chappell, Haydee Kort, Mark Pecevich, and Pat Robb. Savitz and Gerash were now watching me closely, but the more alarmed I sensed they were becoming, the more confidence I felt.

### Unexpected Trouble

The six month review began on Monday, January 23. I was not subpoenaed so I did not have to attend. The defense presented their motions and rolled Jackson out, again. "In essence [Ross] has completed a manslaughter sentence of thirteen or fourteen years with good time," Gerash opened with. "A good part of his twenties has been spent in confinement and he hasn't been convicted."

It was the usual routine. But trouble came from an unexpected

quarter. The most damning witness for the defense was not Newton, Fisch, or Fairbairn, but a hospital worker. The state shot itself
in the foot and revealed the same weaknesses that led the state to
go to court in 1984 with only Fine and Reichlin.

I first learned about it the next morning, on January 25, when I
read *The Denver Post:*

> CASTLE ROCK—. . . Ross Carlson's chief therapist at the Colo-
> rado State Hospital testified Tuesday that he knows very little
> about multiple personality disorder, the mental condition that
> had prevented Carlson from standing trial for his parents'
> murders.
>
> Delighted defense attorneys David Savitz and Walter Gerash
> —who have argued that the institution is incapable of treating
> their client—were so encouraged by the testimony that they
> sent their remaining witnesses home and rested their case.
>
> They want Special Judge Robert Kingsley to dismiss the
> charges because the hospital has not restored Carlson to com-
> petency.
>
> Robert Gonzales, the veteran mental health worker responsi-
> ble for the defendant's treatment, said he sees Carlson daily
> and individually for about an hour each Sunday. But he said he
> knew nothing of Carlson's problems when the sessions started
> last summer.
>
> "I knew he was incompetent to proceed to trial but I didn't
> know why," Gonzales said. "I was told he had an MPD diagno-
> sis and that's what I read in his records. MPD letters meant
> very little to me. I didn't know anything about it . . ."

I was furious. Why was Gonzales, a very nice man, allowed to
testify without having read at least one thing about MPD? He
clearly had not read one word of any of the articles I sent to Pueblo
nor read any of the articles I brought down in December. Had
anyone? MPD or not, everyone treating Carlson should have known
MPD inside and out. And not only had Gonzales not been prepped
about MPD, but the lowest man on the therapist totem pole was
treating the hospital's most complicated patient. Was the hospital
responding to Carlson's imperiousness with an arrogance of its own?

Luckily, MPD was no longer the "official" diagnosis but the defense had been given a hole big enough to drive a truck through. I

had Kingsley's ear but did not want this to go to waste and the case to fall apart because the hospital dropped the ball. Chappell and Pat Robb were also mortified and worried about what Kingsley would do. "This was," said Pat, "a stupid, stupid mistake." She assured me that the staff would be much better prepared in the future.

Chappell told me that Kingsley was visibly upset and that it was lucky Kingsley did not throw out the charges then and there. I called Mark Pecevich and asked that the treatment team do some serious reading. I had no idea whether they followed my advice.

On Wednesday, January 25, after three hours of closing arguments, Kingsley simply said that "the motion to terminate the criminal proceedings is denied." He went on to say that though "the defense attorneys have been most zestful in protecting his [Ross's] rights, the people have certain rights too." When Chappell called me with the news, he thought that my January 11 promise that the competency hearing was near at hand kept Kingsley from siding with the defense. "Now," he said, "we have to get this thing on the road."

### Reluctant Experts

To make sure we got where we wanted to go, I planned to swamp the defense with experienced psychiatrists. Two for one; I wanted to cancel out Fisch, Fairbairn, and Newton. If they had three, I would have six. There would be Orne and myself and, I hoped, at least two or three others in addition to those from the hospital.

When I started to make calls, I ran into problems. Of the local psychiatrists I contacted, no one wanted to sign on. In fact, during February and March, I, like Chappell in 1985, found no one, experienced or not, willing to join me for Carlson Three. No one I asked, it seemed, wanted to get involved. They gave me many excuses, but the circus clearly frightened people off. Some were open; they did not like the publicity and were put off by the case. One was frightened of legal harassment and another mentioned a suit. One had heard that Fairbairn had brought ethics charges against Lori Greene. The case, he said, was too much like a loose cannon; get involved, you risked getting shot.

I was happy when I was able to sign up Jon Bell, someone who once worked on the forensic unit at Pueblo and who was now a full-time faculty member with me. He was the colleague who coined the phrases "Carlsonologist" and "Carlsonology." Now he was about to become a practitioner of that new specialty. I gave Jon one of the four-inch thick books I had made up of Carlson highlights as well as reprints on MPD. Jon graduated fourth in his medical school class. I knew he would master the material well.

I was dismayed when Martin Orne said no. I had assumed he was a given. I could not figure out why he begged off. But Orne told me he had "little experience" with competency; he said that he would consider coming out for the sanity trial if and when it was necessary. I did not argue. He was not a man who you could get to change his mind. That just left me and Jon. I was very disappointed.

Orne suggested I call a well-known forensic psychiatrist, Seymour Halleck, to take his place. Orne had heard Halleck present a paper on MPD. Halleck believed that true multiples should be held accountable for their behavior because they had control over their switching and because their alters frequently were aware of each other. I finally reached Halleck, told him about Carlson, and he agreed to come.

Halleck ended our conversation with what I had grown to expect. "He might be a multiple, you know." Yes, I knew, though I doubted it. Everyone was caught up with MPD, I thought. But the issue now was competency, not multiplicity. I did not say a thing. I sent him one of my books filled with Carlson's records.

On April 14 I wrote to David Savitz that Halleck would come to examine Carlson in the beginning of May. "In the spirit of cooperation and for the best interests of your client," I wrote, "he would very much like to have the defense attorneys and psychiatric team present." I did not hear from Savitz. On April 25, I sent Savitz our itinerary. We planned to meet with Carlson on May 2.

**In Writing**

Finally, after five years, Savitz and Gerash put in writing what I suspected they had told Carlson many years before. Listen to us, Ross, do not talk.

Lawyers, I was discovering, liked to deliver mail in special ways. And on April 21, just days before we were to visit Carlson, Savitz and Gerash sent me an urgent, hand-delivered letter. "We are instructing our client," they wrote to me, "not to attend or participate in any of these outside evaluations. Enough is enough," they wrote.

I thought they wanted to limit who would testify in the competency hearing and, possibly, in the sanity trial. They certainly would not want someone as experienced as Seymour Halleck on the other side.

This was brazen chutzpah, a redundancy. I could not believe they had written it down. But I would now take advantage of it. Carlson had never cooperated and now I thought I had a good idea why. On April 26, I wrote my fourth letter to Kingsley.

"It has now become clear," I wrote, "that Mr. Savitz and Mr. Gerash are *actively* interfering with the evaluation and treatment of Ross Carlson . . . Mr. Carlson is able to work with his attorneys to stymie the State Hospital's attempt to restore him to competency. It is also clear that Mr. Carlson's years of noncooperation have been encouraged by his defense team . . ."

One part of Carlson's charade was over. Carlson was mute, not because of illness, but because of tactics. I no longer had to wonder if he was mute because of Justin, Steve, Norman, or Black. At least with me, Carlson was mute because of David and Walter. Walter was no stranger to noncooperation in these circumstances. I later learned he was involved in a case as early as 1963 where this was the central issue.

## Fifty-Four Minutes of Silence

On April 27, Jon Bell and I drove to Pueblo. Again I met with the treatment team. Carlson still deflected questions about anything of a substantial nature, they told me. Keep at it, I said. Carlson has done this from the beginning. Work with anything he gives you. Work with why he will not talk.

When we walked into the large, shabby day room of his ward, Carlson sat in an overstuffed and overaged chair in the center of the room. We pulled over two other chairs, introduced ourselves, and sat down with him.

Carlson knew who I was and knew why I was there because, as I sat down, he handed me a copy of his lawyers' letter instructing him not to speak to me. I then reread to him Kingsley's order. That exchange over, he sat in his chair, completely silent. Soon, behind his sunglasses, Carlson appeared to fall asleep; for fifty-four minutes he slept. When Jon and I could take it no longer we stopped. We got all of this on tape.

Afterward, Jon and I walked over to the administration building to talk with Pat and Mark. I wanted to make sure everything was on track. As we emptied her licorice jar, Pat again reassured me that this time everyone from the hospital who would testify would be very well prepared.

The next day I received another urgent FOR HAND DELIVERY letter from Savitz. "We thought," he wrote, "that our letter to you of April 21 was sufficient notice and explanation to cancel all such interviews and evaluations. Evidently, you refused to honor our position by virtue of your and Dr. Jon Bell's visit yesterday to the state hospital to interview Mr. Carlson. Please be advised," he went on, "our client Ross Carlson hereby elects to exercise his constitutional and statutory rights to remain silent during the intended interviews of Tuesday, May 2, 1989, with Dr. Seymour Halleck and/or you."

Of course I planned to go anyway and get his stonewall act on tape. Savitz had no right to stop us from attempting to talk to his client. But when I told Halleck of the letter he, too, dropped out because of the "adversarial nature" of the case and because Carlson would probably not talk. I could not believe my ears when he also said he was no longer interested in coming.

Orne gone, Halleck gone; my "panel" had just shrunk to two "outside" experts and three hospital doctors. I had planned to go to court with overwhelming experience, age, and force. It was not going to work out that way. Jon had a few gray hairs and so did I, but we did not match the age and looks of Fairbairn, Fisch, and Newton. I had no choice, however, but to accept those odds. I had become, by default, the main witness for the prosecution.

## Foot of the Colossus

On May 2, when Ross Carlson walked into the room where Jon and I waited he told us in the clearest voice I had ever heard him use that he would not talk. Period. He then turned on his heel and walked out. I got this on tape too. Mark Pecevich had Carlson brought back into the room. For a moment there was a violent scuffle; Carlson was very strong and managed to brace himself with both arms against the doorjambs so he could not be pushed or pulled into the room. I told Mark to let him go. Carlson, Savitz, and Gerash were, I thought, digging their own hole. We did not need to give them ammunition by appearing to abuse their client.

We spent the next hour with Pat and her jar. Pat told me how the evaluations by the state hospital doctors were going. Carlson talked with the other doctors but told them "nothing." In fact, he still held to the story that he could not remember anything before 1985 including when and where he was born. That must be Holden, holding, I thought. Carlson also said that he "doubted" that his parents were dead; he was sure that Bob Chappell had framed him. "Does a child kill his parents?" he asked. "I don't think so. But," Carlson said, "Chappell is tenacious as a bulldog. He just won't give it up."

During many of his sessions, Pat told us, Carlson was irritable and arrogant. Once he verbally attacked his interviewer for having the nerve to try to understand him. "You cannot," he told her, "judge the colossus just by its foot." Ross Carlson was not a modest man.

But by committing to paper the instructions not to talk, the defense had opened themselves to the charge they encouraged Carlson not to cooperate as part of the Jackson defense. Pat thought they had gone "off the deep end" by writing those letters. We hoped the letters would displease Kingsley. The colossus, I told Jon on the way home, had put his foot in his mouth.

### Upon Motion of the District Attorney

On May 31, I wrote my fifth letter to Judge Kingsley. "Mr. Carlson's noncooperation on April 27 and May 2 are repetitions of what happened in the Spring of 1988 and during my December 8, 1988, meeting with him . . . It is clear . . . Mr. Carlson has been instructed to stonewall and to avoid cooperation probably to force the court to find Mr. Carlson permanently incompetent . . ." But I need not have worried about Theon Jackson.

At 3:29 P.M. on April 27—in the middle of Carlson's fifty-four minutes of silence—Governor Roy Romer signed a bill which added seven words to the Colorado Commitment laws. The new law read: "If, on the basis of the available evidence, not including evidence resulting from a refusal by the defendant to accept treatment, there is a substantial probability that the defendant will not be restored to competency within the foreseeable future, *UPON MOTION OF THE DISTRICT ATTORNEY, the court MAY terminate the criminal proceeding . . .*"

For serious crimes, the Jackson defense had been discarded. If there had been the slightest chance that Judge Kingsley was going to dismiss the charges, there was no chance that Bob Chappell would ask him to do so now. Jackson was gone for good. The battle-ground was now competency. For Carlson, there was no other way out.

# BILLY MILLIGAN

I finished my competency report and sent it to Kingsley on July 6. Carlson Three was scheduled for the end of October. One weekend, Susan and I traveled to Steamboat Springs where friends had offered us their lovely log cabin on a ranch overlooking Steamboat. On Saturday morning, we sat in our friends' crowded kitchen in town. When I saw the first page of *The Denver Post*, which lay on their kitchen table, my stomach churned.

CARLSON COMPETENT FOR TRIAL, DOCTORS SAY.

The churning settled out into a mixture of anxiety and anticipation. " 'It's the second psychiatric miracle: the miracle of nontreatment that occasioned competency,' Savitz said sarcastically . . ." My doctor self felt challenged by Savitz's sarcasm; this was a game, I reminded myself for the hundredth time. Our vacation solitude spoiled, I read on.

"Two doctors who went to interview [Carlson] at the hospital April 27 reported that he refused to talk to them and presented them with a letter from Savitz urging him not to cooperate. 'Mr. Carlson knew who we were, knew why we were there, and knew what the letter said. He was clearly able to cooperate with his attorneys,' Dr. Michael Weissberg wrote."

Everything about Carlson ended up in court or in the papers or both and I was preoccupied for the rest of the weekend. In Sunday's *News*, Gerash was even less kind. "I'm outraged," he said. "The doctors are doing another hatchet job on Ross."

## Billy Milligan

On September 14, I walked through the metal detectors and took the elevator up to Chappell's modern brick and glass office at the Arapahoe County Justice Center, a cluster of buildings on the southern edge of the Denver metropolitan area. The thing about metropolitan Denver is that, unlike cities in the east, you can see where it ends, and for the moment it ended right outside Chappell's door.

Bob called the meeting to rethink "the theory of the case" because, he said, he had been "nailed so many times." I did not understand the jargon. The "theory of the case," he said with a chuckle, was the framework of arguments he would use in Carlson Three in front of Kingsley.

Bob motioned me into a small, windowless conference room and walked in after me. There was another man there, Paul King, the D.A. for Douglas County who would assist Chappell. As Bob spoke, I noticed for the first time that at thirty-nine, his hair was thinning and graying at the temples. We all had changed since this began.

Moments later we were joined by Brian, tanned and relaxed, who just returned from Mexico. As always, he wore his service revolver and as always I stared at it before self-consciously looking away. Of the four of us, Chappell was the only one who had not gone away this summer; he was tied to home by his brand-new twin girls.

As I sat down, Bevis started to tell me a story about "a multiple in Guam" he had just heard about; someone who cut up and cooked his mother. But before I could respond, Chappell dropped another bombshell of a "Carlson update," of the kind I had grown to expect.

"Hey, Mike," Bob said, "did you know that Carlson was seen with *The Minds of Billy Milligan* in 1982?" *Milligan* was the book about the only multiple ever to be found insane after he committed a crime.

Chappell sounded tense. An ex-classmate of Carlson's, a guy named Paul Fletcher, placed Carlson with the book *Billy Milligan* a year before the murders, a book which could have served Carlson as his manual on how to fake MPD. The thing that made this discovery painful now, Bevis said, was that Fletcher tried to report the tie between Carlson and *Milligan* five years ago. Five years was why Chappell was fuming underneath. First no one answered Kachel's calls and now Fletcher.

In 1984, right after Carlson revealed he had been invaded by eight different personalities, Fletcher told his father that he had seen his classmate carrying *The Minds of Billy Milligan* in Heritage High School during 1981–1982. Unlike what other parents might have done, Paul's father called the D.A.'s office. Only no one bothered to pass the message on to Chappell; the message was lost in the avalanche of Carlson's growing file.

Five years later, Paul, now a student at the Sheriff's Academy, told an instructor about Ross and Milligan. This turned out to be another break because this particular instructor happened to work with Bob Chappell. This time, the Carlson-Milligan link was not lost.

I did not know a lot about Billy Milligan. Milligan, Chappell told me, raped and kidnapped three women. Milligan was the first—and so far the only—person found Not Guilty by Reason of Insanity because he was a multiple. Milligan's case was never appealed— much to the chagrin of prosecutors like Chappell. And Carlson, Chappell told me, was definitely seen with the book.

## My New "Theory of the Case"

Something else happened over the summer. I had a new idea, a new "theory of the case" and had come to today's meeting hoping to sell it. After we finished with Milligan I began. The longer we waited, I said, the more we found out about Carlson's deception. The black bag, the Hinckley defense, David Kachel, David Bassler and the alibi for the alibi, and now Milligan. But, paradoxically, the more we documented Carlson's deception, the more we fell into the defense's trap.

No matter how tempted, we should avoid calling Carlson a fraud and liar, at least directly. Too much effort had gone into proving he was a psychopath. I told Chappell that the real/fake dichotomy had defeated him twice, in 1984 and again in 1987, and distracted everyone from the key issue, competency, thereby playing right into the defense's hands. Chappell tried two tactics, I said, based on ridicule and both failed. One, he ridiculed Carlson as a fake and, two, MPD as a disease. Both were mistakes. The defense would always find someone to testify Carlson had MPD. Day had thought Carlson and MPD were for real. While Kingsley might not be so sure about either it was, I thought, a mistake to try ridicule a third time.

Why? Because MPD was a diagnosis which stuck like glue. People were drawn to it and MPD, just like possession, befuddled normally reasonable brains. The newspapers and television stations kept box scores. How many personalities did Carlson have? Eight? Nine? Ten? The hype attracted attention and the attention brought with it belief. People were willing to believe anything; once brought up, I told Chappell, it was hard to make MPD go away.

The way Chappell prosecuted the case had spawned a religious argument. Chappell had kept the issue MPD, not competence. And, I told Chappell, he did it because he was frightened of MPD; he wanted it to go away. I told Chappell not to be frightened of MPD. If Fisch, Fairbairn, Newton, Savitz, Gerash, and Carlson wanted to believe that Carlson was a multiple, let them. We had to tell Kingsley what being a multiple really meant. MPD? So what!

Multiplicity did not mean insanity and multiplicity did not mean incompetence. Carlson knew what he was doing when he lured his parents to Cottonwood Road and he knew what he was doing now. He was legally sane then and competent now. Even if he were a true multiple, Ross Carlson was not a house with eight people living inside. He did not really have eight or ten different heads as the defense's "pinwheel" display showed. He had one body, one personality, and one brain.

At the core of MPD was amnesia. Multiples wanted to forget. Even in real multiples, memory problems varied from moment to moment; there was always "leakage" between personalities, and there was always shared memory between all personalities. The "children," Blue or Gray, after all, could still drive cars. Furthermore, the central mechanism of MPD was the abuse of autohypnosis. How much of Carlson's ability to dissociate was under his conscious control? With Fairbairn, Carlson switched personalities at will. Carlson came and went as he pleased.

As to sanity, multiples, just like people who are hypnotized, cannot be forced to do things that they would not normally do. All personalities—even in real multiples—know right from wrong.

Even Fig Newton in a 1984 paper agreed that all personalities in bona fide MPD were able to "test reality," that is, to know the difference between right and wrong. Therefore, even if Carlson were a multiple, all of his personalities were "sane." Carlson might be a multiple, but he was surely a cold-blooded killer. I then repeated the bottom line: multiplicity was not synonymous with insanity and incompetency as the defense had wanted people to think.


## Sixty-Six Percent Chance of Winning

So far Chappell, Bevis, and King sat there and listened. Then I took out a piece of paper and drew a diagram. Give Kingsley three choices, I said. Don't back him into a corner and force him to accept or reject MPD.

Choice number one: Carlson was an out-and-out fake and, therefore, not mentally ill. In that case, Carlson, by definition, is competent.

Two: Carlson might have true MPD but still be competent; I thought we could effectively demystify MPD for Kingsley.

Three: The one Eddie Day picked; Ross Carlson had MPD and, because of it, could not participate in his defense. Two out of three was not bad, I said. We had a sixty-six percent chance of winning right off the bat.

It took only moments for Chappell to like my new approach. "We bit off on the wrong issue," he agreed. To focus on MPD was a "mistake." Eddie Day, like everyone else, thought that Carlson must be sick; why else would he kill his parents? And we forced Day to make sure Carlson got treatment, Chappell said. We forced Day to become an advocate for Carlson because we called Carlson a liar, and we got stuck in that rut with Kingsley in 1987. "With MPD you first fall in love and then you get married," Chappell continued. "Only later do you get divorced." None of us knew where in this cycle of marriage and divorce Kingsley was but we decided to give him as much latitude as we could.

Our new approach simplified things. We would give the defense MPD and just focus on competency in Carlson Three. We could take swipes at MPD but not make destruction of MPD our main objective. Of course, Carlson was abnormal. Normal people do not kill their parents. But Ross Carlson was also competent and legally sane. *Billy Milligan* and my new theory; the three-hour meeting had covered a lot.

## Halls of Justice

The defense pulled out all the stops for Carlson Three. First, Savitz demanded personnel records of all the doctors on my panel. What did he want to know? Did he want to know how much money I made? Or if I was ever in trouble? Savitz also wanted to know if I had a police record, of all things. It seemed that he was desperate for something to impeach us, to keep us off balance. No wonder most of my colleagues had decided to stay away.

I was livid. But Bevis called me for my birth date so he could search for my rap sheet. I had none. Our university attorney said she would fight Savitz on my personnel file. On that, Savitz backed down. By now the halls of justice seemed pretty dirty to me. This was more than a Savitz attempt to establish dominance. He may have just been doing his job, but the game was getting rough.

## Pueblo: October 13, 1989

The hearing was set for October 19. Because I had seen Carlson more than five months before, I planned to visit him one last time. I did not want any surprises in court. On October 12, I got my third, by now routine, "do not bother my client" letter from David Savitz. This time I almost did not go, but Jon Bell and I drove to Pueblo anyway. I assumed Carlson would not talk—but when we arrived I was glad that we had made the trip.

Jon and I waited in the conference room for five and then ten minutes. Finally, a secretary told us that Carlson asked whether he had a choice whether to see us or not. I asked her to relay the message that we would not force him to come, but that it would be in his best interests to attend. He didn't.

I had also arranged a meeting with the treatment team—it was only days until the trial and I wanted to make sure everyone was ready. But instead of Gonzales and the rest walking into the conference room, I met people I had never even seen before.

This was how I found out that Carlson had been transferred to a different ward—his old unit had been moved to a less secure area—but no one had told me. I was to "review" and "report" to Kingsley but here it was, six days before the trial, and a completely new set of staff members were involved with his care and would be witnesses in less than a week. And they knew little about MPD. I was furious but decided not to say anything now because they were nervous enough about court without my criticism. I worried, however, about who would put their foot in their mouth first.

Someone had dropped the ball again. I had recommended that Carlson be treated like any patient, but not like a sack of potatoes. I wondered if now that the hospital administration felt safer than it had in years, whether it was retaliating for five and a half years of paralysis. The only thing which tempered my rage was the conviction that no matter if Sigmund Freud himself had treated Carlson, he would not start talking now, five and a half years after he was first admitted to Pueblo.

I spent the afternoon talking with Carlson's new team about MPD and Carlson. They were clearly scared of Carlson—of working in the fishbowl—and worried about being made fools of in court. I could not blame them.

They did tell me some interesting things. Carlson had become more overtly grandiose. First, he wanted to make a deal with the staff, "to share power" in running the ward. Now on occasion, he compared himself with Alexander the Great who had accomplished so much while still young. "Alexander," Carlson told his new therapist, "has gotten more print than Jesus Christ." First Antichrist, and now Alexander versus Christ. Carlson, it seemed, had it in for Jesus.

On October 16, I wrote my sixth letter to Kingsley and told him about Carlson's sixth refusal to talk. I also sent him a copy of Savitz's letter. My education of Kingsley was almost over.


### Preparation

On the day before the hearing, I met for two hours with Bob Chappell to go over my testimony. "Control the pace," he told me. "Don't talk over Gerash and do insist that he not interrupt you. And whatever you do, do not argue. Be especially aware of his method of asking compound questions. Pick your spots. You will be able to make your points."

Because the state was asserting that Carlson was competent, Chappell was back in his accustomed position and would go first. Chappell wanted me to be his lead witness and lay out our new theory of the case right at the start: one, two, three. A judge, he said could get bored after a few days. Chappell wanted to get me on while Kingsley was still fresh. I was glad to go first.

Later that day, I found a copy of *Billy Milligan* in a used-book store. When I read it, I found it was all there, most within the first fifteen pages: how to act, what to do, how to move your eyes, the fact that multiples lose time. All of Milligan's personalities were listed in the preface: Milligan actually had one personality just like Carlson's street punk, Norman, a rational one like Steve, and he had younger ones, like Blue and Gray. Billy Milligan even had a personality who was The Protector, just like Black.

On page four, there was Billy's Spiegel eye roll. Milligan also wore dark sunglasses, just like Carlson. Milligan, like Carlson, was also panicked about going to jail and being raped. Once he shaved off his mustache—just as Carlson did his eyebrows—and, like Carlson, did not remember doing it. But the thing that I found most interesting was on page fifty-eight: Milligan's lawyer told Milligan that "one of two things can happen. Either, at some future time you will be declared competent, and a trial date will be set; or after a certain period you'll be ruled incompetent to stand trial, and the charges will be dismissed . . ."

I could not be sure how Carlson used *Milligan*. Carlson's experts would probably say that Carlson wanted to read about a disease he thought he had. But I thought that was unlikely. Soon after he read *Milligan* Carlson discussed John Hinckley's insanity defense with David Kachel. Hinckley, they said, should have had people know him as another personality. I would have been surprised if *Milligan* had not played a key part in Carlson's thinking before and after the shootings.

As I read *Milligan* I reminded myself to avoid the seduction of the real/fake issue. But I knew I would use *Billy Milligan* in my testimony. Once on the stand, I would not be able to resist. *Milligan* would make effective theater in court and I wanted to see what Carlson would do.

That night Chappell called. I could hear one of his twins cry in the background. I sensed he had a slight case of the opening night jitters. Everyone was nervous; the play-offs were about to begin. But maybe because of my contact with Kingsley, I was confident. I could not believe that Kingsley would let this go on too long. Something big would be decided by Thanksgiving.

# FOOL ME TWICE

I was still in Denver when Bob Chappell resurrected the command post on the second floor, in the small littered room across the road and dirt lot from the Douglas County Court. I had been nervous before my first appearance in 1988; now I could not wait to take the stand. My last patient left at 9:30. I was on the road five minutes later and in the Castle Rock courtroom at 10:05. But of course there was a delay.

**Outside, Sonny**

Chappell and Gerash were arguing two new defense motions when I walked in. The defense wanted to force us to consider only one diagnosis, MPD, since MPD was what both Day and Kingsley said Carlson had. They did not want us to mention antisocial personality or fraud. Savitz and Gerash wanted to keep MPD on center stage. I did not blame them. The other motion challenged the constitutionality of the new "Carlson law." They wanted Kingsley to find the new competency law, the "Carlson law" they called it, unconstitutional.

When Gerash saw me he asked Kingsley to have me wait, once again, on the hard bench outside. Gerash was forever putting me in my place. I spent my time wandering around the courthouse. During the mid-morning recess, I overheard a white-haired man joking about Gerash with another courtroom denizen who smoked a stubby cigar. Professional jealousy, I wondered?

They argued in court until noon. Finally, Kingsley, with a wave, rejected both motions and I was told I could reenter. As I walked in I recognized reporters from the major Denver papers and was introduced to a new one, a woman from the *Los Angeles Times*. Bevis had already warned me that she had been hanging around with Gerash and not to tell her too much. Loose lips and all that.

No sooner than I sat down, I heard Kingsley call for the noon recess.

## On the Stand

At 1:30 my turn finally came. After I was sworn in, I sat in the box with Carlson and the defense in front of me and Judge Kingsley to my right. Again I thought I saw Kingsley give me a nod. Then Chappell marched me through my findings.

I told Kingsley about my visits with Carlson. Three in 1984 when he talked and said nothing and the six since when he hardly talked at all. I told Kingsley not only was Carlson not cooperating, but he was encouraged to do so. Carlson "was told," I said, "not to talk to me or anyone else I hired." I then read sections of the "do not disturb our client" letters. I implied that I believed Carlson's noncooperation had been encouraged from day one. When I looked over at the defense table, Carlson seemed to be listening when not chatting with Savitz, who now always sat between Carlson and Gerash ever since the "shut that machine down" episode. On occasion, when no one looked, it appeared to me as if Gerash made more faces at me.

## Andy Warhol?

Then in the dark court we watched the tedious two tapes of Carlson not talking. The thirteen minutes of December 8, and the fifty-four minutes of April 27. On screen, I could hear Carlson say: "What is the scope of your interest? My schedule is very flexible . . . I am usually available seven days a week. Call me, preferably a week ahead of time." I heard Kingsley move with impatience. The witness stand was close to him and I sensed that Kingsley was fed up with Carlson, and, I hoped, fed up with MPD.

Then came the fifty-four minutes of complete silence of April 27, 1989. On tape, Carlson sat in the overstuffed chair, fingers pressed to his temple, for close to an hour. In the dark courtroom I could not see Carlson's expression as we watched him sleep. Soon the court reporter, BJ Moody, leaned over and asked me whether these boringly long films were by Andy Warhol. BJ's joke was a good sign. Courthouse rumor had it that she sided with Ross and the defense. It now looked like BJ was swinging our way. We ended the movies with a brief one-minute clip of Carlson's May 2 announcement that he "chose not to talk" to us at all before he walked out the door.

We stopped at 4:45. I expected accolades but Paul King told me to "lay off" constantly suggesting that I believed Savitz and Gerash encouraged Carlson's noncooperation. Kingsley, he said, already had gotten the message. Also, he told me, stop speaking so fast. Slow down. But Chappell was happy. It had, he said, gone well. I then went home to reschedule more patients, since my plan had been to start my testimony in the morning and be finished by now. Instead I had to cancel patients, since I had to be on the stand again in the morning for Gerash's cross-examination.

## Strange Twist

I was in my office at 7:00 before I drove back to court. Waiting for me on my desk was an article from a mock newspaper *The Castle Rock Chronicle* under the heading of STRANGE TWIST IN CARLSON CASE.

CASTLE ROCK—In an unprecedented twist, the expert witness in the case, Dr. Michael Weissberg, head of the Colorado Psychiatric Hospital Emergency Services, was found to be suffering from a rare dissociative disorder, ironically the same disorder that defendant Ross Carlson was hoping to be diagnosed with. Though the details are still sketchy, it appears that Dr. Weissberg, under the stress of cross-examination, began to speak in the voice of Ida Lapidus, an elderly Long Island woman. He began to blurt out recipes for kugle dishes, unique in their simplicity yet which have potential for use as a main dish. Dr. Weissberg was taken back to his hospital for evaluation at their psychiatric emergency services.

Dr. Joel Fine, who assumed control of the emergency room in Dr. Weissberg's absence, attempted to explain the sudden chain of events. "I'm surprised I didn't see this sooner. He had the classic triad of bow ties, Subaru wagon, and empty popcorn bags, which usually means he won't hold up under stress . . ."

The entire courtroom was taken by surprise. The defendant was overheard saying, "Everybody is crazy around here except me." The defendant's attorneys were expected to ask for a mistrial after the judge ordered the courtroom cleared and the bailiff was instructed to check out Dr. Weissberg's pockets for more helpful hints in and around the kitchen . . . The trial is expected to resume tomorrow. See Recipes, page 4.

Joel Fine, no relation to Alan, was my present chief resident and a relentless trickster. Of course, Carlson humor helped temper the grim and tense realities of the case. This morning's article was the best. I laughed all the way to Castle Rock.

When I showed Fine's article to Chappell he coughed, he laughed so hard. "He is damn right," Chappell said, hardly able to get out his words. "Carlson must be saying that 'everyone is crazy around here except me.' Carlson must want to laugh all the way to the bank." I guessed that the pressure behind Chappell's laugh was the six years that had gone on before. He then told me to put the article away.

## In the Gutter

I was on the stand by a quarter past nine. It was now Gerash's turn to examine me. He wanted to talk about MPD and abuse and I wanted to keep the focus on competence. Even if Ross Carlson had MPD, I told Gerash, Carlson is legally competent. "I have never," I said, "seen someone so capable . . . this is not an example of somebody who is incapacitated." He tried to dismiss me with sweeping speculations about Carlson's childhood abuse. He often spoke with his back to me, looking, it seemed, at the reporters seated in the court. As Walter repeatedly raised the issue of abuse, he tried to bring the focus back to MPD just as he had always done.

I would not let him. I was no longer intimidated and had gotten used to asking questions while I was on the stand. Kingsley let me do it. So when Gerash asked about abuse, I asked him what did child abuse have to do with Carlson's competence now? Walter told me that he, not I, asked the questions. He then brought up amnesia. Carlson, he said, could not "recall" the details of his parents' death. How could he help, then, in finding witnesses to defend himself?

Would you recall all the details if you had killed your parents? I wanted to ask. Would you tell your lawyer? I then repeated what Gerash earlier called my "off-the-wall statistics" that forty to seventy percent of killers claim some form of amnesia and/or memory loss about the crime. As I spoke, I could see Carlson lean over and actively confer with Savitz.

Gerash went in circles, as Chappell said he would. Once, Kingsley got cross with Gerash for asking the same question over again. I looked over at Chappell who just raised his eyebrows a notch. As my testimony dragged on, I was reassured when I heard "Jesus, Walter" muttered a few more times from the bench.

As we trooped out of the court at noon, we all tried to keep straight faces. Yesterday, we were cautious, but by now everyone was high. It all burst out when we got to our little office out of sight of the reporters. King felt like he was at halftime of a football game and his team was creaming them. "I am stoked," he said, as he hit his left palm with his right fist. Chappell and Bevis kept smiling and Pat Robb gave me another hug. I had focused on competency long enough, we had decided. I now would make it clear that I thought Carlson was pulling a fast one no matter what his diagnosis.

That afternoon, we were in the gutter. Gerash asked how much I was paid for my testimony. I wanted to answer it in the worst way, since, by now, most of the money I made on the case went to the university and not into my pockets at all. But Chappell objected to Gerash's question and Kingsley sustained. The smear had been made: I, too, was a hired gun and Gerash wanted to remind Kingsley of that fact.

I couldn't resist *Billy Milligan*. The first time I mentioned Milligan, Carlson snapped to attention. I could not see his eyes through his dark black glasses but I had just planted another seed that he was a fake. I was still high when I got off the stand. I thought Walter had a bad day. As I passed him, I told him "nice job, boychik." I also wanted to ask him what he planned to do with my personnel file and "police record" but, of course, I did not.

## Hunters

When I walked back to my car, I saw four men, two dressed in jeans and plaid shirts, standing around a pickup. They seemed to stare at three brown sticks which stuck out at crazy angles out of the back of the truck. When I got closer, the sticks were legs and the legs were attached to two dead bucks. The men were clearly cops, two just back from the deer hunt. They had good luck. Ross Carlson had worn the same outfit, jeans and plaid shirt. But I was sure Ross Carlson did not wear the fluorescent orange hunters in Colorado, by law, have to have on. Carlson hunted in disguise.

The next morning, I hurried, as I always did now to get the papers. In 1984, reporters were enthralled with MPD. On Saturday, I was pleased with what I read.

In the *Post* the lead paragraph went:

Even if Ross Carlson has multiple personality disorder, that does not mean he isn't competent to stand trial for the murder of his parents, a University of Colorado psychiatrist testified yesterday.

Dr. Michael Weissberg of the CU Health Sciences Center said he doesn't believe that Carlson, 25, suffers from the personality disorder.

But the diagnosis is not the issue, Weissberg said . . . "There is no question in my mind that this guy is competent. I've never seen somebody who is so capable . . . This is not an example of someone who is incapacitated," Dr. Weissberg added . . .

That was my message, our new theory of the case. I had gotten it over to the *Post*'s reporter.

## The Justice System

Over the next week, Kingsley watched hours of tapes done by the other doctors. When I spoke to Chappell on Monday night he was worried again. Judge Kingsley had asked Pecevich whether he had been there when Carlson fell on the floor and yelled that the "cyborgs" were eating his brain. Did this mean, Chappell wondered, Kingsley thought Carlson crazy?

On Tuesday, a patient of mine, one who I had to cancel on Friday morning, brought up the story she had also seen in the *Post*. "So that's where you were," she said, "you were seeing Carlson instead of seeing me." She then told me she was scared. As she read the article, she thought that, one day, I might be in danger; that Ross Carlson would somehow get out and kill me.

I made a "standard" psychoanalytical interpretation. She worried about my safety, I suggested, because she was hurt and angry that I went to court instead of seeing her; her fear that I would be hurt was a disguised wish that I would be. When I finished, she said she "appreciated the interpretation, but cut the crap." Carlson was, she said, a killer. As she spoke, I realized that my interpretation was the result of my own denial of Carlson's dangerousness. I thanked her for her real concern.

On Wednesday, during one of our calls, Chappell started to worry again. Kingsley still seemed stuck on Carlson's crazy behavior. Had we, Chappell asked, gotten across the idea that Carlson might be crazy and still be competent? Had we gotten across our new theory of the case?

As Bob and I talked, I had a sobering thought. It was us and them; no one else. Until this moment, "The Justice System" was a disembodied abstraction, wise, fair and, of course, just. The good guys always won, evil always lost, and justice would take care of itself. Now I realized that this was an idea out of tenth grade civics. It dawned on me that what we did mattered very much; paraphrasing Pogo, I now knew that "The System" was us.

### Carlson's Psychotic Personality

The next morning I decided to go to court and ran into Walter in the lobby of the courthouse. After nodding hello he said to me, "Hi, coach. You here to coach Jon Bell?" At least he had graduated me from apple polisher.

During the mid-morning break, the woman from the L.A. *Times* buddied up. I gave her noncommittal answers and learned something from her. She thought that one of Carlson's "psychotic" personalities was the killer. She might have been fishing for a response, but I found this interesting since it might have come straight from the defense's mouth. This must be, I thought, what Gerash and Savitz planned to argue at the sanity trial, if they lost this round. Ross was not psychotic, only one of his personalities was. I did not tell her that Fig Newton admitted that MPD was not a psychotic diagnosis and that all personalities in MPD knew right from wrong. I would save that for the sanity trial as well.

## Perfection

That afternoon, I told Chappell about my conversation with Ms. L.A. *Times*. Chappell told me to be careful. She might talk to Gerash; yesterday Bevis saw Gerash walking with her. But something in my story started Bob on one of his free-form musings. By now, I was used to his thinking out loud.

"In our system of justice," Chappell said, "a defendant like Carlson is entitled to a fair trial, but not a perfect trial." No defendant, for example, has perfect recall. "But, for some reason," he went on, "five years ago Eddie Day started to strive toward perfection. And since then," he said, "we have been in this god-awful mess."

Chappell stayed on perfection. "There was near perfection in what Carlson did," he said. "It was almost a perfect crime. If someone had stolen that Cadillac he left with the window down and keys in it, that person would have been a dead duck." I recalled a note in Carlson's chart on September 8, 1983, well before he thought he would be caught. Teary-eyed, he told a nurse that he thought his parents "had picked up a hitchhiker and something had happened to them . . ." That was alibi number two; Cortez was number one. The tears were from a crocodile.

"What would have happened if the black bag had not been found? It would have been the perfect crime . . ." Chappell's voice trailed off. "And why," he finally said, "why did Carlson's parents just lie there and die? Maybe they thought he had put blanks in his gun and they were calling his bluff."

I then brought up Savitz. I had noticed Savitz redden twice in court that day. I thought Savitz was angry at Gerash. I had shifted in my feelings toward Savitz: I was beginning to like him. He was predictable and he worked hard. Like his clothes and monogrammed shirt cuffs, he was sharp. I did not know what Gerash thought, but Savitz clearly believed that Carlson had MPD and I could not understand why someone like him would go for it.

Then Chappell looked at me with an intensity I had not seen before. "You can't sit next to someone," Chappell said, "someone who has done what Carlson has done without building a shield between you and him. It is too uncomfortable. The shield for Savitz and everyone else who has been with Carlson day in and day out is MPD. MPD takes the monster away from Ross and puts it somewhere else. It's that simple." Somehow, the diagnosis of MPD allowed Savitz to think that Carlson did not do it at all.


## Those People

Over the next days, Jon Bell did well but the mental health workers, in Chappell's words, "again did not shine." This time their failure did not mean as much. Savitz and Gerash also testified. In their direct testimony, their story was the same: The amnestic Carlson could not remember the details of the crime and could not help to find witnesses. He was incompetent.

Savitz kept referring to "those people" for Carlson's alter personalities. Talk about making an abstraction concrete. Savitz really did think that Carlson was different people. Chappell was right: Savitz really had to see Carlson that way.

In our routine late afternoon meeting, Paul and Bob confirmed what I suspected. Prosecutors are better putting on their cases first. They are not, they agreed, good counterpunchers. Again Chappell worried, this time about the sanity trial. "The best of all possible worlds," he said, is "if Kingsley rules that Carlson is a fake and a fraud." Then, Chappell said, he wouldn't worry that Carlson would switch to "Dopey, Grumpy, and Sleepy" in the middle of the next trial in front of a new judge and start this process all over again.

"If Kingsley doesn't rule that Carlson is a fake, then every day," Chappell told all of us, "they will come into court with complaints that Carlson is incompetent once again." Carlson, I thought, could be at this for six more years.


## Fifty, a Hundred More

When the defense put on their men, I came down to listen. When Chappell cross-examined Fisch, Chappell had a headache from an early morning trip to the dentist. But he was good. Chappell told me that he could not wait to get Fisch to admit in court that he believed that patients never lie. "Patients always tell the truth," Fisch dutifully said when he was led to it by Chappell. At that, Kingsley looked at him as if to say "maybe in your office but not in mine." I could not hide my grin as Brian looked over at me.

Well, Chappell asked, which personalities knew about the shooting? Fisch did not know. Well, was the amnesia global or did some personalities know what happened? All I know, said Fisch, was that the personalities "shut down consciousness." But there was, he added, leakage between them. Chappell persisted. Was Carlson's decision to "shut down" memory conscious or unconscious, Chappell asked. Could he control it or not? Fisch surprised me when he admitted that he did not know. Carlson might be able to control it and then again he might not. Score one for us.

Chappell also got Fisch to repeat what he said in 1984; that he had not yet met the killer, "that part of Antichrist" who was still hidden. Fisch then added, as if to lend credence to his assertion, that Carlson may have another "fifty or a hundred different personalities" as yet undiscovered.

If this was meant to impress Judge Kingsley it did; it was too much; multiple overload. Kingsley asked Fisch to repeat himself, which Fisch did, seriously, as if he were divulging an important, scientific fact. Fisch clearly did not understand the effect he was having on the court. "Fifty, one hundred" more, Fisch repeated. Kingsley rolled his eyes, looked at the ceiling, and shook his head. The improbability of MPD was buckling under its own weight. Kingsley seemed to barely suppress a grimace.

Fisch hurt himself when he admitted that he had not examined Carlson in a year. He was basing his testimony on his prior examinations. This time he had stopped into the jail to see Carlson but had not really interviewed him. "Do you mean," the incredulous Chappell asked, "that you just went to see Ross Carlson just to say howdy?" Fisch had to agree.


### Death Threat
Then I learned something else. Carlson had seriously upped the ante and turned my wife into a prophet. During their chat, Carlson had told Fisch that he, Carlson, could not "guarantee Dr. Weissberg's life."

I was listening to Fisch when he said this. Its import took only seconds to sink in and I started to go numb. I imagined that all eyes were now on me and I feigned a nonchalance I did not feel. Everyone else, I thought, must be relieved that it was me and not them. Carlson, even shackled, was a frightening man. When I am nervous I start to make jokes. At that moment, sitting in the Douglas County Court, I wondered what Carlson's threat really meant. When Carlson got out of jail would only one eighth of him kill me? Then I would only be one-eighth dead?

The jokes did not settle me down. If things went poorly, Carlson could be back on the street soon. This fact would not go away. Through it all Carlson sat at the end of the defense table, impassive, eyes hidden behind his black shades. Later, Pat Robb told me that on one of the hospital tapes she had seen Carlson start to rock back and forth and chant: "Weissberg, evil, Weissberg, evil." Carlson's mantra made me feel even worse.

Newton, once again, flew in from L.A. This kind and soft-spoken man did not hurt us. In fact, he helped. He admitted that MPD was not a psychotic diagnosis and that, in fact, all "alters" knew right from wrong. Earlier that day, I heard that after this case was over, he would retire and move to Bozeman, Montana. During Chappell's questioning, Ms. L.A. *Times*, who sat behind me, leaned over and said that she smelled me behind Chappell's questions. No, I said, Chappell did this all on his own.


## Closing Argument

The hearing, which started on Thursday, October 19, was scheduled to end the Friday of the next week. But, as usual, things dragged on and closing arguments were scheduled for Thursday afternoon, November 2, three weeks before Thanksgiving.

On Wednesday night, we sat in our small office and tossed out ideas for Chappell's closing argument. What Bob decided to say tomorrow and what he chose to save for the sanity trial, which we hoped would come next, would be of crucial importance. How far should he try to push Kingsley? Should he stick to our theory of "MPD so what" or should he go for it? Should Chappell try to get Kingsley to call Carlson and his MPD a sham or would that force Kingsley to protect Carlson and rule again that Carlson had MPD?

I thought Chappell should leave the real/fake issue alone. Let Kingsley decide for himself where he wanted to land on MPD. If he wanted to take it further, let him do it on his own. No one, I said, liked to be pushed, especially by someone who once worked for you. As we broke up, Bob said we would probably hear Kingsley's decision in a couple of weeks.

## Children

The late morning was sunny but windy and cold when I returned to Castle Rock at ten minutes of twelve. Chappell was holed up in our small command post, by now littered by the remnants of two weeks of occupation. He worked on a laptop from the notes of the last night's discussions. Out of character, Bob was uptight; he told us to leave him alone; he needed to collect his thoughts before he went back into the arena. Court was to be reconvened at one.

When I later met up with Chappell he looked grim, although I could not believe we would lose. "I thought I would win in 1984, and I thought I would win in 1987. Now, I don't know what to think." I thought he was steeling himself against yet again another disappointment. We entered court a little before one. I left Bob staring at his papers and wandered around the back of the room.

Savitz and Gerash, looking somber and tense, walked in a few moments after we did and put their briefcases on the defendant's table. Gerash took off his blue Fedora. This was an important case for him too. After some forced pleasantries, Gerash went over to talk to Ms. L.A. *Times*. This was, I thought, going to be it. Then Carlson was brought up from the cells below, dressed in his sports jacket, slacks, button-down shirt, and tie. Then we waited.

Instead of Robert Kingsley walking in, thirty seventh graders trooped into court with their teachers and spread out over the wooden pews. Was this a civics class, I wondered? Were these kids learning about "the justice system"? Their fresh-faced innocence contrasted with what they were about to see. Then again, Carlson also did not look evil. He probably looked like one of these children not too many years before he shot his parents. I looked over the packed courtroom and saw the reporters from the two Denver papers and someone from the local *Castle Rock Gazette*. Ms. L.A. *Times* sat down right behind me.

## All the Way

Kingsley was ten minutes late. As soon as the door to the judge's chambers opened we all rose and waited for Kingsley to be seated.

Not one to stand on ceremony, Kingsley motioned for us to sit as he climbed the bench. The courtroom was dead still; the lull before the final storm.

Kingsley settled in his black high-backed swivel chair behind the wooden desk—called "the bench"—on the raised platform on the east side of the room. The low, flat November sunlight filtered through the high courtroom windows. Kingsley adjusted his black robes as he looked over the crowd. With a small nod and, I thought, a glimmer of a smile, he seemed to welcome the kids. His eyebrows were particularly arched. He looked the part.

Kingsley carefully tilted back in his chair and then stunned the court. "I have spent the last three nights going over the evidence," he said. "I won't insult counsels by listening to arguments . . . when I don't think there is anything that will change my mind . . . I have determined what I think is proper."

Not one of us expected this. I did not move a muscle. I could hear the reporters writing furiously.

Then Kingsley, as this dramatic moment in the packed courtroom played itself out, explained his decision. "When I was appointed to this case in 1987, Justice Day had already made an order in which he found the defendant incompetent . . . I went along with the decision of Justice Day," because [I] was "not particularly impressed with the testimony that was presented by the people, and the defense went all out. But things," Kingsley said after a long pause, "changed after that." Which way, I wondered, would he jump?

"The most significant thing to me in this entire proceeding occurred during . . . the attempted . . . questioning of the defendant by Dr. Orne." Then Kingsley started to talk about our April 16, 1988, tape. "I think I have seen almost everything that could take place in a courtroom," but "I have never seen a performance like the one put on by the defendant at that interview . . . I think I will remember it until I die." Stonewall made a big impression; our tape was worth ten thousand words.

Kingsley eased into it. "A great deal has been said about Dr. Orne," Kingsley went on. "To be perfectly honest, I have no conception of what he said or if he said anything. I was astounded," Kingsley said, "when someone told me he weighed two hundred and ninety pounds. I have no more recollection of him than one of the students who walked through that door this morning."

Orne, Kingsley said, tried to talk to Carlson in a very "polite manner." First, Carlson began to "rock back and forth, back and forth, back and forth . . . And after about ten minutes of it I thought, if he keeps this up I'm going to go through the ceiling. [But then] he threw himself on the floor where he laid as though he were dead . . . [then] two attendants . . . carried him out as though he were a dead man. I can see his heels now, the toes going straight up and the heels going down the floor where he was picked up.

"I asked the attendants, what did Carlson do when he got out of camera range? I was informed that he got up and called his lawyer in Denver and talked to him for thirty minutes. And, from that day on, I have been suspect of the behavior of Mr. Carlson." I was now certain we were going to win. But I did not know by how much.

Kingsley continued. "I viewed the tapes and I heard the testimony of Dr. Weissberg [and the rest] and all I saw was a repetition of the same behavior. Dr. Weissberg testified as to his beliefs to the competency of the defendant . . . that the scenes that we saw were not real scenes, but were something devised by the defendant in an effort . . . to keep from answering questions . . . I was amazed he could control the interviews with all those doctors, but he did."

Kingsley looked directly at Carlson. "I'm reminded of the old story," Kingsley said, "fool me once, shame on you; fool me twice, shame on me." Kingsley had just called Carlson a liar, fake, and fraud. Kingsley was going to go all the way.

I was sitting directly behind the prosecutor's table. All I could see was the back of Chappell's neatly combed head; it did not move an inch. I then looked over at Carlson but the lectern blocked my view. I could imagine Carlson sitting there, impassive, as the rug was pulled right out from under his feet. Kingsley had just come off the fence in a very big way.

"I will not comment on the defense counsel," he continued. "I'm sure I have great respect for both of them. They have done a tremendous job protecting their client's rights." Kingsley, I realized, was about to run through the cast of characters. I had more than a professional interest in what Kingsley would say.

"Perhaps the less said about the testimony of Dr. Rewey the better. I can't," he now went on, "help but mention Dr. Ralph Fisch . . . Mr. Carlson described the murder scene to him [in De-

cember, 1983]—it was a bizarre description but a description nonetheless . . . Now Dr. Fisch says the defendant has amnesia for
everything that took place before 1985 . . . But when I asked Dr.
Fisch about Carlson's statements he told me that it was not the
defendant talking! That was another person, that was another ego,
Holden, Blue, or Gray or whoever. In other words, Dr. Fisch has an
answer to everything, however ridiculous that answer may be."

And what of Dr. Newton? "Dr. Newton wavered first . . . there
was complete amnesia between the various alter egos, but then that
changed . . ." The amnesia, we all knew, was the heart of Carlson's case. How would Kingsley deal with it? The issue of amnesia,
of knowledge, and of memory had distorted the case from the beginning. I looked back at Kingsley; I could not tell if he looked at
Carlson or Savitz or Gerash as they sat at the defense table. What he
said next looked as if it was directed at the three. "I very frankly
can't buy this amnesia . . ." Kingsley read, "if it is convenient, he
doesn't remember . . . he can tell just as much as he wants . . ."

My heart raced. Kingsley had just driven a stake through the
central lie of Carlson's incompetence and swept away all the rulings
of the past five years. Carlson was competent and his MPD was as
dead as his parents and was now being buried.

I could hardly concentrate on what Kingsley said; I was too excited. But I heard his final words. "I do not have to decide on this
defendant's guilt or innocence, his sanity or insanity at the time of
the crime . . . I have only to determine whether or not the defendant is competent to proceed." But he had already made the decision.


### Abomination

In those ten minutes Kingsley undid years of legal paralysis. When
it was over and Kingsley had left the court, the reporters hurried for
the telephones, just like in the movies. Life imitating art. The theatrical image of the reporters racing for the phones was probably lost
on Carlson. But this had turned out to be a big story; bigger than
anyone had expected.

When he stood, Carlson showed no emotion. His face behind his
glasses was sallow, kind of pale. Always in sunglasses, he hadn't
been in the sun for years. Savitz was pale for another reason. Gerash

turned to no one in particular and called the ruling "an abomination."

I walked over to Chappell and shook his outstretched hand; as much as he tried, he could not hide his glee; an ear to ear grin kept popping out on his face although he tried to wipe it off while we were still in the presence of Carlson, Savitz, and Gerash. We then walked into the fresh November air. Bob kept thanking me as we headed to our little office across the street. "Getting you to work with us on Carlson," he said, "was the kind of lucky break which has always characterized this case." But then Chappell added something that clearly had been eating at him for years. "You should have become involved sooner, when I came to talk to you in 1985."

### Sixty-Eight Days

My excitement lasted only a short time. Ahead lay the sanity trial. Because of Carlson's right to a speedy trial, it would have to be scheduled very soon, probably within a month. The murder trial would follow right afterward if Carlson were ruled sane. Chappell would finally be able to lay out the damning facts, six years after the murders. Those trials had better, I thought, go as well as today. Behind his wooden stare, Carlson must really be enraged.

Chappell told me something else which, until moments ago, seemed far in the future. Even if found sane, there was an outside chance Carlson might only be convicted of second-degree murder. Then he could conceivably be out after serving twelve years, counting good time. Carlson, Chappell reminded me, had already been in custody for five. Carlson could be out pretty soon. But if we didn't win the sanity trial Carlson would be back in Pueblo, be fused, and could be out even sooner.

I called my wife with the news of our victory and also called Jim Shore, my chairman, who got me into this in the first place. While I was on the phone, Paul and Bob figured out that they had sixty-eight days to complete the sanity trial and begin the murder trial, if necessary. That meant, Bob said, that he would have to put off a trip to Nebraska so his ninety-six-year-old grandmother could see his twins for the first time. Susan and I had planned a trip to Vienna, Czechoslovakia, and Israel for December. That trip was, Chappell told me, out of the question.

Sixty-eight days; not much time to savor the victory. Six-year-old files had to be reopened, witnesses tracked down, police reports dusted off, and the evidence lined up. Bevis was already making calls. On Friday, the trial dates would be set by Judge Turelli, the original judge got off the case by Chappell in 1984. Chappell would be in the same courtroom where he did not want to be in the beginning, over five years before.

Before I left, Chappell also told me he worried the defense would try to exclude all psychiatrists who evaluated Carlson after Eddie Day's 1984 ruling from the upcoming sanity trial. I would be barred and that would leave Chappell with, once again, only Reichlin and Fine. Chappell did not know if Turelli would go for it. It was then that I realized that Robert Kingsley was done. We would have to educate a new judge all over again.

# · C H A P T E R ·
## T W E N T Y - O N E
# RETRIBUTION

Friday was a gray, dismal day and I felt a posttrial depression setting in. The first-page headline CARLSON RULED COMPETENT TO STAND TRIAL was nice, but Susan and I were unhappy because of our trip. I also began to worry about Carlson's sanity trial, the last hurdle before his trial for murder. There would be a new judge and a jury. That morning, the *Post* published another list of Carlson's personalities in big, black letters: JUSTIN, STEVE, BLUE, GRAY, NORMAN, STACEY, BLACK, ANTICHRIST. Even defeated, MPD did not go away.

Later on Friday, Bob called me. Turelli had set the sanity trial for December 5 and the murder trial for January, 2, 1990. Our trip out the window, Chappell heard my disappointment because he added that "it was lucky that my loss in front of Kingsley in October 1987 led to you. Imagine," he said, "if that did not happen." I thanked him. Luck comes in funny ways.

Bob then said that the defense had told Turelli that the trust was almost empty. They wanted, Chappell said, the state to begin to pay for Carlson's defense. Chappell laughed. "Those guys won't say how much was in it but I bet it was pushing five hundred thousand." Savitz admitted that Carlson's defense had cost "hundreds of thousands of dollars." And, Chappell added, "that guy has cost the state of Colorado well over half a million and we have not yet gone to trial." When Chappell said he was still figuring out how to get me into the sanity trial, I could not imagine missing it. I had a personal stake in the outcome. I did not want Carlson walking around on the streets.

I called Sue, who tried to be understanding, but her irritation came through. Ross Carlson, she said, had interfered enough with our lives. Legal cases, I told her, took on a life of their own. There was nothing I could do about it.


## Bad Blood

Sue and I were out early on Sunday morning. When we returned, the light blinked on our answering machine. It was Chappell. "Mike, give me a call. I have some unbelievable news." I thought I heard pressure in his voice. As I punched in his number, I wondered why he had called so early. I was still so keyed up from Thursday I had the thought that Carlson had somehow escaped and Chappell wanted to warn me to watch out.

I was wrong. Chappell picked up the phone after only one ring. "Sorry to call you so early, Mike. But we have reason to believe that Ross Carlson has leukemia." It sank in slowly. I had a hard time believing the words. Then I thought of Carlson's sallow face right after Kingsley ruled. It was not a lack of sun or the loss; at that moment insane white blood cells were overrunning his body.

Bob told me what he knew. Thursday, Carlson developed a nose bleed, common at our altitude, but this one did not go away. Friday, the jail nurse saw Carlson was pale and had unexplained bruises. She drew blood and sent it off for tests, which showed too many white blood cells and not enough red blood cells and platelets, findings compatible with leukemia. Saturday, he was rushed to a hospital in Littleton and given four units of blood.

But now, Chappell told me, Carlson refused treatment. Nothing was ever straightforward with Carlson and I suddenly wanted Carlson to be in my hospital so that I could watch him. I asked Bob to find out if he could be transferred. "Out of my hands," he told me. "He is the prisoner of the Douglas County Sheriff. I will pass along your suggestion." Before I hung up, Chappell jokingly bet the defense would say Carlson's leukemia was due to his MPD. I then asked Chappell to check whether all his personalities were sick.

This was an empty joke. For two years, I had worked to have

Carlson put behind bars. Six days ago, I was frightened when he threatened my life. Three days ago we won a complete courtroom victory. Now I heard that Carlson might die. Shaken, I felt relieved and I felt guilty because of my relief.

Bob called me that night. Carlson would "accept" treatment only if his metal cuffs were replaced with leather restraints. The imperial Carlson; first, he thought he could kill with impunity, then he controlled the state hospital, and now he wanted to dictate the treatment for his leukemia. What about the transfer, I asked. Chappell said he would see what he could do.


**Monday**

Carlson's leukemia made the evening news and the front pages of both papers the next morning. He was getting more press than Alexander and Jesus combined, but not in the way he wanted. When I got to work, Imogene, my secretary, asked me if Carlson's illness could be fake. I told her no. I did not tell her that when Bob Chappell first called me, I had the same idea.

She then wondered if Ross Carlson had gotten leukemia because he lost the trial. I also said no. He had, I now knew, been tired for weeks. But, I added, stress could disrupt immune functioning. The night before, my sister had a different explanation. "Carlson was an extremist," she said. "He got angry at his parents, so he killed them. He lost big in court, he got leukemia."

A few moments later, I called Chappell, who told me that it looked like I would get my wish; Carlson was being shipped over. Then we talked about the timing of the sanity trial. Even if Carlson recovered quickly, I thought Chappell should postpone it. "Carlson will look weak, sick, and helpless, no matter what," I said. "He will be missing his hair. He will look pale. The jury might have a hard time with that, and sympathy for Carlson will not help." Chappell agreed and then added that it was "crazy for Gerash and Savitz to allow their client to cook more cancer cells while they encourage him to fight the shackles."

At 11:35 A.M., Ross Carlson was finally admitted to University Hospital and our cancer unit on 6 East, two floors below the psychiatric unit where he went on August 19, 1983, after he killed his parents. He started here; he might end here. I thought that was fitting.

**Shackles**

6 East is an open unit, not a prison ward. Carlson was, therefore, shackled and guarded by a sheriff's deputy. But the nurses were worried. This was no ordinary patient; 6 East had just gone through the wringer with another famous patient. The star quarterback of the University of Colorado's football team had just died after weeks of agony and publicity. The nurses had a terrible time watching him die. They did not want another public patient so soon again. Some of the nurses made jokes about being sued—jokes that no one thought were funny. I did laugh when someone asked me if Carlson had "Multiple Myeloma."

I got my first call at 1:00 P.M. from the hospital chaplain and at 2:00 P.M. from Ginger, the head nurse on 6 East. We decided to meet on Tuesday to discuss managing Carlson. As of now, he was being kept in a single room at the very end of the hall. Carlson's white blood cell count was now over 200,000, twenty to forty times the expected 5,000–10,000 range. His platelet count was only 25,000, a very low figure which meant he could bleed at any moment. He was also severely anemic.

A bone marrow biopsy confirmed the diagnosis: Carlson had Acute Lymphoblastic Leukemia, ALL. He was in a new fight for his life. With ALL, seventy percent in Carlson's age group died within two years and ten to twenty-five percent within the first one hundred days. But no sooner was Carlson admitted, than the legal routine began, again.

**Hospital Policy**

Carlson agreed to chemotherapy, but when the moment came to begin, he refused. He would not, he said, "consent" to treatment if kept in restraints which were, ironically, like those used by Fairbairn five years before which Black broke out of so theatrically. It was policy to restrain prisoners on open wards. But if restrained in "two points," Carlson would refuse treatment. Wrist shackles "reminded" Carlson of childhood abuse, Savitz told the nurses, doctors, and the court.

I should not have been surprised when Savitz and Gerash swung into action. It did not matter that this was a different hospital, a different situation, and a different disease. This was how it was from the start. All of Carlson's care had been contested and nothing could be done without threat of court action. Why, I thought to myself, should this be any different? Savitz filed a motion with Turelli.

On Tuesday, the conference room was packed with Ginger the head nurse, the doctors who were responsible for Carlson, our chaplain, a representative of the university police and, of course, our legal counsel. I gave them a brief version of what I knew of Carlson. Except for the need for security, treat Carlson, I said, like any other patient. I then learned that Carlson had been checked into our hospital under a false name, Nicholas Douglas. Of all the patients to give a false name to, Carlson, I said, was the wrong guy. Change that to Ross Michael Carlson. And apparently, the Douglas County Sheriff's office left a tape recorder running in his room at all times. Some regular patient.

Everyone was frightened of Carlson, of his attorneys and what they might do. Escape was also a major concern. I told the staff that, no matter what, Carlson had to always remain in restraints. He was, I reminded everyone, after all, a killer. They needed no reminding. We decided to meet daily. As I walked out of the room, the chaplain wondered "Does he have the inner strength to withstand the onslaught of chemotherapy?" The way she asked it provided the answer. No.


### Divine Retribution

I did not know if we would ever find out. Savitz subpoenaed Carlson's medical doctors to court to justify the wrist restraint. The doctors were furious; they had other patients to care for and no time for what they felt were frivolous attacks. Some of the doctors told me in private that they were so angry that they wanted to send Carlson back to jail, untreated, where he certainly would die.

On this, Savitz and Gerash were out of their league. In 1984 Chappell's judgment had been dulled by the overwhelming evidence he had of Carlson's guilt. Now the defense was blinded by habit. Did Savitz and Gerash really believe Carlson would beat a murder rap and now leukemia? Could Carlson dispense with leukemia just like he thought he could pull off the perfect crime? Ginger told me in her droll way that Carlson's leukemia would not be cured "just because those lawyers were involved." I agreed.

On Wednesday, I talked to Pat Robb at the state hospital. This was, she said, "divine retribution" if she ever saw it. "It was a good thing that he started to bleed on Friday and not before Kingsley ruled. If he had bled earlier, we might never have finished the case."

Later on Wednesday, as his fever rose, Savitz argued about the conditions under which Carlson would "accept" chemotherapy, while Carlson was being riddled by his sick, leukemic cells. It was as if Carlson had all the time in the world.

## The Resurrection of MPD

On Thursday, one week after Kingsley's ruling, Gerash told Judge Turelli that it was MPD which made Ross Carlson refuse treatment. One of his "alters," said Gerash, had told Carlson to reject chemotherapy unless the wrist cuff and the long chain attached to it were removed. It was an unexplained "phenomenon" of his childhood. "For some reason, he was bound at one time," Gerash said. "He can't take the shackle on his right hand." It must have been abuse.

Carlson did not mind, said Gerash, leg restraints. Besides, said Savitz, only University Hospital wanted to keep the wrist cuff on; the sheriff's office did not care. Judge Turelli ordered the hospital police chief to court on the following Monday to tell him why a wrist shackle was necessary. Had Turelli forgotten why Carlson was arrested in the first place? Would he want to work next to a partially restrained Ross Carlson who had lost the trial of his life and had nothing to lose? Turelli might be the judge for the sanity trial; Savitz and Gerash were already educating him.

I was concerned about the hearing for another reason. I worried that Savitz or Gerash would raise competency again. Were they going to argue this time that Ross Carlson was not competent to refuse treatment? I knew that Carlson should be restrained in two points, both wrist and leg, but I wanted to avoid a hearing in front of Turelli even more. So I called the chief of our university police and tried to talk him into removing the wrist shackle. He told me about an inadequately restrained prisoner who shot one of his officers. He was worried about Carlson's potential to kill again. "If he was so suicidal in 1982 when he tried to buy the dynamite," he asked, "why did he also want to buy an untraceable gun? What would he care if it were traceable or not if he just wanted to kill himself?" Good question. He refused to remove the restraint.

Our hospital attorney, an ex-army prosecutor from Kalispell,

Montana, also wanted to go to court. He worried about the liability to other patients and staff. But, I thought, he enjoyed the prospect of a good fight and of putting the defense in their place. When I kidded him about that he said no. "We are just following our rules."

That afternoon, the doctors looked glum. Carlson was worse; his white cells were multiplying and looking younger, uglier, and disorganized. The doctors were furious they could not begin to stamp them out. Ginger said they could not wait much longer. Carlson's tumor mass was expanding, she said. With more cells to kill, Carlson would be sicker when treatment began and could "blow out his kidneys." She then told me something I already knew. "Those lawyers and that doctor are way too involved." That doctor was Fairbairn. No kidding. "Carlson thinks he has control here, but we cannot afford to wait."

That night, Chappell could have cared less about the restraints and was not worried about Carlson escaping. "He cannot check into any hospital in the United States without getting arrested. He would die on the run." But then Bob added with concern, "Maybe he would kill again before he died or was found."

**Friday Compromise: "Is Everyone Happy?"**
On Friday, I planned to convince our attorney to compromise. But when I found he had just left for some early season skiing, I talked to his boss who agreed with me and called Savitz. Would Carlson "submit" to treatment if he were secured only in leg hobbles attached to his bed? Yes. We faxed Savitz the agreement. From now on, Carlson's ankles would be shackled to his bed, but his still powerful arms would be free. When I saw Savitz, he was relieved. "I am so grateful," he said. "Now we can start treating him," as if he had no part in the delay.

When Ross was told, he responded with "Is everyone happy with this? Now, I don't want this to happen unless everyone is happy." He spoke barely above a whisper; his mouth was inflamed and lymph nodes in his neck had, by now, gotten very large, packed full of leukemic cells.

I worried about how secure this really was. Much had changed in the last few days. Carlson had lost a lot since last Thursday; he first lost his legal battle and now his health. Our police grumbled but the

Douglas County Deputies had known Carlson for years. The deputies thought Carlson would be safe.

Carlson's chemotherapy began at three, Friday afternoon. Chemotherapy means poison, poison that kills all the living cells in the body. Only, the fast-growing leukemia cells are supposed to die first. The side effects of this particular treatment are horrendous; the drugs, like the leukemia, could kill Carlson.

## Nurses

In hospitals, doctors prescribe tests and treatments but nurses take care of the patients and have to deal with their nausea, vomiting, sores, pains, and fears. And the nurses on 6 East began to have trouble with Carlson. They were, they told me, trained as caretakers. Many were parents with teen or young adult sons, Carlson's age, and felt conflicted when they had tender and sad feelings for a murderer. Ginger told me she had a twenty-five-year-old son and she thought of her son each time she walked into Carlson's room. "There is a part of me," she told me, "that thinks that he is hurting and there is a part of me who says who gives a shit. He killed his parents, after all."

Two nurses asked me if Carlson had been adopted, a question I did not understand. Were they interested in the genetic transmission of sociopathy? I finally realized what it was. Everyone who came into contact with Carlson had to come to terms with what he did. These women could not conceive of a child who killed his parents. Therefore, they thought, he must have been adopted. Adoption, like MPD, was a shield. If adopted, Carlson did not, after all, kill his own flesh and blood. But it was true: Carlson had killed his biological mother and father, the two people he now needed the most.

Ginger, who had seen many people riddled with leukemia, told me that in order to survive this harsh ordeal, patients had to have unusual inner strength. She had the same impression that the chaplain had; Ross did not have it. The weakness of character which allowed Carlson to kill his parents—his lack of inner strength—might lead to his death now.

On Friday, November 17, one week after his treatment began, Carlson complained of severe pain in his jaw and stomach. The poison was killing Carlson's cells, all of them. X rays showed that his colon was massively distended, a side effect of the medicine. Surgery was contemplated but rejected as too risky. His body crumbling, Carlson was in great distress.

Sunday the *Post* ran a column about the cost of Carlson's treatment, $1180 a day, paid by Douglas County citizens. The $1180 did not include the costs for the twenty-four hour security, another $453 a day. The columnist asked whether the charge was for eight rooms —one for each personality—or just one dormitory? How much, he asked, do we have to spend on the Eight Faces of Ross Carlson?

## The Gun

A sick killer, one who might die, does not always look dangerous. Familiarity had bred a sense of security. Carlson's friends were not searched when they visited and his shackles were not always on. The Douglas County dog catcher took the night shift, more than once.

On Sunday night, November 19, Carlson asked to go to the bathroom. A small, female deputy removed Carlson's shackles so he could move more easily. This was against procedure but this was not the first time Carlson had been totally free.

As he stood up, Carlson lunged for her gun. Carlson was strong enough, despite his debilitating disease, to get it free. But as he grabbed for it, the deputy jammed her finger between the trigger and the trigger guard. As long as she kept her finger wedged in there, Carlson could not pull the trigger and the gun could not be fired. At least not that way; the hammer could still be fanned. The deputy could do little else as the much heavier Carlson knocked her to the ground.

In hospitals, evenings are for catching up on paperwork. As the struggle began, two interns sat in the doctor's station down the hall, writing their notes behind closed doors. But they heard something through the glass. First it was a woman's voice screaming "Stop it, stop it." And then "Help. Help." They ran past other hospital rooms full of startled cancer patients and their visitors. When they got to the end of the hall they turned right and burst into Carlson's room. As soon as they did they, too, were in immediate, mortal danger.

They saw the deputy and Carlson on the floor, thrashing about, both with their hands on the gun. The pistol waved wildly around the room. But within moments, the two interns and the little deputy pinned Carlson and pulled the pistol from his grasp.

Rumors flew around the hospital. Before she knew the full story, a psychiatry resident called me at home. "Carlson got a gun," she started with. For a split second, I pictured Carlson as he raced down the same darkened back stairs he eyed so often in 1983 and then bolted out the side door into the street. I breathed a sigh of relief when I heard that everything was under control and no one had been hurt. Twenty minutes later I arrived on 6 East. Ginger was already there. I wanted to talk with the nurses, doctors, and Ross.

By now, Ross was shackled; both wrists and both ankles securely locked to his bed. When I walked into his room, he would not open his eyes. He lay there, pajama top off, in his black sunglasses. Half-naked, he emitted a posed, languid, insouciance, even now, so close to death. It was: "Ross Carlson on his death bed." Nothing about him seemed real. He then told me, eyes still firmly shut, "I want to die." I told the nursing staff and guards to keep him in four point restraints until further notice.

That night, two nurses were too scared to go into his room. But the young doctors, a man and a woman, acted as if what just happened were all in a night's work and as if nothing were wrong. It was every day that they wrestled a leukemic murderer for a gun.

In fact, the only thing which worried them was that Carlson, because of his low platelets, might bleed from this violent struggle. They examined him and found no evidence of bleeding. He did need a transfusion but he refused and said, instead, "David will take care of me."

## It Must Have Been Black

Carlson's escape/suicide attempt was all over the news. The next morning I listened to the radio as I drove to work. "Ross Carlson had gotten a gun at University Hospital. It was wrestled away. A hospital spokesman did not say which personality made the grab."

David Savitz was clearly upset when I met him on 6 East at 7:45 A.M. "I have tried to be his friend, his therapist, and his lawyer," he told me. "But it has been very hard." It was definitely not an escape attempt, Savitz said. But, he added, he did not know "which personality" tried for the gun. Carlson, Savitz began to explain, "attempted suicide" because he was very upset about "losing"

Bernauer Newton. Ross had believed that the fatherly Newton would treat him after he got out of the hospital but just learned that Newton wanted to retire.

I left Savitz talking to one of the interns about the timing of the gun-grab. Savitz was trying to figure out which personality tried for the gun. As I thought about what Savitz just told me, I realized that Carlson still expected to get out. A little later, on hematology rounds, Bob Fairbairn told the assembled doctors and nurses that "it must have been Black who grabbed the gun." But to Ginger the guy sure looked like Ross Carlson. The defense did not give up easily; everything Carlson did was explained by MPD.

I did not know what Carlson wanted to do with the deputy's gun. It might have been a suicide attempt, but others might have died with him. If it suited him, I'm sure Carlson would not have hesitated to take a few doctors, nurses, or even patients along.

We held a press conference at noon. In a room crowded by cameras and reporters, the head of University Hospital talked only in generalities and wisely did not say if it was a suicide or escape attempt. "It was," he said, "a very dangerous situation." He reassured the press that we would do everything to protect patients and staff. We were, he said, all very lucky. Prisoner policies would be changed. The little deputy would not be on duty again and neither would the county dog catcher who had also covered a few overnight shifts. Deputies would also not be allowed to carry guns onto the hospital ward.

But no guns made our chief nervous. What would happen, he later asked me, if one of Carlson's friends tried to bust Carlson loose? You traded one problem for another, I told him. From a medical standpoint, this was the right place for Carlson. We were expert in the treatment of leukemia. But hospitals like ours were not designed for killers.

On Monday night, Carlson had no normal white blood cells left in his body. Savitz helped convince Carlson to continue his treatments. The next day, when the news of his attempt, whatever it was, left the front pages, Carlson sulked. He asked one of his nurses, "What is all this stuff about the Berlin Wall? Why am I not on the front page of the paper?"

## The 2,290th Day

The inevitable happened the day before Thanksgiving. At four in the afternoon, Carlson's body, which was in high-speed decay, could no longer stand the strain and now splintered, this time for real.

Carlson was reading about King Herod when he began his descent into death. He bled into his eyes, so he could not see and bled into his lungs, so he could not breathe. "I cannot," he told a nurse, "get enough air." Like his mother, Ross Carlson was drowning in his own blood. He was quickly transferred to intensive care, but this was the end. When I hurried over to the intensive care unit, with its single rooms of high-tech suffering, I ran into David Savitz, who stood vigil in front of Carlson's door as his doctors huddled around their patient inside. But it was like giving medicine to a dead man. Savitz, close to tears, told me that "they don't teach you this in law school." He looked beat and completely worn out.

Savitz said he felt closer to Carlson than to any other client. He found it "spooky" that he developed leukemia following the hearing and talked as if Carlson's leukemia had something to do with his MPD. It felt odd trying to help Savitz deal with the death of Carlson. Finally, Savitz admitted Carlson was "like a son." I did not remind him what Carlson did to his last father. On a nearby desk was an elegant fruit basket Savitz brought for the nurses to thank them for taking care of Ross. As I left, Savitz sat alone in the ICU and waited for Ross Carlson to die.

At 8:52 A.M., on Thanksgiving morning, the quintessential family holiday, Carlson died alone. Ginger called me. When I heard that Carlson was dead, I had an empty feeling tinged with sadness and relief. Arrested on Yom Kippur, he died on Thanksgiving. In the abstract, I am against capital punishment. But it had taken 2,290 days. After 2,290 days, justice delayed, in my opinion, was justice finally done.

I then called Chappell. It was over, I said, when he picked up the phone. Chappell was quiet; we both could not believe that it was the end. Here we were, driving for the final touchdown when they turned out the lights. We had lost a golden opportunity to nail the multiple personality defense in court. I said that it was too bad that anyone had to die. Chappell grunted what sounded like agreement. But at that moment, I was not sure that either of us meant it.

Even after Ross's death, Gerash argued for MPD. On the evening news Gerash told a reporter that all of Carlson's personalities had died in the Intensive Care Unit today; all of Carlson's personalities, Gerash said, were finally "fused" in death. "Nature is cruel," he told another reporter. "The only thing crueler than nature is man." I did not know if Gerash fully understood what he had just said. Ross Carlson had been a very cruel son. The next day, Savitz told a reporter that when Carlson died "he knew that I loved him. He knew that I cared."

In his handwritten will, Carlson asked to be buried next to his mother and that a flower be placed on her grave every Friday. After his autopsy, Ross Carlson was interred next to his mother and father at the Sunset Memorial Park, Minneapolis, Minnesota. Of the three- to five-hundred-thousand-dollar trust, the papers reported that only twelve thousand dollars remained. The report went on to say that Ross wanted that money to be donated to a fund for abused children.

That weekend, as I started to pack up the boxes of notes and records I came across a letter Ross wrote on December 15, 1983, to people who befriended him after he killed his parents.

"The Lord's hand moves with reason," Carlson wrote in his cramped hand, "though we do not allways understand his reasoning . . . It is strange that we fear death. Dose not the Christian faith promes us a better place . . . How lucky we are to be Christians! For the Lord provides for us . . ."

# 4

## THE FIRST SIN

# ENIGMA

The emptiness stuck with me, but the end of the battle was not the only reason why I felt a void. My memories of Carlson quickly became a jumble of snapshots; his was a story without coherence. When the hunt was over, Carlson disappeared into thin air. For six years, despite the plots and subplots in and out of the courtroom, Carlson lacked a center. He was all flash and show; razzle-dazzle. Now that Ross Carlson was gone, the question of who he was and why he did what he did remained.

### Real or Fake?

I was convinced that Ross Carlson was a fake. Multiple personality disorder was Carlson's fallback position when his movie alibi crumbled; *Billy Milligan* was just part of his many months of preparation. The day after he killed his parents, Carlson blew off Dr. Wilets with "ask Justin" when Wilets asked Ross who had killed Rod and Marilyn. Public Defender Craig Truman then had Carlson examined by John Macdonald and Sy Sundell. What Macdonald and Sundell learned convinced Truman not to file an insanity plea. Carlson replaced Truman with Gerash.

Three months later, Carlson told Fisch about Antichrist and Justin; then came the February telephone calls and collage. Aided by the questioning of Ralph Fisch and Bob Fairbairn, he refined his roles and may even have come to believe that he was a multiple. Then, with the help of his money and lawyers, he played a six and one-half year shell game and finally lost. Carlson brought out Steve, Blue, Norman, Black, whenever he wanted to. The *A*-plus actor used altered states to his own end. Carlson knew what he was doing when he did it.

But multiple or not, it took me five years to understand that MPD was beside the point; it did not explain Ross Carlson's motivation. Multiples do not routinely execute their parents. Ross Carlson was a real killer and killed his parents because of who he was. And, once stripped of his multiplicity, the central question remained. Who was Ross Carlson and why did he break the fifth and sixth commandments? Honor your father and your mother; thou shalt not murder. For me, the linchpin of his case was still missing.

## How and Why?

I did not feel that way in the beginning. When I first went to see Carlson in 1984, two things were on my mind: how and why? His plan revealed a cold, calculating, predatory creativity, almost the perfect crime. I marveled at the fact that Carlson missed his goal by the errant kick of a football.

The second thing was: why? My knee-jerk answer was that Ross Carlson had been severely physically abused. Many people still said that when they first heard about Carlson. What I learned, however, of the outlines of the Carlsons' life did not make them much different from any other of a million young families. Except that Ross blew his parents' brains out all over Cottonwood Road.

Ross was the only child born to a young couple in Minneapolis, Minnesota. According to his mother, Marilyn, Ross was a "good baby," an "active toddler," a precociously "verbal boy" who grew into a man with good looks and a quick mind. Until he was two and a half, both parents attended school two nights a week. But, Marilyn was quick to add, she spent days at home with Ross playing, reading to him, and caring for her son. Ross, Marilyn once explained, was asleep by the time the sitter arrived. Ross talked at twenty months and spoke in sentences at two. At four he campaigned for Hubert Humphrey. A year later, the family moved to Colorado.

Ross did have some difficulties. At nineteen months he sustained the wrist burn, which required a two-day hospitalization for skin grafts. At three Ross had bouts of bronchitis. And despite his obvious intelligence, first grade was "disastrous." Ross had to take special reading classes and had trouble with spelling. While not a behavioral problem, Marilyn said, "We never heard positive things from the teachers . . . until the fifth grade when the teacher commented on his superior verbal ability."

What was of more importance, according to his mother, was that for most of his life, Ross had no close friends. He had, in Marilyn's words, "several friends, but no 'best' friend." That changed in the tenth grade when he began to lift weights and, in his mother's words, "the girls began to call." Marilyn thought that "things were going well during his senior year." She felt "quite blue about the prospect of him leaving home . . ."

## Abuse?

What about physical abuse? During their odd December 1983 interviews, Fisch and Carlson had the following interchange:

FISCH:    Now, hear your parents' voices. Do the voices seem meaningful, or are they merely patterns of sound in the air?

CARLSON:    . . . I hear things like—brush your dog, take out the trash . . . commands . . . I    guess.    Ah . . . My mother has a Margaret martyrdom-type sound to it. "It's okay. You do what you need to do. I'll take care of all the dishes by myself." . . . My mother used to use guilt very expertly, to move me to action . . . I still get a very strong sense that I am being held in some kind of contempt. Ah . . . a feeling of "You lazy scumbag. Why don't you do any work?" That's, that's what I get . . .

Brush your dog and take out the trash are not exactly abusive commands. Carlson did tell Fisch of his father's feces-filled-diaper attack. "I sat there and cried," Carlson remembered, "and I decided to control my internal functions so that would never happen again." Carlson also told Dr. Greg Trautt that his father once lashed out at him with a knife when he refused to take out the garbage. Were these self-serving reports or true? Carlson knew that his lawyers and psychiatrists wanted to find abuse; who knew what to believe? Though Brian Bevis found no confirmation of abuse, it might have happened.

But even if Ross Carlson was "abused" by the diapers-in-the-face and by harsh ridicule, that was not enough to explain why he killed his parents when he was nineteen. Though the issue of abuse lingered, the "why" question soon dropped away, coopted by the chaos of legal maneuvering. The *why* had been replaced by another, *how;* how to put Ross Carlson in jail.

### The End of the Hunt
But when Carlson died, the hunt was over. With each day, I could take a broader view of Carlson because I no longer planned testimony or strategy. As Carlson faded from the front pages, I no longer looked for advantages and handholds. The blinders imposed by courtroom tactics fell away. I could now consider questions—and answers—I had set aside.

That was when I had the good fortune to meet Michael Batagglia. I knew Carlson as a murderer, but Batagglia knew him as a friend. What he told me made Carlson more real; Michael gave me a glimpse of Carlson before he was distorted by the harsh glare of homicide, MPD, the courts, and the law. He thought that "it was financial," "one of his deals" gone bad, but Batagglia had no clear idea why Carlson killed his parents. I was relieved when he told me that he was sure "that nothing was wrong with him other than what he did." I had worried how the battle had distorted my own objectivity. Batagglia's assessment, as an outsider, helped.

Because I found my meeting with Michael useful, I decided to revisit other important people in Carlson's story. I wanted to hear if their views had changed after the battle had cooled and they had time to digest and to think. I wanted to hear how they would put things together now.

**Other Voices**

Late in the spring, 1991, I called Bob Chappell. When I told him about my chance meeting with Michael Batagglia, he revved up as he did when Carlson was alive. "Wasn't Michael one of Carlson's early personalities? He always had," he said, "somebody in mind for each personality, someone he could pattern himself after. We found the small child Blue, we found the weight lifter Stacey. Now here is Michael. We found someone he knew for almost all of his personalities . . ."

When we met, Chappell looked relaxed in a way I had not seen before. I told him I was interested in his views on the whole case. Chappell began with Kingsley.

"You see, you did not know the whole story, but I met him in 1975. He was chief judge and I was his clerk. I worked for him for thirteen months and knew that he was fond of me. And I know I was fond of him. But we drifted apart. It was my fault. I should have stayed in touch. The longer I stayed away, the more I hoped that I would not run into him. When I decided to get rid of Eddie Day— that was the hardest decision of my life—I worried we might get Kingsley. It was uncomfortable when we did. I explained our past to the defense but they did not object. I could not talk to him during the trial and I have not talked to him since.

"When I worked for him, Kingsley would say things which would stick with me. I remember once when a deal fell apart he said that 'once there was a time when a lawyer's word was good enough. Now, everything has to be in writing.' You told me that I should have been more suspicious and devious with the Carlson case, but if good lawyers these days have to be tricky then I will never be a good lawyer . . .

"At first, when the sheriff brought the case to us, we declined it. Not enough evidence. I drove to Carlson's house and I saw him being taken away. I saw Kenny Cortez come over and questioned. I watched the autopsies. I got a real sense of how cold-blooded this was. They were good shots. What Carlson told Alan Fine was true. It was like this: Bang. Bang.

"The bullet he shot into Rod's head went around and around and scrambled his brains. The bullet he shot into his mother's head did not kill her right away but tore away part of her jaw and she drowned in her own blood. No, I don't know what would have happened if we had not found the black bag. Carlson would have gotten out and had a chance to destroy the evidence.

"Why did I lose in 1984? A lot of reasons. Inexperience. At that time I thought it was all my fault, but we lost because Day was vulnerable to the seductiveness of MPD. I fought against MPD and that was a mistake. I was totally stunned when we lost . . .

"I could not find any experts. Once I got out the phone book and started to call but I got the most amazing excuses. I remember when Gerash made that comment in April 1984, that Carlson might sue anyone who he thought had broken the doctor-patient relationship. Dr. Wilets would never talk to us. Sundell and Macdonald could not talk. It was obvious to me why Gerash would not want them to see the inside of the courtroom.

"I knew Gerash would always hire someone with more experience and have one more expert than me. No way could we win a battle of money. But I thought that reason and common sense would prevail. I always thought that you present the facts and it would come out right." He shook his head.

"Even you said no in 1985, but you had a strong effect on me anyway. I remember your words exactly. You said 'I don't want any part of it.' What you said after that told me that I was doing the right thing. You said, and this is an exact quote, 'This is the most dangerous person I have ever seen.' After that, I decided to stay on track and not plead the case out.

"So when Savitz and Gerash came to my boss, Bob Gallagher, after Kingsley's 1987 ruling and wanted Gallagher to roll over on the insanity plea, no way that was going to happen. Over my dead body. I told Gallagher that you were now involved and were bringing in Orne. Gallagher agreed with me completely.

"You were the turning point. No doctor, no matter how qualified, from the state hospital would be believed. They needed to get someone between the state hospital and Carlson, to buffer them, and you did it. The letters you wrote to Kingsley were significant. I know that from the response we got from the defense. The reason I know he read them was when they objected he said 'There is nothing wrong with them.' "

Chappell then mentioned Carlson's first lawyer, Public Defender Craig Truman. Truman, Chappell had told me in the past, learned something from Carlson that had a lot to do with the case. Somehow, Chappell knew what it was but would not divulge it since he was sworn to secrecy. "Maybe," Chappell said, "Truman will tell you about it. If true, what I learned tells me that Carlson perpetrated one of the biggest frauds on the justice system ever . . .

"Why did he kill his parents? I am not sure that I know the answer to why he killed them. He put together an execution plan and laid the foundation for a mental defense a long time before he did it. We know that he was strongly motivated by the prospect of inheriting money but I have trouble making that my sole explanation. How far back in his life do you go to search for the answer to that kind of question? Pretty far.

"Why Antichrist? We wondered how much a play religion had in his life. His parents practiced religion constantly. He was required to attend church regularly. In regards to Antichrist, it just occurs to me, it may have some significance in relation to Frank Christianson, the name he wrote on a piece of paper the night he killed his parents. We never knew what Frank Christianson meant. I really don't know why he did it . . ."

Chappell might be on to something, I thought. I, too, had recently begun to think that there was a connection between Antichrist and Frank Christianson.


**Kingsley**

I then met with Kingsley. With trepidation I had called him, but I need not have worried. "Can I collect anything that will be of help to you?" he asked. "No," I replied. "I just want to hear you talk."

I easily found Kingsley's house in a pleasant south Denver neighborhood. He greeted me with a handshake and the raspy voice I had liked the moment I met him. We walked into the paneled family room, which overlooked a tidy patio. Kingsley pulled out newspaper clippings and asked if I wanted them. No, I told him, I had them all. I then asked him if he would talk about Carlson. He, like Batagglia, needed no prompting.

"He fooled me completely . . ." Kingsley was silent then sat up suddenly. "Did they do an autopsy? I am sure he did something to himself . . . maybe poisoned himself." Kingsley seemed disappointed when I told him that Carlson died of leukemia. "I was sure he had done something . . ."

"Chappell? Nice kid and a good lawyer. But during that first hearing Bob did not have the ammunition. The weight of the testimony the defense produced outdid anything he was able to come up with . . . he had not come close to matching the testimony that Gerash was able to produce.

"So long as Carlson remained devoid of any personality he was safe. But when he started to act up, like on the tapes or in court, he made a fool of himself. What was the thing that changed my mind? It was something that he did with his eyes . . . What was it? . . . Jesus, I can't think of it.

"I started to think that guy was a hell of an actor. I watched him in front of me every day. Everything that he did was to impress me but had the opposite effect. I began to change my mind early in the second hearing in 1989. I watched his gestures, his doing this and that, until I was sick. He was so phony. I wish I could remember what he did with his eyes that tipped me off . . .

"Carlson had a tough break when I got assigned to the case. I had been involved with more bizarre cases than anyone around. Carlson could have gotten a young well-meaning judge and he would have been home free. Now Carlson was up against someone who does not trust anything anyone says in a courtroom . . .

"I always liked Eddie Day. He was a good judge, perfectly honest. I never was going to dismiss those charges. Walter was just making words with all those motions . . .

"I'll never forget. Carlson took off his glasses—he had these dark glasses you could not see through—I was watching him all the time. The eyes . . . What in the hell—I can't remember. He was so well controlled. It just seemed to me all his gestures were exaggerated. He overdid it." He thought for a moment. "That was it," Kingsley said as he suddenly sat up. "That was what it was he did with his eyes. When he would change personality he would do all that blinking. He wore those damn glasses and I could not see his eyes. But once he forgot to do the Spiegel thing." Now Kingsley was very excited. "It was the damnedest thing. I was looking right at his eyes and he switched personalities. That is what changed the damn thing for me. He made the mistake of changing personalities with his glasses off and he forgot the old Spiegel. That clinched it for me." Kingsley smiled and sat back.

"Why he did it, why he killed them, I do not know. No, I do not think that people are evil. They are just stupid. They don't think about the consequences. But Carlson did not fall into that category. He was not stupid. There was no evidence about why he did what he did or at least I did not ever get the prosecution's viewpoint. I don't know why he did it, but I don't think it was for the money . . .

"What did I learn from Carlson? To be skeptical. Never believe anything you hear. Or see."

### Truman

I saved Craig Truman for last. When I called him, he, like everyone involved with Carlson, wanted to talk and would not put down the phone.

"It is an odd situation; the attorney-client privilege goes on after death but I will tell you what I can. I represented Carlson early and had my good friends John Macdonald and Sy Sundell see him. I also evaluated his situation while he was at your hospital. As a result of our investigation we decided the multiple personality disorder defense was not the way to go. It was a red herring. Yes, Carlson started to talk multiple talk right away. Ross was nobody's fool . . .

"I can't tell you specifics, but I was surprised when the D.A. did not find out that Carlson checked out books on multiple personality disorder. If they had checked the city library and the school library . . . If you found those records, you might find that he was very interested in MPD before the murders. He also talked to one of his friends—his partying friends about MPD. But the friend lied like the dickens to the police."

So Carlson had read more than just *Billy Milligan*. For not talking, Truman had told me a lot.

"John and Sy cannot talk. Walter objected to it. Dr. Wilets? A bright guy. You can guess why Walter would not have wanted Wilets to testify. . . ."

When we met, the ex–public defender greeted me at the door of his spacious, high-ceilinged office, water cup in hand, and motioned me to a seat as he sat down behind an enormous desk. He looked like his picture: aviator glasses, thinning hair, pale skin. His face told me that he had put in his time in the trenches.

"We got a call from the coroner the morning the bodies were found. They told us that it was a 'tough one,' a double homicide. It was a tough one because of the nature of the killing. It looked like an execution. We got involved right away.

"The defense had a lot of money. Walter would spend what it took. Chappell needed to come into court with more experience but he did not. From the beginning, all the danger signs were there, but the D.A. missed that this was a major case. In terms of style, the defense and the prosecution were antithetical. You are right. But Chappell does not need to learn to be more devious. He needs to learn to be more antidevious.

"Chappell had a hard time getting experts. It was a high-profile case. The experts knew they would be ripped apart on the stand. They knew the case could go on forever. The MPD stuff was pretty speculative and slippery—all smoke and mirrors . . ."

"Are you talking about Carlson?" I asked.

"Attorney-client privilege lasts forever, so I can only speak in general terms. But MPD is a boutique diagnosis. Some defense attorney decides that MPD is the way to go. They think it is a perfect defense. You can't see it, smell it, or touch it. You can't prove that it is there. In a case where there is no other defense, some defense attorneys might seize on it. I can find psychiatrists to say anything . . .

"But practicing law that way leads nowhere. Juries usually do not buy hogwash, especially in Douglas County. The way I do it is first talk to my client and ask if they think they are insane. I tell them if they say yes I will get them the best psychiatrists. Over the years I have learned the way to win is to get people such as Sy and John. If they say yes, my client is insane, then I know the D.A. will usually go along. But if I don't have a good insanity defense, I say let's get on with it . . .

"When Walter called and told me that 'the bread was loose' I asked him to come over so I could turn over all the stuff and transfer the case. Walter came down, not David, just Walter. I spent an afternoon telling him everything we had, written and not. I told him all I knew." Truman paused and let that sink in. "He knew everything I knew but I never talked to Savitz about it. There are people who still believe that Savitz never knew everything. David was a true believer. If that scenario was correct, it broke David's heart. . . .

"We don't trust anyone in this business." Truman picked his words carefully. "We don't like surprises in court. So when a client tells us something we investigate our clients. When our clients start talking in sophisticated ways about this symptom or that symptom we want to know where they got it from. You can assume we investigated what Carlson told us. John and Sy know what we found. Walter also knows what we found . . .

"Why did he kill his parents? I believe that Ross had become a party boy and his parents had indulged him but things were about to change. They were going to set some strict rules for old Ross and he was going to be sent away to school. He got angry and got carried away with the circumstances. The next thing you knew it got set up." Truman paused. "The crime scene was a picture of particular cruelty . . ." There it was again, Carlson's rage.

"The underlying reason why he did it I don't know. He was narcissistic. In a way, he was charismatic. Ross had groupies, all these girls, sort of like Charles Manson. After he was in the hospital, they would ask me if he could have a tape deck or sound system. They loved him. In a funny way he was a charismatic guy.

"Abuse? One of the things that I felt terrible about was all this abuse talk and dragging his parents through the mud. If there was any abuse going on it was Ross doing it. His parents were doing back flips to make his life perfect . . .

"Did he start talking about Antichrist right away? I can't tell you about Antichrist. That is privileged information. No, I also cannot tell you whether his grandfather thought he was possessed by demons. That is also privileged. But when I think of Carlson I think of Banquo in *Macbeth*. 'He urinates congealed ice.' He was inaccessible. I never was able to interview him; he always interviewed me and only told me what he wanted to tell me." Congealed ice comes from *Measure for Measure*, appropriately enough, not *Macbeth*. Ice, however, fit Carlson to a tee.

"From the beginning, this was a very interesting case from a negotiation point of view. Clearly, it was not a 'who done it.' From the start, everyone knew who did it. I thought there was something available to work out—a deal to be made—but it never got on that track after I left the case. If our justice system works, people have to be redeemed for what they did. After all, that is the goal of the criminal justice system. And criminals often want to be redeemed and pay the bill. Criminals, you know, often return to the scene of the crime. They want to be caught; they want to be redeemed.

"I think," Truman went on, "at the end, Carlson craved redemption. I heard that after he was diagnosed with leukemia he tried to talk to David about it but David did not hear him. Even at the end, David thought it was this personality or that who was talking, not Ross Carlson. But, I think, at the very end, as he lay near death, Carlson wanted to be redeemed . . ."

# ·CHAPTER·
## TWENTY-THREE

# THE HEADS OF THE BEAST

But his wish for redemption did not tell me why Carlson did it.

The defense tried to mitigate Carlson's murders with MPD and abuse; but they also never offered an explanation. Michael Batagglia said it was financial, a scam gone awry; Brian Bevis also bet on money. Carlson killed his parents shortly after his mother discovered he ran an escort service. Carlson liked money and wanted his parents' life insurance and the equity in their house, a jackpot Bevis quickly pointed out estimated at half a million dollars. Though greed was one facet of Carlson, I was not satisfied with this at all.

Truman thought it was because Carlson, the "party boy," was about to be kicked out of the house. He murdered them the day they raised the money to send him away to college. While this spark may have ignited the fuse, the explosion was waiting to happen for a long time. As Chappell said, for something like this how far back did you go?

I was surprised when, at the autopsy, it was discovered that Rod Carlson, the Littleton schoolteacher, had liver disease; the kind frequently found in alcoholics. This was unusual for a strict Baptist. While this suggests that there are things about what neighbors called the "all-American" Carlsons we will never know, an alcoholic father does not explain murder at all.

And so on.

I had spent years with Carlson, interviewed him eight times and tried a ninth, read thousands of pages of reports, testimony, and evaluations, and saw him in court for days on end. I spent hundreds of hours on his case, but for months after he died Carlson's motive was as obscure as it was the night he killed his parents. The three people who could possibly shed light on this question were dead and buried. I got nowhere.

Ironically, clues were in view from the start. The night of the crime Ross Carlson, like most criminals, gave the world a glimpse of his motives, only I had not seen the clues. My consolation was that no one else saw them either. Almost by luck—again—four details from the day of his birth, the night he killed, the moment before his death, and the Bible illuminated the enigma of Carlson's homicidal rage. But it took me a long time to catch on.

## Child of Sin

I reviewed what I knew. It was not love, but blind groping that led to Ross Carlson's birth. No one disputes that Ross was conceived out of wedlock; he was a mistake, an unwanted child. His story started in some furtive, dark place full of shame and guilt.

I do not know at exactly what age Carlson was told about the moment of his conception but I am convinced he grew up with this knowledge. Perhaps this is why Ross said his parents held him in contempt. During his early days in Pueblo, Ross said he was unwanted, a "burden" to his family. His birth, he said, made it hard for his parents to accomplish their "goals." He knew, he said, that they were angry at him for it.

Before he stopped talking, he told Greg Trautt that he grew up in a two-faced, dissociated household. To everyone, his parents were "perfect." His father, Carlson said with ridicule of his own, even cut the lawn in shorts and Florsheim shoes. But, in private, things were different. For instance, when as a child he got angry, they put a paper bag over his head. Trautt's inkblots agreed. His tests showed that the Carlsons hid their rage; they operated with the unwritten rule not to express their true feelings. Like with Ross, they bagged them.

**Predestination**

For the Carlsons, a brand of rigid Christianity provided the rules of the game. It formed the boundaries for the Carlson family and the bedrock of Ross Carlson's psyche. Ross went to church, Sunday school, youth groups, Bible study, and retreats. There was, for instance, ample evidence that Carlson was preoccupied with religion after the murders. In January of 1984, he wrote to his mother's parents, the Reverend and Mrs. Hill:

> *"Until recently I did not understand what it was like to be believed in and loved unconditionally. For [my new friends] I did not have to jump through any hoops or preform [sic] at a certain level. I just had to be me . . . I believe that was the message God wanted me to get . . ."*

God's "message" to Carlson; "I just had to be me." After his arrest, Carlson told Trautt that events were "predestined"; he was destined to be in "this" situation. Everyone was born with a script which unfolded until death. Carlson hinted there was meaning to his act. I began to think that somehow Carlson felt predestined to kill his parents. "I just had to be me." I knew this but had not yet put two and two together. I had not yet asked myself why Carlson chose Antichrist as the killer.

**"The Antichrist Is Evil Like the Devil . . ."**

Carlson first revealed that Antichrist killed his parents to Ralph Fisch in December 1983. Carlson's MPD was not yet in full bloom —he had yet to call Fisch with the list of his personalities and send Fisch his collage. Carlson told Fisch that "my parents made my life miserable. I don't know why—mother was religious—why Antichrist killed them. My grandfather wants me to become a minister. Religion helps me some now . . . My mother felt God was punishing her for having me. Their love was conditional, depending upon what I did. They never touched me. I went with a girl who touched me. She touched my leg, I craved it . . .

"The Antichrist is evil like the devil. Family are all Baptist ministers. It blows your mind . . . you need a bible to tell them what to do. I get sick of my relatives. Hate them. So religious and biased . . . I craved being touched."

Religion and punishment, conditional love, Antichrist is evil like the devil. My mother felt God was punishing her for having me. They never touched me. Nevertheless, despite what I knew of the fundamentalist context of his life, I thought Antichrist was just another one of his names which Carlson pulled out of his hat. I should have known better. The hat was his unconscious and Antichrist was the clue.

## Herod, the First Antichrist

I only began to understand the importance of Antichrist after Carlson died. And, only because of an accidental clue, Herod the Great.

What someone chooses to read at the end of his life says a lot about the man. After he died, Ginger, the head nurse on the cancer ward, told me in an offhand way that the last book Carlson read was about Herod the Great. As he began to bleed into his eyes and lungs, Carlson read *The Sins of Herod* by Frank G. Slaughter. Carlson, the voracious reader, chose to read about Herod and his doomed descendants, knowing full well that this might be his last book.

Herod stayed in my mind. A few months later, while in a used-book store, I remembered Herod and found Slaughter's book. As I read about Herod in Slaughter, and then in Josephus and finally in the Bible, I was reminded that luck always characterized Ross Carlson's story. It was luck that Carlson was caught, and it was luck that I now read about Herod.

First, there was an uncanny likeness between Herod and Carlson. It was as if Ross Carlson read about himself as he died. Herod the Great was one of the cruelest tyrants who ever lived. He, like Ross, murdered his family. Hardly a day passed without Herod putting someone to death. Herod murdered two brothers-in-law, his wife, his mother-in-law, and three of his sons, one just days before he died.

Five days before Herod died a terrible death, he, like Carlson, tried to kill himself. Herod wanted to die because he suffered from, in the words of Josephus, distemper, great fever, excruciating pains in his colon, and an inflammation of his abdomen. At the end, Herod could not breathe. All like Carlson. Herod also brought me to Antichrist.

The story of Herod begins on page one of the New Testament

and, of course, is intimately intertwined with the attempted assassination of Jesus Christ. Every Christian knows the story well.

I found parallels between Carlson and the story of the birth of Christ too. Jesus was conceived out of wedlock, as was Carlson by Marilyn, whose name means descendant of Mary. Here the stories diverge. Joseph refused to disgrace Mary and would have chosen to quietly end their betrothal had he not dreamt that Mary had conceived by the Holy Spirit. Marilyn—the irony of her name could not have been lost on her pastor father nor on her—and Rod were forced to confess publicly and seek Marilyn's father's congregation's forgiveness.

After Jesus was born in Bethlehem, Herod was outraged that his power would be usurped. He tricked the three wise men—the Magi —to search for Jesus by telling them that he wanted to worship the child when, in fact, he wanted Jesus dead. The Magi, however, saw through Herod's duplicity and did not return. Another angel appeared to Joseph during a second dream. "Get up," he said, "take the child and his mother and escape to Egypt. Stay there until I tell you, for Herod is going to search for the child to kill him."

The climax of the story was on the overleaf of Frank Slaughter's book, one of the last things Carlson read: "Herod was furious when he realized he had been outwitted by the wise men, and in Bethlehem and its surrounding district he had all male children killed who were two years old or under, reckoning by the date he had been careful to ask the wise men. It was then that words spoken through the prophet Jeremiah 31:15 were fulfilled:

*A voice is heard in Ramah,*
    *weeping and great mourning,*
*Rachel weeping for her children*
    *and refusing to be comforted,*
*because they are no more."*

In a rage, Herod wiped out the male babies of Bethlehem in a bloody psychopathic attempt to kill Jesus, a true murder of the innocents.

As I read this, it dawned on me that Herod—literally—was the first Antichrist. In fact, early Christians referred to Roman rulers as Antichrist. Ross Carlson knew that Herod tried to kill Jesus: I wondered if Carlson thought of Herod as the first Antichrist and of himself as Herod's reincarnation, the Antichrist who murdered Rod and Marilyn Carlson.

Herod convinced me that it was not a pure Carlson fiction that Carlson placed Antichrist at the very center of his night of slaughter. I then recalled Carlson's abhorrence of pork. Perhaps Carlson thought that Antichrist was, as depicted in the New Testament, a leader of the Jews. Truman might have been right: At the end of his life, when Carlson read about Herod, he returned to the scene of his crime. At the end, he might have sought redemption.

I put my books down and there Antichrist sat. I guessed there was more but I remained stuck until I went to the Bible. When I found a note in Carlson's chart that he had a Bible with him in September 1983, just days after his arrest, I decided to renew my search for Antichrist. "The New International Version is incredible," Carlson wrote to friends.


### The Book
The Bible, for the Carlsons, was The Book. They went to church regularly, often three times a week: always on Sunday mornings, usually on Sunday evenings, and often to prayer meetings on Wednesdays. They came from a culture preoccupied with evil and redemption, sin and punishment, with its own rules and its own values. What I discovered about Antichrist in The Book, the three Carlsons surely knew by heart.

The idea of a mighty ruler who will appear at the end of time, whose essence will be enmity of God, was taken over by the Christians from the Jews.

The Old Testament Book of Daniel paints a chilling picture of the apocalyptic struggle between good and evil at the end of time. Four beasts came out of the sea and the fourth beast was terrifying, "It had large iron teeth; it crushed and devoured its victims . . . It was different from all the former beasts, and it had ten horns." Each horn would be a ruler, but at the end yet another ruler would arise. This evil ruler would appear with large armies and would persecute the saints and destroy the temple.

I found the first Christian view of Antichrist in 2 Thessalonians. In his letter to his new converts, Paul warned against deception by "the man of lawlessness" and "the man doomed to destruction." "Don't let anyone deceive you in any way. For that day will not

come until the rebellion occurs and the man of lawlessness is revealed, the man doomed to destruction . . ."

John also warned against dangerous, "false" teachers, those who
said that Christ was not the Messiah. John's prose is powerful and
evocative. "Dear children," John wrote, "this is the last hour; and as
you have heard the antichrist is coming . . . They went out from
us, but they did not really belong to us. For if they had belonged to
us, they would have remained with us . . ."

By now I sensed it was very important that Carlson had called
himself Antichrist, the man of lawlessness, the false prophet, the
man doomed to destruction. But, I still did not know why Ross
Carlson chose Antichrist as his signature; I still did not have the link
that tied Carlson to Antichrist.

## The Mark of Antichrist, the Head of the Beast

I remember the exact moment when, while sitting in the same chair
where I first watched Fairbairn's tape so long before, I found the
answer to Antichrist.

Antichrist has different meanings in the Bible. Sometimes
Antichrist means the devil and sometimes it is a distinct concept.
So, after thumbing through the concordance for Antichrist, I
searched for the quintessential Antichrist: Satan.

I turned to Revelation 12:3, Christ's mystical picture, delivered
through the mouth of the Apostle John, of the end of the world.
There I found the classical tradition of Antichrist; the Antichrist of
the two beasts:

> . . . a woman . . . was pregnant and cried out in pain as she was
> about to give birth. Then another sign appeared in heaven: an enor-
> mous red dragon with seven heads and ten horns and seven crowns on
> his heads . . . And there was a war in heaven . . . The great
> dragon was hurled down—that ancient serpent called the devil or
> Satan, who leads the whole world astray . . .
>
> And I saw a beast coming out of the sea. He had ten horns and
> seven heads . . . The dragon gave the beast his power and his throne
> and great authority. One of the heads of the beast seemed to have a
> fatal wound, but the fatal wound had been healed . . .

At that moment, I knew that this was Carlson's head, the head of the beast. In my excitement, I tried to focus on the paper and read and reread that passage to make sure I got it right. ". . . a fatal wound, but the fatal wound had been healed . . ."

In 1982, Marilyn—descendant of Mary—wrote that "Ross is our only child. He was born with a spot on his head about the size of a nickel that skin had never grown over. This seemed extremely unusual to our family physician who kept Ross in the hospital for nine days after his birth . . ." Carlson's scar, the ugly white scar at the top of his head.

The beast came out of the sea with ten horns, seven heads, and a fatal wound which had been healed. The childbirth metaphor was obvious. But the beast came out not of the sea, but out of the womb of Marilyn Carlson. "One of the heads of the beast seemed to have had a fatal wound, but the fatal wound had been healed . . ."

Then a second beast came to help the first. The second beast "made the earth and its inhabitants worship the first beast whose fatal wound had been healed . . . it could cause all who refused to worship the image be killed . . . If anyone has insight, let him calculate the number of the beast, for it is a man's number. His number is 666." All those who refused to worship the image of the first beast, whose fatal wound had been healed, the second beast killed; just like Ross Carlson.

Here was, I was certain, the reason for Marilyn Carlson's preoccupation with her son's defect, his hole in the head; it was Ross's stigmata, his scar, and their sin. Marilyn's son was not Jesus, the Messiah; Marilyn had given birth to the beast. Ross's grandfather—the pastor—seemed to agree. After the murders he announced that yes, his grandson was "possessed by demons as stated in the Bible."

The beast formed the core of why Ross Carlson killed. Ross Carlson, conceived in sin, was born with the mark of Satan. Marilyn, the seventeen-year-old, devout, and now-despoiled young fundamentalist Christian girl, must have tragically thought she had given birth to the devil. Ross was unplanned, unwanted, defective, marked, and he knew it.

## The First Sin

Ross grew up knowing of his sin. Ross, through no fault of his own, was sin reincarnate. He felt defective, in part because of his dyslexia and undescended testicle, but mainly because of how he was conceived. His very existence was proof of his parents' evil. He was their failure and his scar a daily reminder of their shame. Ross Carlson's first sin therefore was not his sin at all, but his parents' sin. Their sin was obvious for all to see when Ross was born with the mark of the beast.

Six sixty-six. No one knows why John chose 666 as the number of the beast. Some believe that he did because it fell short of the holy number 7 in every way. Six sixty-six was trapped by its birth, like Ross Carlson. I was not surprised when I found out that Ross Carlson chose 666 as the combination for his briefcase: Ross Carlson had learned that 666 was his number too.

## Soul Murder

Now Ross Carlson's story fell into place. On the night of the murders, Ross Carlson called himself Antichrist because his parents taught him that he was the beast. The fact that Carlson chose to clothe himself as a multiple was likely also an outgrowth of his satanic Antichrist persona. He transformed the heads of the beast into his personalities: Steve, Justin, Stacey, Blue, Gray, Norman, Black.

For the first time, I felt sympathy for Ross Carlson. Because his parents knew Ross was their sin, they unwittingly murdered his soul. By the time we met, Ross Carlson had grown into who his parents thought he was—the man of sin, the man of lawlessness, unwanted, an outcast—the very image they had of themselves and of him.

Carlson, always exquisitely alert to the moods of others, said something interesting to a nurse on November 27, 1984. He said he could always tell what people wanted, he was "tuned in" to them as if he had ESP. He could finish sentences spoken by others as if he were in unconscious communication with them. This seemed accurate: and undoubtedly, he was tuned in to his parents' guilt and shame.

Soul murder is the most subtle—and malignant—form of child abuse. It is subtle because soul murder does not depend on physical harm or neglect. Souls are murdered by glances; souls are murdered by ideas and distorted feelings. On the surface, parents who murder their children's souls often appear normal and good.

And soul murder is malignant because parents who murder their children's souls are unable to see their children as they are, only as they expect them to be. Soul-murdered children, as they grow, come to believe that they are who their parents think they are. They do not have their own identities. As Erik Erikson wrote over forty years ago, it is this very deprivation of identity, not frustration, which leads to murder. Physical evidence of child abuse is often sparse because, when a soul is murdered, there is no dead body.

Fisch and Fairbairn missed soul murder because they did not know where to look. They searched for secret sexual and physical abuse. I did not find soul murder until Ginger told me about Herod and I read the Bible.

Though I cannot prove this, I firmly believe that Ross Carlson—enthralled with Kathleen Turner in *Body Heat*, a seductress and murderer, and Richard Gere in *American Gigolo*, a prostitute and hustler—accepted his parents' accusation of sin and became their sin. Because of this, Ross Carlson, like Antichrist, was a man doomed to destruction. This was Carlson's belief in the Lord's hand, his belief in predestination.

### ". . . as special as Ross . . ."

I think Marilyn Carlson knew that something was wrong from the day of Carlson's birth, if not before. When Ross was arrested for trying to buy dynamite—and a gun—she wrote a four-page single-spaced letter to the probation department on December 21, 1982. There is an unsettled tone in her description of the Carlson family:

> *As Ross's parents, we have an outstanding relationship with each other. We were only seventeen and eighteen when we got married, but we feel we have a lasting marriage. Ross may well have felt badly or lonely because we get along so well that we have spent a deal of time together in various pursuits. We love Ross dearly and had no more children because we knew that we would never have another one as special as Ross.*

We did not have another because no one could be "as special as Ross"; especially evil and bad. It sounded to me as if his parents had no room for Ross in their lives. He "may well have felt," Marilyn wrote, "badly or lonely . . ." Marilyn seemed to know that she and Rod resented Ross, his intrusion, his mark of evil, and shut him out. Each of Marilyn's loving glances must have been tinged by knowledge of their shame.

And, perhaps, with just a little bit of hate.

I do not know for sure what it was like for Ross Carlson to grow up other than what he told others. He felt, he said, ridicule, contempt, unloved. But I was reminded of something Michael Bataglia told me. "I asked my girlfriend about Ross," Michael said. "Mr. Carlson was her fifth grade teacher. She remembered when Mr. Carlson once told the class that 'my son could not do this math problem.' Christie thought that was an odd and insulting thing to say. She also remembered that in the fifth grade, Mr. Carlson lost it with a student in the cafeteria. I don't know what the student did, but Mr. Carlson started to shake him for it. Ross was real secretive about his parents. . . ."

Marilyn and Rod likely loved their son, but they despised their sin so much that they could not help but hate him as well. As he grew from infant to child to man, Rod and Marilyn infused their sin-child with their hate. And, because he was not loved enough, Carlson could love no one, not even himself.

Carlson was starved for what he called unconditional love. He tried to build himself up with narcissistic mechanisms: karate, weight lifting, *American Gigolo*-type suits, his groupies. When I saw him first in 1984 he treated my words like gnats and me like a doorknob. Now I knew why. Treated like a thing himself, he also treated others like objects and thereby missed a chance for sustained and true human contact.

Therefore, Ross Carlson was nothing, if not, at his core, excruciatingly lonely. And full of rage.

## Frank Christianson

Soul murder also cleared up the mystery of Frank Christianson. All this about Herod and Antichrist looped me back to the last clue, "Frank Christianson," the phantom name from the night of August 17, 1983. Frank Christianson confirmed my new understanding.

When Carlson went to meet Frank Christianson, he became the epitome of Antichrist.

Until now Frank Christianson was a question mark. No one knew why Carlson wrote down the name Frank Christianson right before he killed his parents. In seven years no Frank Christianson has come forward or has been found.

I now suspect that no one has come forward because Frank Christianson did not exist except in Carlson's fantasy. Carlson pulled his name out under the pressure of Ken Cortez's questions and the excitement of the moment; it came from the darkest recesses of Carlson's mind.

"Where are you going? Who are you going to meet?" repeated the worried Cortez. Finally, Carlson wrote "Frank Christianson" on a scrap of paper which, although Carlson destroyed, Cortez later recovered.

On August 17, on the way to the movies, the last thing Carlson wrote, two hours before he killed his parents, was "Frank Christianson." Frank Christianson was Christ the Son. When Carlson wrote "Frank Christianson" he wrote: "Frankly, I am going to meet Christ the Son." On Wednesday night, August 17, 1983, in Northern Douglas County, Ross Carlson killed Christianson, Christ the Son, just as Herod tried to do two thousand years before.

Ross Carlson murdered his parents in his ultimate act as Antichrist. Carlson's first sin was his parents' hate and shame. He *was* their sin and shame. His second sin was their murder. On one level, Ross Carlson felt predestined to commit his second sin because, in that terrible moment, he fulfilled the role his parents had assigned him at birth. Ross Carlson became, as he pulled the trigger, the beast, Satan, the Antichrist.

Thus he brought his parents to justice. In this twisted way, Ross Carlson absolved his parents of their nineteen years of guilt as he meted out their ultimate punishment.


**Absolution of the Lambs**
People are still puzzled by another thing: Why did the Carlsons lie there like lambs to die? It was, in Craig Truman's words, a picture of particular cruelty.

Some people who investigated the case think that Rod and Marilyn did not believe, until too late, that they were in danger. They must have thought that this was another of their son's scams, a trick. Or that his gun was loaded with blanks. But most people are not sure.

I think there is another explanation for the Carlsons' paralysis on Cottonwood Road. I believe that the Carlsons, like their son, wished for absolution.

Rod, big and strong, was capable of putting up a fight. Only he didn't. "This is hell," Ross reported his mother saying right before he shot her, "I don't want to live. Just go ahead and shoot me." She succumbed without signs of having struggled at all.

Was this because they did not believe that their danger was real? Or did the Carlsons think they deserved to die? By August 17, 1983, they must have felt doubly guilty. First, because of their son's illicit conception and now because of their resentment and hate. In some ways they may have yearned for this satanic epiphany, this celebration of Antichrist, their punishment and their execution. And in this, Ross Carlson did not let his parents down.

## The Terminal Sin

His birth scar, Antichrist, Herod, Frank Christianson, 666. Nevertheless, when all is said and done, nothing fully explains the horror of what Ross Carlson did and why he did it. My explanation should be seen for what it is: informed speculation. Ultimately, we can never really understand the tragedy of murder; we only know what things are associated with killers. And explanations always pale next to the reality of the crime.

Carlson's matricide and patricide were humanly inhuman acts; explanations are used to mitigate this horror. They are for us, the survivors; they lend coherence and create order where there may be none. They may satisfy the mind but should not be mistaken for the truth. Long before child abuse, poverty, biology, or bad genes were offered as explanations, murderers were morally condemned. Ross Carlson deserves condemnation, soul murdered or not.

As I again thought of Carlson's craving for redemption, I was reminded that he must have known that in the New Testament there is one sin which can never be redeemed, a sin beyond forgiveness, the terminal sin. Only the New Testament never specifically identifies this "sin that leads to death . . ." And, as he struggled to catch his last breaths, Ross Carlson must have wondered whether matricide and patricide were indeed unforgivable sins. For all his agonal suffering, he must have doubted whether he could ever achieve salvation. ". . . Whoever blasphemes against the Holy Spirit will never be forgiven; he is guilty of eternal sin." Ross Carlson must have felt this too.